# This Sticker GUARANTEES

POLICY AND POLITICS IN AMERICA

# TOP CASH

## for your used book anytime

This book belongs

To _____

_____

# Blue Raider Bookstore

When you buy from us you get even more!

Edited by *Allan P. Sindler*

University of California, Berkeley

Contributors

*Edward C. Banfield*   University of Pennsylvania

*David L. Kirp*   University of California, Berkeley

*Theodore R. Marmor*   University of Minnesota
and *Martin Rein*   Massachusetts Institute of Technology

*Jerome T. Murphy*   Harvard University

*Jack H. Schuster*   University of California, Berkeley

*Allan P. Sindler*   University of California, Berkeley

# POLICY AND POLITICS IN AMERICA

## SIX CASE STUDIES

LITTLE, BROWN AND COMPANY  BOSTON

# PREFACE

It is no secret that public confidence in the capacity and competence, and even at times in the credibility and good faith, of America's government to act effectively to remedy stubborn social problems is on the decline. The heady optimism of the 1960s, which spawned many and varied policy assaults on social ills, has given way to a sense of public confusion and malaise, amid judgments that the Great Society programs of President Lyndon Johnson have had mixed results at best. These feelings are by no means universal or uniform among all sectors of America's citizens; they appear to be especially pronounced on college and university campuses.

The "reasonableness" of that decline of confidence has itself become a major issue on and off the campus. Has government been performing less effectively? Or has government done about as well or better, but expectations and the basis of appraisal have shifted? Has our political rhetoric become too inflated, promoting unrealizable policy objectives and hence disillusionment? Or can our political system or ideology or values be deficient in critical ways? Our social science knowledge remains as yet quite limited, while the severity of our problems is perceived as increasing. Does that unhappy combination mean that government should intervene less often and less massively, or the reverse? Is the complexity of assessing the effects of policy a sufficient reason to go slowly, or is it mostly a mask for inaction or ineffective action by government? So the questions go, all too often couched in these mutually exclusive, either/or terms of debate.

So framed, the controversy is often too slippery to be grappled with by means other than rhetoric and ideology. In the case studies in this volume, we have elected instead to supply evidence germane to the dispute, but drawn from careful examination of the interplay of particular policies and the political process. That evidence, not surprisingly, is mixed, reflecting not merely the absence of any party line among the contributors, but the face of reality as well. Student readers are encouraged to work our studies over to extract from them the diverse evidence on both the strengths and weaknesses of the American political system. In that way the seductive simplicity of "Are you for or against the System?" can be rejected in favor of the more fruitful though difficult task of concrete analysis and contextual understanding.

The coverage of our case studies includes the major political institutions — Congress, the presidency, courts, federal and state bureaucracies, interest groups, and elections. Important contentious policies are emphasized, such as the failing attempt to date to correct "the welfare mess" by adopting a Family Assistance Plan; the effort to substitute direct election of the president for the present indirect procedure; the judicial attack on the continuance of local school financing inequities based on variable school district wealth; the conception and implementation of Model Cities legislation intended to reverse urban decay; and the working relationship of federal and state administrators in shaping the operation and effects of Title I compensatory education funds of the Elementary and Secondary Education Act. In addition, one study treats the reelection bid of a congressman closely identified with education legislation, and his efforts to make use of the education constituency in his campaign.

While concentrating on a particular policy and sector of the political process, each study is also sensitive to the broader and continuous political interplay that marks the making of public policy in America. The pervasiveness of politics as a determinant of policy formulation, enactment, and execution is amply reflected in each contributor's account. Three of the studies — the ones on the courts, intergovernmental politics, and elections and interest groups — have a special focus on educational policy and politics. Further, several case studies examine policy implementation — a critical stage of policy-making which has been unduly neglected in the literature — from realistically political perspectives.

In treating our respective subjects, each of us has sought to raise general questions to stimulate student response and classroom discussion. The analysis and interpretation we offer aim to inform that discussion, and not to dampen it by too obtrusive an evaluative role by the author. Lively student discussion and not so occasional disagreement with some of the writers' observations are what we hope and expect will occur, especially in light of the complexity and controversiality of the policies and processes treated. Only students and instructors will know how well our expectations have been realized, and we would welcome their feedback comments.

A final word on who is responsible for what in this book. The editor conceived of the volume, recruited the contributors and studies, set the broad format of each study, and related the parts to the whole. Each contributor chose his topic and developed his study, being guided by a common awareness of the volume's purposes and of the coverage and emphases of his co-contributors' chapters, and by consideration of the editor's suggestions on successive drafts. Although the responsibility of each author is limited, therefore, to his own study, the collective cooperation of all underlies the coherence and completion of the volume. As editor, I should like to express my gratitude at working with such congenial colleagues on this collaborative venture.

*Allan P. Sindler*

# CONTENTS

*the most popular votes. The winning candidate should
have a minimum level of vote support. Protecting and
promoting two-partyism. Maintaining checks and balances. Reflecting federalism? Political feasibility.* Evaluating the present system. *Why the electoral vote
distorts the popular vote. Relative advantage. The politics of relative advantage. Majority, plurality, and
nonplurality presidents. Two-partyism and third parties.* The district plan. The proportional plan. Direct
popular election. *Congress's growing receptivity to
altering EC and to E. A redistribution of relative advantage. The 40 percent minimum support level. The
contingency procedure. The runoff and third parties.
Alternatives to the runoff election.* Congress disposes.
*Pre-1969 momentum. President Nixon intervenes. The
House acts. Getting E to the Senate floor. The Senate
blocks reform. Analyzing the votes.* Concluding observations. Sources and readings.

*building. A gloomy prognosis?* Will the courts push into the "educational thicket"? *The equal protection precedents. Proximate means versus ultimate ends. The educational thicket. Proximate means and symbolic consequences.* Intradistrict and interstate fiscal inequities. Will the "no wealth" standard be extended to other government services? Concluding observations. Sources and readings.

administration of Title I: 1965–69. *USOE: a state-oriented agency. An avoidance of evaluation. Inaction on audits of abuses. USOE's timidity. Resisting USOE's initiative: concentrating the funds. Resisting USOE's initiative: local parent advisory councils.* State administration of Title I. *Management of Massachusetts' Title I. An explanation of the Massachusetts pattern.* A turning point in Washington? *Another try to establish parent councils. A new face for USOE.* Massachusetts revisited. New Title I enforcement: a post mortem? Concluding observations. Sources and readings.

STUDY SIX 200

## ELECTIONS AND INTEREST GROUPS

An "Education Congressman" Fights for Survival: Congressman John Brademas' Bid for Reelection, 1968

*Jack H. Schuster*

Brademas: the man, the politician. 1968: a foreboding year for Democrats. Brademas' difficulties in 1968. *Indiana congressional redistricting. The new Third District. Intraparty dissension. Nixon's coattails. The Wallace problem. The Republicans' choice.* Campaign strategies: images and resources. *The incumbent's edge. Mobilizing allies. Image and party. An exhausting pace.* Mobilizing the education community. *The Washington "education lobby." The "education congressman." Education as a campaign issue. Cultivating the education interest groups. The federal educators — legislative-executive coordination. Rallying the local educators. Seeking an "education community-at-large." A well-timed education conference. Recruiting student support in the year of disaffection. National mass media endorsements.* The election outcome. Concluding observations. *Postscript. Some larger questions.* Sources and readings.

Notes on the Contributors 243

POLICY AND POLITICS IN AMERICA

# STUDY ONE

# THE CONGRESS

Origins of welfare reform. *Inadequacies. Inequities. Inhumaneness. Fiscally burdensome. Intrusive administration. Urgent reform.* Welfare policy during the 1960s. *The 1962 amendments. The 1967 amendments. Nixon's alternative: 1969.* Nixon's choice. The provisions of FAP: a political account. Apparent contradictions and anomalies. *Summary.* FAP's fate: 1969–72. *Becoming unstuck. The debacle of 1971. Reform in 1972: "Reform is dead, but who killed it?"* Concluding observations. Sources and readings.

# Reforming "The Welfare Mess":
# The Fate of the Family Assistance Plan, 1969–72

*Theodore R. Marmor and Martin Rein*

President Richard Nixon's plan for welfare reform — announced before a nationwide television audience in August 1969 and sent to the Congress as a bill in October — was to become for three years the subject of serious consideration by the financial committees of the Congress. The Nixon initiative, known generally as the Family Assistance Plan (FAP), called for the most extensive structural changes in public assistance since the original social security legislation of 1935. When the plan was introduced, initial reservations were voiced by some, but most commentators were strongly favorable. Indeed, what was almost a mood of euphoria enveloped FAP, seen by many as *the* turning point in welfare reform. Three years later, after political and technical considerations had substantially altered the original proposal, the elation of August 1969 was considerably eroded. Not only were there doubts that the bill which had evolved was such a bold new departure after all, but support was insufficient to enact it or any other alternative major reform.

The Family Assistance Plan suggested changing American public assistance in two central respects. First, it proposed a wholly federal program of cash assistance for all poor families with children, guaranteeing $1,600 per year per family of four, administered by the Social Security Administration, uniform and nationwide in scope and standards of eligibility. FAP would thus constitute a substantial transformation of the existing federal-state programs of family assistance. It would partially replace the program of Aid to Families with Dependent Children (AFDC) and it would make mandatory state aid to unemployed parents. Second, the Nixon plan would enlarge the role for the federal government in the other programs of public assistance to adults (aid to the blind, the disabled, the aged) by altering the federal-state sharing formula: for the first time the states would be required to meet nationwide standards of eligibility and administration, a national minimum benefit would be established, and state compliance with the new federal requirements would be rewarded by fiscal relief to state budgets. Broadly stated, the plan represented both a major expansion of coverage (to working-poor intact families) and increased federalization of the standards, benefits, and financing of the widely diverse federal-state programs.


Origins of Welfare Reform

To explain the origins of Nixon's initial proposals for welfare reform requires answers to three questions:

1. Why was structural reform of welfare on the agenda of American politics by the election of 1968?
2. What determined the range of alternative reforms out of which the Family Assistance Plan was framed?
3. What accounts for the choice of features from among these alternatives which comprise FAP?

The rediscovery of widespread and chronic poverty in America during the early 1960s made certain that public assistance programs would be critically evaluated. But the public discussion was far more adverse than might be anticipated in a political climate which accepted a commitment to reduce poverty. Public assistance became a policy area without defenders; the existence of a crisis in welfare emerged as the common theme among a disparate collection of critics and criticism. It was to this widespread sense of crisis that President Nixon appealed when justifying his reform before a mass television audience:

. . . whether measured by the anguish of the poor themselves, or by

*Theodore R. Marmor and Martin Rein*

the drastically mounting burden on the taxpayer, the present welfare system has to be judged a colossal failure. . . . and the tragedy is not only that it is bringing states and cities to the brink of financial disaster, but it is also failing to meet the elementary human, social, and financial needs of the poor.

The common verdict that American welfare policy had failed obscured the considerable disagreement over the precise character of its ills and the appropriate remedies for them. But by the middle 1960s the welfare system came to be widely regarded as *inadequate, inequitable, inhumane,* and *fiscally burdensome.* The responses to these interlocking claims constituted the range of relevant alternatives available to President Nixon when he took office in January 1969.

*Inadequacies.* American public assistance is most obviously inadequate because payment levels are lower than what states define as subsistence needs and lower still than what the federal government regards as the poverty line for families of different sizes.* In April 1968 an AFDC family of four recipients received an average $194 per month. Had the fifty-one states (including D.C.) met their own need standards, average expenditures would have been $237 per month, or 22 percent more than was actually expended.† The welfare system is inadequate because it fails to rescue recipients from what either the states or the federal government regard as impoverishment.

*Inequities.* The welfare system is also regarded as inequitable. Regional variation in welfare benefits account for many inequities. Public welfare recipients in similar financial circumstances but living in different regions of the United States receive dramatically different benefits which far exceed differences in the cost of living. In 1969, for example, a family of four in Mississippi received an average $39 a month on AFDC; a comparable family in New Jersey received $263 a month. Some critics argued that such regional discrepancies promote migration from the South to northern industrial states, though the evidence for such migration is extremely inconclusive.

Inequities also arise because nearly two-thirds of the poor are ineligible for the existing categories of public assistance, which limit benefits to widows, orphans, abandoned families, the aged, sick, and disabled. In those

---

* The poverty index, or "poverty line," is set by the Social Security Administration and represents the minimum income which a household of a given size and composition will need to subsist. The index is adjusted yearly to reflect price changes. In 1971 the SSA poverty line was approximately $4,000 for a family of four, or $335 per month for a nonfarm household.

† An extreme example is California's AFDC program where in 1971 the amount budgeted for the "basic needs" of a family of four was $380; the maximum payment, however, was $221, or 58 percent of budgeted need.

states which do not have an AFDC–Unemployed Parents (UP) program, aid is restricted to female-headed families (except in the case of the aged, blind, and disabled), thus providing a self-evident financial inducement for fathers to leave or to appear to leave the home. Many have argued that such eligibility requirements mean that our public policy encourages family disorganization.

Finally, inequities arise because the welfare system fails to help the working poor. Nearly two-thirds of America's poor do not receive aid from the existing categories of public assistance, and many of those are from families in which at least one adult member is working. Yet they remain poor because the family income is not sufficient to support them above the poverty line. In those states with AFDC–UP programs, where it is possible for intact families to receive assistance on condition of unemployment, it is often the case that benefit levels are higher than some wage levels, and a man earning the minimum wage or below may be better off unemployed and on welfare than employed and off welfare. (It should be noted here that welfare recipients are entitled to work without losing all their benefits and that many recipients do indeed work to supplement their welfare income. Before 1967 it made no financial sense for a recipient to work since every dollar earned meant a dollar less in AFDC benefits; even then, in 1961, 40 percent of all black and 26 percent of all white AFDC families had a full- or part-time worker. A 1967 study suggests even higher proportions of AFDC recipients in the labor force. Hence the view of the welfare population as the nonworking poor may be misleading. Still the fact remains that many of the working poor are ineligible for any sort of welfare assistance.)

*Inhumaneness.* Inequities in the treatment of the poor raise more than moral questions, for they bear upon broader social issues of migration into the cities, family disorganization, social cleavages, and disincentives to work. A concern for such problems made certain that welfare-reform discussion would highlight interstate and interprogram variation and, in the process, emphasize the perverse and often inhumane treatment which followed from the restrictive eligibility features of AFDC and AFDC–UP.

*Fiscally Burdensome.* The fiscal burdens welfare has placed on city and state budgets have been a prominent cause of complaint about public assistance. The welfare system has increased substantially in cost over the past decade, most obviously in the controversial AFDC program. Expenditures for AFDC increased from slightly less than $1 billion in 1960 to an estimated $3.3 billion in 1969. The number of AFDC recipients during the period rose from 3 million to 6.5 million persons, and even this understated the growth. In fact, 8 million different persons received AFDC benefits sometime during the course of 1968. Moreover, a growing proportion of the total child population is receiving public assistance. In 1955, 3 percent of all

*Theodore R. Marmor and Martin Rein*

children received such aid; by 1968 the proportion had doubled to 6 percent. In thirteen years AFDC recipient rates had doubled and costs had tripled.

The growth in the scope and cost of welfare must be separated from the increased fiscal burden this growth created at the state and local levels. The federal government financed an increasing proportion of total costs; by 1968 it absorbed more than half the costs of public assistance as compared with only 40 percent in 1945. State and local expenditures continued to represent a substantial political and financial burden on these governmental units, although the state and local *share* of total expenditures for public assistance has in fact declined during the post–World War II period. When federal reimbursements are taken into account, states and localities contributed a decreasing proportion of their own resources for welfare. A neglected technical paper prepared for the President's Commission on Income Maintenance shows that while the proportion of states' own budgets devoted to welfare has increased in recent years, it has still not caught up with the relative importance of welfare in the state budgets of the 1940s and early 1950s. A review of recent trends in the New York City budget showed that the city laid out only about 7.3 per cent of its own tax levies for public assistance in 1968–69. (See Table One.) During the next five years, when welfare reform was at the center of the national public debate, the fiscal burden of welfare, i.e., without considerable state and federal reimbursement, remained surprisingly stable, and a decrease was projected for the 1972–73 budget.

Public assistance costs are more usually presented as aggregate figures.

---

*TABLE ONE*

Comparison of Total Tax Levy Expenditures and Tax Levy Expenditures for Public Assistance in New York City, 1968–73

| Fiscal year | Total tax levy (in millions of dollars) | Tax levy for P.A. (in millions of dollars) | P.A. tax levy as a percentage of total tax levy |
|---|---|---|---|
| 1968–69 | $3,688[a] | $267.9[a] | 7.3 |
| 1969–70 | 3,992[a] | 266.4[a] | 6.7 |
| 1970–71 | 4,253[a] | 315.1[a] | 7.4 |
| 1971–72 | 4,581[b] | 335.9[c] | 7.3 |
| 1972–73 | 5,022[d] | 326.1[d] | 6.5 |

Sources: [a] Annual Report of the Comptroller of the City of New York: FY 1968–69, 1969–70, 1970–71.
[b] Expense Budget as adopted, FY 1971–72.
[c] Bureau of Budget Estimate of Expenditures.
[d] Expense Budget as adopted, FY 1972–73.

---

By this measure, in New York City total costs for public assistance have in recent years, for the first time, exceeded those for public education. Thus, it is the absolute size of the welfare program and its relation to other public expenditures rather than its relative bite out of state and local funds that gives rise to controversy, outrage, and bitterness. The AFDC program also raises social issues as sensitive as race (half the beneficiaries are black), religion (family planning), illicit sex, and family responsibility. The wealthier states which have high recipient rates and high benefit levels — and hence high total expenditures — have successfully made fiscal relief an urgent political issue, although the relative burden of rising welfare costs seems less dramatic than the absolute rise in total costs.

*Intrusive Administration.* The public welfare system is costly in human terms as well. Many critics believe that the discretion exercised by local administrators is one of the most pernicious aspects of current welfare programs. In many communities public assistance is associated with intrusions into personal privacy, arbitrary treatment of clients, and the use of social services as a form of control, where moral fitness requirements are imposed as a condition of aid. Administration of public welfare may be both harsh and humiliating to the recipients. In recent years there has been an expansion of legal-service programs for the poor, funded by the Office of Economic Opportunity; representatives of welfare clients have challenged established state welfare regulations in the courts with considerable success. Residence requirements and the "suitable home" provision have, for example, been overturned by the U.S. Supreme Court. These changes make the system more liberal and point up the arbitrary, capricious, and harsh pattern of its previous administration.

*Urgent Reform.* These problems of public welfare comprise the central issues with which major change of the welfare system must deal. They also suggest the disparate groups with a stake in change: the present recipients, the poor not presently aided, state and local governments, and the taxpayer. And these problems comprise the objects of concern which commission after commission highlighted in the mid-1960s: The Advisory Council on Public Welfare (1966), The National Commission on Technology, Automation, and Economic Progress (1966), The Advisory Commission on Rural Poverty (1967), and the Kerner Commission on Civil Disorders (1968).

Not only governmental commissions demanded welfare reform. The riots of 1965 pressed officials to think of ways in which the plight of the poor might be alleviated. Militant welfare rights organizations disrupted, protested, and castigated the present welfare system.

One response to the anxiety about growing disorder in cities was to liberalize the administration of the system, a task the courts assisted by repudiating practices which restricted access to welfare. This partially explained

*Theodore R. Marmor and Martin Rein*

why in some states first a higher proportion of applicants were accepted for welfare and then more eligible persons applied, further expanding the growing welfare rolls. Administrative liberalization and more humane practices thus heightened the sense of crisis.

The presidential election of 1968 provided the link between the growing concern about the malaise in welfare and the precipitants of the Nixon Family Assistance Plan. The campaign had called forth from the Republicans expected criticism of the growth in public assistance and casual claims about transplanting persons from the "welfare rolls onto payrolls." In office, President Nixon had to turn from complaint to remedy. There he found substantial constraints on what might be done to satisfy the criticism which had so successfully discredited public assistance.

To understand the alternatives put before Nixon when in office and the choices he made, it is necessary in at least a broad outline to examine the reforms which preceded the president's initiative. Was Nixon's proposal for reform a bold departure from the past or a continuity of it?

## Welfare Policy During the 1960s

A review of national welfare policy from 1962 to 1969 suggests that three strategies have been pursued: a service strategy, an income-incentive strategy, and an administrative strategy. Each of these elements can be identified in the two major amendments to the Social Security Act of 1962 and 1967, which preceded the Nixon administration's 1969 proposals for the Family Assistance Plan.

*The 1962 Amendments.* The 1962 amendments were heralded as the "services" amendments. They emphasized problem identification, the availability to welfare recipients of information, advice, and referral to other community resources, and direct help through specific services such as day care and training. These activities were designed to encourage "prevention and rehabilitation" as a way of reducing the size of the case-loads. Casework (diagnosis, advice, and referral) was featured prominently in this early service strategy; however, an emphasis on manpower training and job creation was by no means neglected, as attested to by the creation of a Community Work and Training (CWT) program.

The beginnings of an income-incentive strategy could also be recognized: Congress required states to allow for work expenses to encourage welfare mothers to seek employment. States were also permitted to disregard income set aside for children's future needs, such as education. The incentive principle was in turn related to a broader income strategy that emphasized wider coverage of all those with economic need in less restricted program categories, with larger cash grants and a major simplification of eligibility determination. Essentially, an incentive and income approach sought a less conditional claim to assistance, emphasized uniformity in the treatment of clients, and aimed at economic improvement by combining employment and welfare.

An administrative strategy was also evident. This took several forms. One was quality control; a new method was devised to review a random sample of the eligibility decisions made by caseworkers, and thus determine the percentage of incorrect decisions. Here it was assumed that rolls could be reduced if the eligibility decisions were more stringently examined. The Senate Appropriations Committee in the spring of 1962 demanded that a survey of the rates of ineligibles on state rolls be completed by the following fiscal year. The Department of Health, Education and Welfare (HEW) had simultaneously to make plans for a national eligibility survey while it was drafting the service regulations — illustrating, as political scientist Charles Gilbert points out, the "program's basic ambivalence." A second aspect of the administrative approach was to make it more difficult for deserting fathers to avoid supporting their children; this would take the financial reward out of desertions and reduce the number of families eligible for aid. Third, provision in the CWT program contained the beginnings of a new type of compulsion; a client who refused a bona fide job offer or refused to undergo work training would forfeit eligibility for the new AFDC–UP program Congress had just extended for five years. This latter program, initially passed in 1961, authorized federal participation in state AFDC programs for families in which the father was unemployed. The CWT program also made available federal funds to communities which created work-relief projects. The introduction of work relief for unemployed fathers was a sharp departure from the accepted principle that recipients need not work off the value of the grants they received. But work relief now seemed justified because of inclusion of employable men and the belief that such a program would preserve work-motivated behavior and deter would-be loafers.

The creation of the AFDC-UP program was in part designed to reduce family breakup. President Kennedy's 1961 speech to Congress on economic recovery and growth pointed out that "too many fathers, unable to support their families, have resorted to real or pretended desertion to qualify their children for help." The new UP program was seen as an important approach to eliminate the financial incentive for desertion. The UP program also significantly contributed to a redefinition of AFDC recipients as potentially employable persons, rather than individuals who, by definition, were outside the labor force.

*The 1967 Amendments.*   In 1967 much more attention was given to the incentive strategy. The incentives were contained in the $30-one-third rule (which permits recipients to keep the first $30 per month in earnings plus one-third of the balance) and in the expansion of deductions for work-related expenses. The services approach was not neglected, as Congress

*Theodore R. Marmor and Martin Rein*

established a work-incentives program to help mothers on welfare become self-supporting through job training. The service and incentive strategies were to reinforce each other.

Congress once again extended the range of services for which it would match state payments. It lost heart in the contribution of social work services as means to reduce the rolls but kept its faith in prevention and rehabilitation. States were required, for example, to offer voluntary birth control information in the hope that such a measure would decrease the future growth of the program. The federal government would also reimburse states for 80 percent of their expenditures on job training and day care up to a maximum federal contribution of $130 million and $35 million, respectively. Day-care funding was increased from $10 million per year to support both the incentive and administrative strategies: day care, if available, would aid mothers seeking work or training; at the same time, it would enable states to require mothers of preschool children to accept these child-care arrangements and find jobs.

The 1967 legislation also called for new restrictive features. It required compulsory work-training programs for AFDC mothers and older children out of school. Those judged able to work or qualified for training were required to accept jobs (if any were available) or placement in the Work Incentives program (WIN). Welfare authorities were given power to withhold payments from AFDC heads who refused work or training. These compulsory work requirements were the result of congressional frustration over the failure of services and the inability of welfare administrators to reduce welfare rolls. Intent and practice diverged, however, as voluntary requests for training under the Work Incentives program exceeded the available supply and compulsion became unnecessary.

In addition, the law established a freeze on welfare expenditures. The freeze limited federal support for recipients eligible through family breakup to those in the AFDC case-load in the first quarter of 1968. This policy was designed to encourage states to develop manpower and service programs — that is, to take positive action to reduce their AFDC case-loads. But the freeze never went into effect. The Internal Revenue Service was required to give the states information that would help locate fathers who had deserted their families.

*Nixon's Alternative: 1969.* For all the discussion of welfare reform during the 1960s, a very limited pair of alternatives was considered by the Nixon administration in the first half of 1969. The Republican party was far more expert at complaint than solution in public welfare. The experts who dominated the design of alternate programs were disproportionately Democrats, which helped assure continuity with past perspectives. The result was consideration of two plans, initially within HEW, and then within the White House, the Urban Council, and finally the Cabinet.

One proposal — the product of a postcampaign task force headed by the assistant director of the Bureau of the Budget, Richard Nathan — concentrated on the interstate inequities in the treatment of current welfare recipients. The Nathan task force argued in January 1969 that to reduce disparities of welfare payments in different parts of the nation and thereby relieve the economic motive to migrate, the federal government should require all states to pay at least $40 per person per month, and then itself provide three-fourths of that federal minimum and half of the next $40. The Nathan plan also suggested that AFDC–UP be made mandatory in all states, and that the most "deserving poor" — the blind, disabled, and aged — be incorporated into the social insurance system with increased benefits. None of these proposals dealt with the inequities between the welfare and working poor; indeed, it exacerbated those inequities. Consider the effect of the $40 per capita reform in Mississippi. A mother with three children would get $1,920 annually and under the 1967 AFDC rules could keep $574 if she earned $1,000 annually. Her total income from earnings and welfare would be $2,494, an amount substantially higher than many workingmen could command in Mississippi.*

Concern about this inequity dominated the other major alternative available to the Nixon administration, one developed within the office of the HEW secretary but shaped primarily by hold-over bureaucrats from the Johnson administration who for years had been pressing for sweeping welfare reform. These officials, within both HEW and OEO, seized upon the Nathan task force's failure to deal with the working poor and thus deal with the increasingly black composition of the AFDC program. They recommended reforming welfare by extending it, and extending it by applying the principles of negative income taxation to a group among the poor excluded from federal public assistance: working poor (largely white) families with children. It was in the clash over these two proposals that the Nixon administration developed the Family Assistance Plan, a program for the working poor combined with other proposals to make the existing adult programs less inequitable and more adequate. Both proposals represent an attempt to extend the income and incentive strategy and to deemphasize services and administrative approaches to containing the welfare case-loads.


Nixon's Choice

The full explanation of the Nixon decision to assist the working poor is impossible without attention to the details of bureaucratic bargaining, chance, and the needs of a new president to establish his identity with reform initiatives. Accident played a role. The Nixon administration did not have an

---

* This example is drawn from Joel F. Handler, *Reforming the Poor* (New York: Basic Books, 1972), p. 75.

*Theodore R. Marmor and Martin Rein*

entourage of new appointees within HEW to evaluate the Nathan task force plan. Instead, in the transition period of January and February 1969, HEW Secretary Robert Finch* relied on economists he inherited from the Johnson administration (and soon lost), and they trotted out their favored negative income tax ideas. Within the White House, Daniel Patrick Moynihan, the lone Democrat among the president's staff advisers, favored breaking up the AFDC program and assisting the working poor.

Moynihan, an influential supporter of the Family Assistance Plan, had been predominantly identified with efforts to introduce universal child allowances as a partial remedy to the ills of AFDC. "The family allowance," he wrote in 1968, "would seem an ideal solution [for] problems of social welfare." As "a system for redistributing income in such a way as to benefit the child-rearing" population, it would appear as a unifying program at a time when "race relations and the mounting radicalism on both the left and right" made income-conditioned proposals seem so divisive. He went on to suggest a program paying $8 per month for children under six and $12 for those between six and seventeen at an estimated net cost of some $9 billion. The estimated cost placed this plan far beyond the $2 billion to $3 billion cost constraint which the Nixon administration used in considering welfare reforms. For that reason alone, this alternative was never seriously discussed within the Nixon administration. Moreover, the goal of moderating racial antagonism was served by FAP's coverage of the working poor, which meant that family assistance programs would not continue to be more than half black. Fifty percent of current AFDC recipients were nonwhite, while about 70 percent of the working poor were white. The income-conditioning of the grant did not prevent Moynihan from becoming one of the FAP's most vocal advocates; FAP became for him an income-conditioned family allowance. He viewed the reform as a sharp discontinuity with the past, for to him the essence of the new scheme, whatever its protective rhetoric, was a guaranteed income for all families with children. No one in the administration, he argued, took seriously the incentive features, nor did anyone believe that the program would in the end reduce welfare rolls or cost. (Moynihan's interpretation of Nixon's reform was and continues to be disputed and controversial.)

That the framework of Nixon's reconsideration of welfare policy was dominated by constraints of cost and past failures is perhaps self-evident to those who accept an incremental approach to policy development. The question was not what would a reasonable welfare-reform plan cost (problem-

---

* Later, the dispute over the possible appointment of Dr. John Knowles as HEW's assistant secretary for health gave President Nixon reason to give special weight to the policy preferences of Secretary Finch. Finch's staff developed the alternative to the Nathan plan and, when Finch's choice of Knowles was publicly repudiated by President Nixon in an embarrassing episode, the choice of the Family Assistance Plan soon followed. But these important details on why a particular combination emerged can be separated from the reasons which explain the programmatic features of the plan Finch, among others, advocated.

solving without constraints), but what kind of welfare reform was possible within a ceiling then defined as between $2 billion and $3 billion. What changes might be introduced that would reduce the inequities and inadequacies of the present system and yet gain substantial political support? The origins of this budget constraint are not clear, but its impact was evident in program design.

The other important constraint was the necessity of radically changing the AFDC program, or at least appearing to do so. This was of urgent concern because of congressional action taken earlier to curb the size and cost of welfare. States were obliged to accept a work-incentive plan which would raise the earnings level for AFDC eligibility and consequently increase the number of future beneficiaries. These amendments, which went into effect in July 1969, gave urgency to the AFDC reform in early 1969.

The Nixon administration responded to the problems of welfare within the limits of these constraints. The choices made represented "trade-offs" among competing goals of improved adequacy, increased work incentives, wider coverage, fairer and less demeaning administration, and others. The welfare-reform plan's principal provisions could be thought of as a series of answers to questions about what sacrifices in one area were worth what gains in another, given the two constraints — to limit costs to about $2 billion and reform the structure of the AFDC program. They represented as well a continuity with past objectives (cutting welfare rolls and costs) and past strategies (incentives, services, and administrative requirements).

## The Provisions of FAP: A Political Account

The Nixon Family Assistance Plan constituted a low-benefit negative income tax for families with children. Its coverage excluded childless couples and the single poor, and its guarantee level ($1,600 per year for a family of four) was 45 percent of the official social security poverty line. The plan would not reduce benefit levels for the first $720 of earnings, and thereafter all work and nonwork income was subject to a 50 percent tax rate. Disregarding food stamps, taxing benefits at a zero and then at a 50 percent tax rate creates a point where all benefits fall to zero at earnings of $3,920. (This is referred to as the break-even point.)

The plan was manifestly an attempt to make public assistance more acceptable by extending to the families of the poor transfers once reserved for fatherless families and, in half the states, families with an unemployed parent. But why, it may be asked, were benefits restricted to families with children? Why was the $500 per year per adult guaranteed income floor not provided for all citizens? One interpretation is that the problem to which the Nixon administration addressed itself was the crisis of public dependency, not poverty. Where poverty has been the focus — as with the Kerner Commission

*Theodore R. Marmor and Martin Rein*

(1968) and the President's Commission on Income Maintenance Programs (1969) — universal coverage for all the poor was proposed.

The problem of encouraging work was, as in the past, dealt with in two ways: through positive incentive and negative sanctions. The usual method of determining benefits in welfare systems is to discover the difference between available income and some accepted definition of need. As income increases, benefits are reduced by an equal amount. This procedure creates a 100 percent tax on earned and unearned income; beneficiaries are no better off for working until their earnings or benefits exceed the need level. It has the obvious advantage of distributing benefits only to those who fall below the level of need and of reducing the additional costs which such allocations must require. In the new plan an incentive to work was added: the first $720 of earned income was exempt from reductions as a special incentive to begin earning. This extended the break-even point from $3,200 to $3,920.

Only eight states paid benefits below FAP's $1,600 federal minimum. These states could under the Nixon proposals have completely discontinued their AFDC program and had the new federally financed program cover complete costs. But forty-two states would have been required to supplement families above the minimum floor. What earnings-disregard and tax rates would apply to these supplementary benefits? States would be required to exclude the first $720 a year of earnings, but they could subtract as much as 17¢ for each dollar of wages above this level. The net effect of this dual system of tax rates on both the federal minimum and the state supplement was to raise the effective tax rate on total earnings above $720 but below $3,920 to about 67 percent, or a rate roughly equivalent to the work-incentive provisions of the 1967 AFDC law.

The Family Assistance Plan stressed negative sanctions as well as positive incentives. In drawing them up the administration ignored the very preliminary results of a graduated work-incentive experiment in New Jersey, sponsored by the government and administered by Mathematica Inc. and the Institute for Research on Poverty at the University of Wisconsin. A report of their early findings stated:

> Payment levels have been remarkably stable over the course of the experiment, and earned income has risen at approximately the same rate for both experimental and control families, apparently reflecting the general rise in wage rates. Both of these measures, then, indicate no perceptible reduction in work effort as a result of the transfers.

Thus the decision to require work and training tests was not supported by the best information then available, but rather by the belief that in order to win political support for FAP, the administration had to include in it sanctions as well as incentives.

The Nixon proposal included the requirement that unemployed Family

Assistance Plan recipients accept "suitable" work or training or the fourth person's allowance ($300) would be deducted from the grant. The work and training test must be seen as part of the strategy of increasing the political acceptability of the Nixon plan, especially to the chairman of the House Committee on Ways and Means, Wilbur Mills (D., Ark.).

Public opinion polls have shown that overwhelming majorities of Americans support guaranteed employment plans, but guaranteed income has not commanded majority approval in any national polls. It was not surprising, therefore, that HEW Secretary Finch insisted in his explanation of the Family Assistance Plan that it "does not guarantee benefits to persons regardless of their attitudes; its support is reserved to those who are willing to support themselves." In fact the Nixon program was a guaranteed income plan, since failure to comply with the work test would result in a denial of only one family member's share of the guarantee.

The emphasis on work and work training made it difficult to limit program costs, at least in the short run. Training and child care are expensive; child care alone was more costly than the basic guarantee of $1,600 per year for a family of four people. The plan sought a compromise by providing $600 million for the training program, which at the most could reach 150,000 welfare parents and provide child-care services for about 450,000 of their children. To have provided training and child care for all eligible poor families would have meant totally abandoning the $3 billion cost constraint. Of the anticipated 9 million adults eligible for the new program (leaving aside for the moment their 16 million children), 1.1 million were able-bodied adults who would have been required to register for work or training. In addition, there were 1.8 million family heads already at work full-time. The House Ways and Means Committee modified the administration's bill by requiring that the working poor had to register for work or training. Available training and child-care facilities fell short of the anticipated needs. The insistence on compelling recipients to accept work or training increasingly appeared a gesture.

The low benefit level itself, 45 percent of the accepted poverty line, was also part of a work-incentive strategy. The lower the basic income support, the more powerful the incentive to seek supplementary income.

The totally federal financing of the new category of assistance served a variety of political purposes. It would have raised benefits for present AFDC recipients in eight states, almost all in the South. Any federally financed program of poverty amelioriation involved such regional redistribution of income because 40 percent of the poor were in the South and they constituted the worst off. But raising the benefit levels of public assistance in the South was directed at supposed problems of migration rather than income redistribution. Setting a federal payments floor would, in the words of a White House staff report, "have [had] the effect of inhibiting out-migration of the poorest blacks and whites from the South."

*Theodore R. Marmor and Martin Rein*

## Apparent Contradictions and Anomalies

Even the most cursory review of the main provisions of the Nixon proposal suggests some apparent contradictions. It was hoped, for example, to reduce costs by expanding them dramatically in the short term; the program primarily provided aid to southern communities, while northern states experienced the worst financial crisis; it provided an income guarantee to families with children (only the breadwinner's grant could be eliminated if he refused to work or accept training), while it was characterized as a work program.

Although FAP sought to reduce inequities between the working and welfare poor, the constraints of cost and the problems of overlap between the AFDC supplementary program and FAP created new inequities. Medicaid treatment was not available for the working poor nor were the states required to supplement these benefit levels, but supplementation of the present AFDC program was mandatory when state levels were higher than the FAP minimum. Moreover the definition of "suitable work" was likely to vary in different regions, because it would be responsive to political pressure and to professional discretion. Thus regional inequities reinforced categorized inequities. Finally, there was a large "baby bonus" built into the program, creating an inequity between the childless couple and the family with children. This meant a couple without earnings could have received $1,300 with the birth of their first child.

More intractable problems were inherent in the strategy to use low marginal tax rates to encourage work, relieve distress, and reduce the fiscal burdens of states and localities. For example, the more adequate the basic allowance at which economic insufficiency is met, the more demanding the task of encouraging self-sufficiency. Again, the more attractive the incentives (the proportion of benefits retained as earnings rise), the steeper the cost and the larger the program. How were these conflicts to be resolved?

These contradictions help in understanding the nature of the Family Assistance Plan because they reveal the priority of problems towards which the program was directed. Clearly, the desire to increase work incentives, to reduce the fiscal burden of states, to discourage migration and to compel people to work as a condition of eligibility appeared as the central themes. These features helped make the program politically acceptable to Republicans whose support for the Nixon bill was a necessary condition for its congressional enactment.

More important, these contradictions illustrate the different sources of political support for one or another feature of the proposal. The plan appealed to social work professionals who favored more impersonal, more universal, and more humane income maintenance policies. They opposed the work test because it required substantial administrative discretion and contributed to stigmatizing applicants, but they were attracted to other features which promised greater fairness and more sensible incentives. Reform Democrats who desired income redistribution supported FAP insofar as it would increase resources for some of the poorest groups and, by covering the working poor and male-headed households, would reduce the incentives for family dissolution. They worried less about work incentives but accepted the work and training test as a trade for other desired benefits.

Republican conservatives celebrated the work requirements and took seriously the promise of future reductions in the cost of welfare. They assumed present recipients would increasingly depend upon the labor market and not on the benefit structure for income maintenance, and saw employment as a substitute for cash transfers which would acquire a more residual role.

State governors and city mayors were attracted to the program's promise of reducing their fiscal burdens. Urban-industrial states were disturbed that FAP promised so little relief. The strength of this pressure group was demonstrated as Congress modified the bill in its favor. (House Ways and Means Committee changes in 1970 increased fiscal relief for the higher-benefit states; the House-passed bill provided that 30 percent of the state expenditures between the federal guarantee and the poverty line of $3,500 would be financed by the federal government.)

Through all the debates, the one element of enduring consensus was the call for state fiscal relief from the burden of welfare expenditures (the states then paid an average 50 percent of the costs of welfare).* The Nixon administration took up this banner in the beginning and conceded further relief as the states insisted that the federal government assume some of the costs above the basic federal payment of $2,400 per year for a family of four. In addition, when the states complained in 1969 that a federal freeze on payments for new AFDC families would bankrupt them, the Ways and Means Committee relented, under pressure, and removed the freeze.

Many business leaders who had long demanded a more efficient welfare system supported FAP as a first, yet inadequate step. They doubted whether the economic system could by itself provide adequate income for low-wage earners with large families and hence they hesitantly accepted the necessity of a system of wage supplementation.

Finally, the president, apart from the substantive justifications for changing public assistance, found welfare reform one prominent area in which the Republican party could take positive initiative in domestic policy without being open to the charge they were expropriating old Democratic reforms. The president could assume a posture of decisive leadership through the proposal of dramatic structural reform, not tinkering with the present system.

*Summary.* The conflicts between fundamental reform and cost constraints, between the will to change and the requirement of keeping bipar-

---

* Under H.R. 1, 30 percent of the increased $6.1 billion in federal costs was allocated for state and local savings, according to the estimates of the Urban Institute's Jodie Allen in 1970.

*Theodore R. Marmor and Martin Rein*

tisan supporters, were not candidly and openly admitted. Four programmatic goals came into sharp conflict — adequate relief in distress; effective (perhaps punitive) work incentives; substantial state and local financial relief; and reduced federal cost over the long run. The efforts to harmonize these objectives proved unworkable, and the problems raised were not clearly delineated. They were patched over, and the patchiness was revealed as special-interest groups reviewed with the Congress one or another program feature. The patching arose from Nixon's attempt to win support from conflicting groups, which pressed contradictory criticisms of welfare. As long as policy discussion focused on the "need" to structurally "reform" welfare, the underlying incompatibilities within the Nixon plan could be avoided. But, in the end, the bid for political support from ideologically antagonistic sides exacted its price: after a promising beginning, legislative stalemate ensued.

### FAP's Fate: 1969–72

The introduction of the Republican initiative had proceeded from a simple but impressive political strategy: steal the liberals' thunder by introducing a Republican version of negative income taxation (few enemies to the left); impose claims of party loyalty to win Republican votes in the Congress; throw sops to the right-wing conservatives with slogans like "from welfare to workfare"; wrap it all up in the liberal reform rhetoric of the past decade, concentrating on what's wrong with welfare; and leave difficult choices and administrative problems to technicians or later discussion.

*Becoming Unstuck.* The strategy almost worked in FAP's first congressional review. Sixty-seven percent of those Americans polled after President Nixon's August 1969 speech approved of the Family Assistance Plan. The normally conservative House Ways and Means Committee steered the bill easily through the House of Representatives in 1970, adding restrictive frills to dress up the package for conservative approbation.

Only in the Senate did this lightly glued welfare-reform package come apart. In the summer of 1970, the groups that had for conflicting reasons coalesced behind FAP discovered how much they disagreed with one another. Within the Senate Finance Committee liberals flayed the bill as inadequate and inhumane, using as their standard a generous income guarantee which the majority of American voters would surely have rejected. The conservative senators on the committee, led by the soon-to-retire Republican John J. Williams of Delaware, devastated FAP's pretension to consistent welfare reform. They dissected the process of compromise by which conflicting program features were fused and structural reform frustrated. "Work incentives?" exclaimed Senator Williams, "what work incentives?" And he proceeded to show the administration how FAP, when joined to other means-tested programs like public housing and Medicaid, subjected beneficiaries to marginal tax rates greater than 100 percent. "How to be on the breadline and pay surtax as well," was the way one English critic lampooned such perverse work incentives.

The outcome in the summer of 1970 was FAP's humiliating defeat. The Senate Finance Committee rejected the House-passed bill (H.R. 16311) and even refused to "experiment" with alternative negative income tax schemes. What *The Economist* termed the "most significant policy proposal since the 1930s" had become an embarrassing and frustrating defeat for the Republican administration and its welfare-reform allies. But at least the process of criticism had been comprehensible, so that if the Senate criticisms were met by a new bill, a reassembled liberal-conservative coalition might emerge in 1971.

*The Debacle of 1971.* The hope for a victorious coalition in 1971 proved fruitless. A new bill — H.R. 1 — was introduced, but both the administration and the chief House actor, Wilbur Mills (chairman of Ways and Means), tried to mold the coalition by continual compromise, not thorough revision. But standard compromising tactics fail when ideological principles are at stake, and the 1971 bill was only a slightly altered replica of its ill-fated predecessor.

The 1971 modified version of FAP was introduced by the House Ways and Means Committee, placed first on the congressional agenda, and, like its predecessor, passed the House. It increased the guaranteed level from $1,600 to $2,400, raised the marginal tax rate from 50 to 67 percent, established a fixed amount for work-related expenses and eliminated the earlier practice of paying social security and income taxes for welfare recipients who obtained employment.

The Ways and Means Committee, irate over the past reluctance of HEW and state welfare departments to implement the work-requirement provisions, in 1971 insisted that families with different employment possibilities be administered separately. An employable adult member, according to H.R. 1, made a family eligible for the Department of Labor program, Opportunities for Families (OFF). The AFDC program (at least for families with children under six) would be in a new division of HEW and renamed the Family Assistance Program (FAP). Ironically, the complaint that fragmented local-state-federal administration had bedeviled the past was now met with new fragmented federal arrangements as proposed in H.R. 1:* FAP-OFF.

The result was a repeat of the 1970 experience. In June 1971, the House

---

* It may seem unbelievable (besides the pun), but the Department of Labor was planning a contract with HEW for cash payments to the employables under the OFF program. This splintering of responsibilities between HEW and DOL left unanswered the question of how persons would move between unemployable (FAP) and employable (OFF) categories when their status changed (for example, the birth of a child). The pursuit of simplicity thus conflicted with the desire to categorize finely the poor for different treatment with respect to work.

*Theodore R. Marmor and Martin Rein*

of Representatives passed the welfare-reform bill, but by a narrow margin, and even that victory had required the most extraordinary efforts of Mills. The House Rules Committee — reflecting conservative opposition — took the unprecedented step of permitting floor amendments to a bill passed by Ways and Means. Chairman Mills himself came before the House to plead that it not amend the bill his committee had reported. He claimed an amendment would shatter the intricately balanced committee product and frustrate any reform of the acknowledged welfare "mess." Mills went on to chastise the congressional black caucus for demanding less punitive and therefore less popular welfare-reform provisions. He criticized others for insisting the plan be made even harsher than it was. Most of all, Mills fumed at the challenge to his leadership and to the tradition by which the Committee on Ways and Means works out compromises on controversial legislation which the House then routinely approves.

One of the bill's major problems arose, as we have seen, from the attempt to solve a long-standing anomaly in the American welfare system: the welfare poor have often been better off financially than the working poor. Hence Nixon's initial proposal to expand the welfare system to include the working poor. Yet to do so, to raise the income guarantee and to maintain the same tax rates as proposed in FAP, required extraordinarily large budgetary outlays. As Republican Senator Curtis (Neb.) pointed out during the 1971 hearings, a third of America's families would receive welfare payments by 1977 if the guarantee suggested by Senator Ribicoff ($3,000 per year) were enacted into law. Work incentives, equitable coverage, adequate income guarantees, and low governmental costs could not (and cannot) be combined as a welfare package.

The Senate response repeated that of 1970 and for much the same reasons. To make individuals better off when at work, Nixon urged modifying the requirement that all cash recipients had an automatic passport to Medicaid, America's means-tested health program for the poor. The administration called for a new medical deductible scheme. The scheme would work as follows: one-third of earnings which a family retained above $720 would become the Medicaid deductible, i.e., the amount of medical costs per year the family had to cover before the federal government subsidized medical care. Assume a family had a $600 medical bill. On that assumption, the family would not be entitled to any subsidized medical care until its earnings equaled or exceeded $2,520. Such a scheme would leave present welfare recipients less well off than under the Medicaid program in force in 1970, in which poor families received free medical care until their earnings made them ineligible for welfare. This anomaly resulted from the effort to reduce the value of the welfare medical insurance as income rose. (Present recipients with some other income would receive less than the full Medicaid subsidy while at the same time no one would suddenly lose full medical benefits because of earning an extra dollar. The solution to this latter problem (the "notch") required graded benefits in health. Graded benefits meant less benefits if eligibility was not to be massively expanded.) The efforts to eliminate the anomalies of FAP simply created new anomalies in H.R. 1.

While the Ways and Means Committee followed the norm of compromise, the Senate Finance Committee gave play to divisive ideological conflict. Its liberals, typified by Democrat Fred Harris of Oklahoma, insisted that welfare reform be generous and humane. The Committee's conservatives, led by Chairman Russell Long (D., La.) and including southern Democrats and Republicans, insisted that reform "tighten up" welfare and keep in check those Long called "the black brood mares of AFDC." In the middle, senators like Abraham Ribicoff (D., Conn.) remained committed to help those on welfare. Anxious to avoid the punitive programs pushed by a Long, they also worried that the result of too generous a bill would be no action at all. The differences in the micropolitics of committee consideration were of great consequence, but did not arise from different views on welfare. Rather, the traditions of committee management of conflict — controlled in Ways and Means, freewheeling in Senate Finance — determined the opposite responses to the same bill.

Action in 1971 was indeed minimal. The welfare-reform bill as a whole flopped. During the crowded pre-Christmas schedule the Senate grafted onto existing welfare programs some of the "workfare" features of the larger Nixon plan, such as amendments by Senator Talmadge (D., Ga.), which made registration at state employment offices a mandatory qualification for AFDC recipients. Such changes would have little substantive effect but presumably much political appeal.

*Reform in 1972: "Reform is dead, but who killed it?"* The frustrations of backers of President Nixon's welfare reform were if anything heightened during the first nine months of 1972. "Welfare reform," reported Wilbur Mills in a *New York Times* interview in mid-September 1972, "is dead as a doornail." He warned, with respect to 1973, that "I don't want to ask the House to go through this a third time without some assurance the Senate will act."

The Senate had not acted because no clear majority had emerged for any of the three versions of welfare reform before it. The Senate Finance Committee rejected overwhelmingly both Nixon's H.R. 1 plan and the more generous version which Senator Abraham Ribicoff had offered for administration backing. Instead, what *New York Times* columnist Tom Wicker called the "Scrooge-like" Senate Finance Committee had added to the omnibus social security bill a "guaranteed employment program" which, in Wicker's words, "virtually abolished welfare as such and would force family heads to work at substandard wages, and would set up a Federal Employment Corporation to provide jobs at $48 a week for those who could not find them elsewhere." Only mothers attending school full-time or with children under six would be exempt from the "must work" requirements. Thus 1.2 million of the estimated 3 million female heads of families would automatically be dropped

*Theodore R. Marmor and Martin Rein*

from the welfare rolls and required to work. Three types of benefits would be provided. A federal employment corporation would be created to develop guaranteed jobs for those unable to find work in the private sector. The "make work" jobs would pay $1.50 per hour or $2,400 per year for thirty-two hours of work per week. Those working at the minimum wage would get a wage bonus equal to 10 percent of the wages covered under social security, with a maximum of $400. Those working below the minimum wage would get a federal wage supplement equal to three-quarters of the difference between the actual wage paid and $2 per hour. In addition to requiring work, the bill penalized states that failed to set up adequate birth control programs and authorized $800 million a year for child care and day-care centers for children of working mothers. The work-relief projects of 1962 were reviewed on a grand scale and introduced as the central principle of more coherent legislation committed to work incentives.

Unlikely to win Senate acceptance, the Long plan had sufficient support to preclude a majority for either the administration or the Ribicoff alternative. Within the Finance Committee there was the predictable reluctance of small-state, rural, western and southern senators to reform welfare by making it more generous and equitable. Not one of the major welfare states — New York, California, or Illinois — had a senator on the committee. The composition of the committee, shown below, made plain why even the pleas for state fiscal relief fell on deaf ears.

*Members of the Senate Finance Committee: 1971–72*

| *Democrats* | *Republicans* |
| --- | --- |
| Clinton Anderson, New Mexico | Wallace Bennett, Utah |
| Herman Talmadge, Georgia | Carl Curtis, Nebraska |
| Vance Hartke, Indiana | Jack Miller, Iowa |
| J. W. Fulbright, Arkansas | Len Jordan, Idaho |
| Abraham Ribicoff, Connecticut | Paul Fannin, Arizona |
| Fred Harris, Oklahoma | Clifford Hansen, Wyoming |
| Harry Byrd Jr., Virginia | Robert Griffin, Michigan |
| Gaylord Nelson, Wisconsin | |

Within the Senate itself a small, bipartisan liberal minority followed Ribicoff in insisting on a set of amendments to H.R. 1 designed both to undo some of the worst features of Nixon's bill (stiffened work requirements, invasion of civil liberties of recipients, an increased bureaucratic complexity) and to raise the basic minimum guarantee to $3,000 for a family of four. With only some thirty backers, the Ribicoff amendments were doomed to failure on the Senate floor. The H.R. 1 plan thus fell between critics who charged it with excessive generosity and those who condemned it for insufficient humaneness. With the 1972 election imminent, moderate Democrats had partisan as well as policy reasons for not wanting to let President Nixon win on his much-vaunted, much-criticized scheme for "cleaning up the welfare mess." What was FAP's flop in 1969 became H.R. 1's failure as well in the 1971–72 period.

The details of welfare reform's demise were worked out during the first two weeks of October 1972. First, the Senate consecutively rejected the three possibilities that the Senate Finance Committee had considered. The committee's own proposal — the Long "workfare" scheme — never had a chance. Senator Ribicoff introduced a more modest version of his alternative — with the guaranteed level of $2,600 per year that he had advocated in the spring — but lost on a 34–52 vote. The closest vote came on an amendment by Democratic Senator Stevenson of Illinois. By a vote of 44 to 41, the Senate tabled his amendment, which would have made the Nixon plan of $2,400 a universal one — an attempt to bridge the gap between the financial provisions of the administration plan and the eligibility desires of the Ribicoff scheme. In the end, the Senate proposed "experimenting" with these alternatives and in the meantime transferring the deserving adult programs (aged, blind, and disabled) to the Social Security Administration. On October 16, the House-Senate conference committee completed its work on H.R. 1. Only the transfer of the adult programs to social security survived this final review. Welfare reform was dead. Testing of alternatives was dropped. The euphoria of 1969 had given way to almost complete stalemate despite the constant refrain that the present welfare system was a "hopeless mess."

## Concluding Observations

This essay has developed two quite different themes: the political stalemate which characterizes America's efforts to enact welfare reform and the anomalies and conflicts that are expressed in the reform plan itself. The connection between the two is political and causal: the underlying incompatibilities were accepted to avoid political stalemate. In 1970 there was a period when such a weakened program appeared close to enactment. As time passed, the forces which united tenuously behind a compromise welfare plan discovered their differences more clearly. The story shifted from agreement over the crisis in welfare to disagreement about a sensible remedy. Congressional actions in 1972 did not resolve these disputes; they revealed them. What President Nixon had termed "the most important single piece of social legislation in decades" died in 1972, in part a victim of the president's unwillingness to compromise with the bipartisan group of Senate liberals led by Ribicoff.

What can one learn from this complex happening, enthusiastic presidential endorsement of reform and three years of frustrating struggle in the Congress? The first point is that no overarching explanation will make sense of the complex events of the 1969–72 period. The reasons which led President Nixon to propose welfare reform cannot account for its fate in either the House or the Senate. We need to ask (1) why the president decided to urge an innovation in welfare policy, (2) why his FAP scheme was acceptable to the House Committee on Ways and Means and the House of Representatives, and (3) why the Senate Finance Committee rejected "liberal" reform and the Senate all versions of reform in 1972.

President Nixon's decision to propose the Family Assistance Plan proceeded from the initial assumption that "tinkering with the present welfare system" would not control its rapidly growing costs. Some of his advisers persuaded him that considerations of fairness and adequacy demanded a clear break with the New Deal's legacy of categorical assistance. In this, President Nixon may well have been bolstered by the appeals of his urban expert, Daniel Patrick Moynihan, to act in the image of such English Tories as Disraeli by furthering liberal ideals of social amelioration. What is more, the amelioration Moynihan and others urged had the glamour of efficiency. The idea of a negative income tax had been urged by economists of all political persuasions and had gained the support of many business leaders, including such prestigious organizations as the Committee on Economic Development. All these claims had easier access to a president at the beginning of his term, when the White House was not yet so shielded from departmental entreaties by a practiced staff. Finally, the fact that Congress would be compelled to take up welfare changes in 1969 lent urgency to the president's need to propose a defensible change in the much-maligned present system.

The decisions in the House of Representatives depended partly on this new executive resolve. The Ways and Means Committee faced the choice of supporting (not necessarily approving) the president's bill or not. Two political factors combined to make that support sufficient. The Republicans, led by Congressman John Byrnes of Wisconsin, have traditionally stuck together and had additional party reasons for following the lead of the president. Chairman Mills, able to count on Republican support, easily formed a winning coalition when he became convinced FAP made sense. The tradition of Ways and Means is consensual; with a majority of its members for FAP, the committee devoted its efforts to making the bill palatable to the House as a whole.

Once reported favorably by Ways and Means, FAP's acceptance by the House was almost a foregone conclusion in 1970. The House typically endorses the suggestions of Ways and Means; an extraordinarily active opposition would have been required to repudiate the committee's work, and the committee would not have reported a bill had that opposition been evident. FAP's support by Ways and Means, not the arguments for and against welfare reform, was decisive for purposes of subsequent House endorsement.

No such traditions mark the relationship between the Senate Finance Committee and its parent body. The committee suggestions have less binding power than those of Ways and Means. But, equally important, the committee itself had less reason to respond favorably to a fairer and more generous welfare system. Urban representation on the committee was, as noted, weak.

The ideological divisions within the committee polarized the question of FAP as approval for the principle of a guaranteed annual income. Viewed in this way, the debate opened to the adequacy and legitimacy of the plan, not simply whether FAP was an improvement over the present welfare system. Three contending blocs emerged, each short of a majority within the Senate: those condemning the president's plan as too generous, those willing to support it, and those attacking its shortcomings and punitive rhetoric. Only the most extraordinary efforts by Nixon could have drawn together the latter two groups and that, as we saw in 1972, was not forthcoming.

Welfare reform in the United States is many issues, not one. Politically, it presents many "faces" to a confused and largely unsympathetic public. The strongest constituency for reform is the states and localities, but their interest is fiscal relief, not alleviation of poverty (except that of their treasuries). Other interest groups compete with one another to define the issue of reform in favorable terms. But no version could avoid stalemate within the micropolitics of the American Congress. Without a mass constituency committed to amelioration, the despised welfare population and the working poor now have punishment more than stalemate to fear.

## SOURCES AND READINGS

This policy study drew upon a wide variety of sources in interpreting the character and fate of welfare reform: congressional hearings and interviews, newspaper and journal accounts, scholarly and popular articles, and a variety of books and interviews with government officials. The sources cited below are a small sample of those consulted, but ones the interested student might pursue with substantial benefit.

For information on American poverty and alternative income maintenance plans, the most helpful source remains the three volumes published by the President's Commission on Income Maintenance Programs. Published by the Government Printing Office in 1970, they include the Commission report (vol. I), *Poverty amid Plenty*, the *Background Papers* (vol. II) on the variety of government programs dispensing income in cash or in kind, and a compilation of *Technical Studies* (vol. III) which include scholarly articles on special topics such as welfare and work, trends in state and local government support of welfare programs, and comparisons of income maintenance program experience abroad. A particularly helpful summary of the pre-1968 critique of public assistance is Daniel P. Moynihan, "Crises in Welfare," *The Public Interest* (Winter, 1968), pp. 3–29. For a

fuller presentation of the authors' views on welfare, income mainte-
nance, and public policy choice, see Martin Rein, *Social Policy:
Issues of Choice and Change* (New York: Random House, 1970) and
Theodore R. Marmor (ed.), *Poverty Policy* (New York: Aldine-
Atherton, 1970). For the history of public assistance experience, we
relied heavily on Gilbert Y. Steiner, *Social Insecurity* (Chicago: Rand
McNally, 1966.)

Congressional hearings provided us extensive information on welfare proposals, pressure groups' views, and congressional responses,
but they represent a formidable and sometimes indigestible array of
facts, opinions, and arguments. The House Ways and Means Committee published hearings and reports in 1970, 1971, and 1972; the
Senate Finance Committee published hearings in the same years, but
a committee report in 1972 only. As a guide to congressional deliberations, the reader might consult the *Congressional Quarterly*'s review
of welfare reform's fate in October of 1972: "Social Security Increases; No Welfare Reform," October 21, 1972 (vol. XXX, no. 43),
pp. 2765ff. For House action in 1972, see the essay in the *National
Journal*, "Administration-Senate Rifts Endanger Welfare Reform
Bill," June 10, 1972 (vol. 4, no. 24). An earlier *National Journal*
article reviews the first congressional response to the Family Assistance Plan (December 6, 1970, vol. 2, no. 49).

For weekly coverage of welfare reform we relied on reports of the
*New York Times* and the *Washington Post*. The *Times'* index, *Weekly
Reports*, permits readers to use that source conveniently.

No book has yet been published which covers the whole of the welfare reform effort in President Nixon's first term. There are two works
now available, however, that offer sharply contrasting perspectives on
welfare reform. Joel Handler, *Reforming the Poor* (New York: Basic
Books, 1972) is critical of the extent to which reform plans perpetu-
ate and in some instances extend the discretion and uncertainties of
traditional welfare administration. Whereas that study emphasizes the
punitive rhetoric that came to surround FAP and H.R. 1, Gilbert
Steiner's *The State of Welfare* (Washington, D.C.: The Brookings
Institution, 1971) concentrates on the central role of the presidency in
proposing FAP and making it a legislative possibility. It offers a
better guide to why welfare reform got as far as it did than why it
ended in legislative stalemate. Steiner's book is highly useful on the
details of public assistance, housing, and veterans' programs and is to
date the most extensive scholarly explication of the origins and early
history of FAP. Readers will have to wait for the forthcoming study
by Daniel P. Moynihan for an insider's account of welfare reform's
fate.

By 1972 congressional disputes over welfare reform gave substantial
attention to the administrative dilemmas that arise in trying to make

welfare more efficient, more equitable, and more work oriented. These administrative issues are the main concern of a continuing congressional investigation by the Subcommittee on Fiscal Policy of the Joint Economic Committee; the subcommittee has already published extensive hearings from its field visits, a handbook describing the rules of operation of public income transfer programs, and will finish its report by June 1973.

# STUDY TWO

# THE PRESIDENT

The options before Congress. Some useful perspectives
on the problem. *Little reliance on the intent of the
Framers. Indirect election methods must distort the
counting of the popular vote. A large scope of analysis. Election methods are not neutral in effects. The
play of interests. The burden of proof.* Choosing among
relevant criteria. *The winning candidate should have
the most popular votes. The winning candidate should
have a minimum level of vote support. Protecting and
promoting two-partyism. Maintaining checks and balances. Reflecting federalism? Political feasibility.* Evaluating the present system. *Why the electoral vote
distorts the popular vote. Relative advantage. The politics of relative advantage. Majority, plurality, and
nonplurality presidents. Two-partyism and third parties.* The district plan. The proportional plan. Direct
popular election. *Congress's growing receptivity to
altering EC and to E. A redistribution of relative advantage. The 40 percent minimum support level. The
contingency procedure. The runoff and third parties.
Alternatives to the runoff election.* Congress disposes.
*Pre-1969 momentum. President Nixon intervenes. The
House acts. Getting E to the Senate floor. The Senate
blocks reform. Analyzing the votes.* Concluding observations. Sources and readings.

# Basic Change Aborted: The Failure to Secure Direct Popular Election of the President, 1969–70

*Allan P. Sindler*

A constitutional amendment replacing the electoral college method of electing the president by direct popular election overwhelmingly passed the House in 1969 but foundered the next year on a filibuster in the Senate. Despite near-unanimous support for reform of the present method, two-thirds support in the Senate for any specific reform was not forthcoming. The legislative mood and quandary were aptly summed up by Congressman William McCulloch (R., Ohio) at the House Judiciary Committee hearings in 1969: "The disease is clear, the remedy is not."

This analytic case study concentrates both on major problems of presidential election methods and on the strategy and politics of the 1969–70 controversy. Some readers initially may view the first emphasis as quixotic. Given the populistic and equalitarian spirit of our times, how much more need be said than that the president should be directly elected by the people?

That a great deal more can and should be said is the premise of this study. The first step in grappling with the complex subject of electoral reform is to shed intuitive notions that it is a nonproblem with but a single, simple answer.

### The Options Before Congress

Basically five options faced the Congress — and confront the reader:

1. *Retention of the present electoral college system (EC).* Each state is awarded a number of electoral votes equal to its combined U.S. House and Senate representation. Citizens vote within states for electors morally obligated to vote for designated presidential candidates. The electors of the candidate who has the most popular votes in the state cast all the electoral votes of the state for that candidate (the state-unit rule). The candidate who wins a majority of the total electoral votes is declared the president. If none so qualify, contingency procedures mandate the U.S. House to select the president by majority vote from among the top three candidates, with each state having an equal vote.

2. *Automatic plan (AP).* The office of elector would be eliminated, but the present electoral system of allocating and casting votes would be retained. The contingency arrangements would be altered to provide for a joint session of Congress, with each member having one vote, to select by majority vote one of the top two candidates as president. The state-unit rule would be fixed in the Constitution, instead of leaving it to the discretionary authority of each state as under the present system.

3. *District plan (DP).* Each state would establish as many electoral districts as it had U.S. House districts. Each district would cast one electoral vote for the presidential candidate with the most popular votes in that district. Each state additionally was assigned two electoral votes to be awarded, in the manner of EC, to the statewide popular vote leader. The proportion of the total electoral vote required to win varied in different versions of the plan from 40 percent to a majority. The first two features of AP, cited above, were incorporated into DP.

4. *Proportional plan (PP).* Each presidential candidate would receive the same share of the state's electoral vote as he had of the state's popular vote. The proportion of the total electoral vote required to win varied in different versions of the plan from 40 percent to a majority. The first two features of AP, cited above, were incorporated into PP.

5. *Direct popular election (E).* The present system would be eliminated entirely. The candidate with the most popular votes would win, provided he secured at least 40 percent of the total vote. The contingency procedures initially involved Congress and were identical with those of the AP, cited above, but then were changed to provide for a runoff election between the top two candidates.

Two of these reform themes represented long overdue "housekeeping amendments" of EC so widely endorsed that they may be disposed of at the outset.* The Constitution's grant of full voting discretion to electors was clearly incompatible with their changed function. If electors merely registered the popular-vote verdict, as they should, then who needed them? And if electors chose to depart from that verdict, as they should not, then who could tolerate them? Never a serious problem historically, it became salient to Congress in the 1960s because southern third-party activity had produced unpledged electors and an occasional "faithless" elector. The obvious remedy was to eliminate the post or, if it were kept to provide ceremonial party rewards or to discourage third parties by complicating access to the ballot, to mandate electors to vote for the presidential candidate of their party. All four reform plans cited above chose the first alternative.

The second noncontroversial correction ended the provision for state voting equality in the House when selecting the president. All reforms diluted its underlying federative principle by infusion of the population principle. The major reform plans except the later version of E (direct popular election) provided for a joint session of Congress, with each member having one vote. The inclusion of Senate members was intended, presumably, to sweeten the kitty for less-populated states whose power would be greatly reduced by the change.

Notwithstanding broad support for these two moderate reforms on their merits, including the backing of EC's supporters, strategic considerations precluded their passage as a separate constitutional amendment. Lesser reform was viewed as the enemy of greater reform. Rather than support AP, reformers embedded the two revisions under discussion in their own respective plans. Effectively, then, four basic alternatives were up for resolution. Congress's failure to settle on one or a variation of them reflected a division of views which, it is assumed, has its counterpart among readers of this study. There were differences on perspectives and criteria for electoral change, on values, on interests, and on estimates of the effects of institutional revision. Dissecting these disagreements provides not only an explanation of what happened in Congress but also the information needed for the reader to come to an informed personal judgment on how best to elect the president.


Some Useful Perspectives on the Problem

*Little Reliance on the Intent of the Framers.* Promoters of major institutional change are often handicapped by having to justify deviation from the intent of the Framers. Likewise, defenders of the status quo still

---

* Others in this category not mentioned here include new provisions to cover the death or disability of the winning presidential candidate prior to his inauguration and to run a presidential candidate and his affiliate on a joint ticket.

criticism by riding the coattails of those who fashioned the Constitution. Controversy over presidential election methods differs because EC has never operated as the Framers planned. The story should be familiar enough to permit summary treatment here.

The early rise of parties and partisanship thoroughly changed EC's operation, though not its form. Electors became merely agents of the authority designating them, whether state legislature or voters. By the 1830s each state's exclusive authority to determine how to distribute its electoral vote became hollow. The dynamics of the state-unit (or general-ticket or winner-take-all) device, whereby all the state's electoral votes went to the popular-vote leader, coerced all states to adopt that method. That change in turn regularly gave an electoral majority to a candidate, negating the expectations of many Framers that the House, voting by state equality, ordinarily would have to select the president from among the candidates who led in the election. A similar turnabout occurred on the Framers' tidy plan for the selection of the vice president. The intention to award that post to the major losing presidential candidate, rather than to have a direct contest for it, was rudely undercut when partisan electors distinguished sharply between candidates for the two offices. This new practice required formal change by means of the Twelfth Amendment in 1804. Overall, the politicization of EC greatly modified its indirect character, though it remained significantly different from direct popular election.

*Indirect Election Methods Must Distort the Counting of the Popular Vote.* Newcomers to the subject of electoral reform often are morally outraged upon learning that EC distorts the counting of the popular vote. They seem to have assumed that EC should reproduce faithfully the underlying popular-vote division. Yet what would be the point of restating popular-vote distributions by another measure which exactly mirrors the initial figures? Take a two-candidate race, for example, in which the vote split 40 million to 30 million. Why devise a system in which, say, 2 million votes equaled 1 VM ("vote mass"), and then go on to report the election results as 20 VM to 15 VM? Similarly, when electoral- and popular-vote divisions differ, some popular votes in effect must count differently from others, i.e., some degree of vote inequality must exist. These characteristics are not peculiar to EC, but attach to any indirect election method, such as PP or DP.

*A Large Scope of Analysis.* Any and all indirect election methods are rejected by some precisely because they inaccurately translate the underlying popular-vote divisions. This study's perspective differs by recognizing that other significant political questions are involved. The presidency is the preeminent national political institution, and the way the president is elected helps determine his legitimacy, leadership, power, and policy directions, as well as his relations with other governmental officers and levels.

Further, the election method has consequences for the separation of powers, federalism, the party system, voter behavior, and the like. Only a wide-ranging inquiry, then, can answer how best to design the method of electing the president.

*Election Methods Are Not Neutral in Effects.*    A broad inquiry is required because choosing among alternative election methods is not a technical matter of institutional tinkering, essentially neutral in its larger implications. Quite the contrary. Election methods differ in the values they stress, how they distribute power, what interests they advantage and disadvantage, and how well they satisfy diverse criteria. The problem of retaining, modifying, or supplanting EC should not be cast in terms of "bias versus neutrality," but rather of weighing combinations of different biases.

*The Play of Interests.*    Since the subject of election methods is profoundly political, not primarily technical, its determination in good part by the customary play of political interests should be expected. Doubtless a concern for democratic norms per se and for "what's best for the nation" should be present and influential within the Congress. But it should neither surprise nor dismay that the reaction of legislators was often grounded on calculations of constituency and interest advantage.

Such interests are all too often derogatorily labeled as parochial motivations. Yet they are, after all, what fuels political conflict and resolution in a representative democracy. Further, is there, as the disdain for the play of parochial interests implies, an external, objective and independent standard which unambiguously defines for all "the one best election method" for president? The boundaries of what we call "democracy" seem to be broad enough to accommodate many kinds of institutional arrangements. Should, for example, city council elections be based on at-large or ward districts? Should the U.S. House be elected by proportional representation? Should the U.S. form of government be cabinet-parliamentary rather than a separation of powers? The expectation that reactions to these questions will be animated by considerations of political advantage should apply to our subject as well.

*The Burden of Proof.*    The standard posture of lawmakers, as of most of us, is "why change?" rather than "why not change?" The more extensive the proposed change, the greater the burden of proof on its advocates, especially when it takes the form of an amendment to the Constitution. As Richard N. Goodwin, a high aide in the Democratic administrations of the 1960s who opposed E, put it:

> . . . the single most important rule of constitutional amendment: if something is working, don't change it. We have never before amended the Constitution in anticipation of possible abuse or on the basis of

abstract theory. Only after an abuse has manifested itself, and usually after considerable public pressure, have we acted, and even then with reluctance.

In Viscount Falkland's well-turned phrase, endorsed by young Senator John F. Kennedy (D., Mass.) in a Senate speech in 1956 against replacing EC by PP: "When it is not necessary to change, it is necessary not to change."

Despite these attitudinal barriers to major institutional change, the EC proved a pushover to attack. Six conservative members of the Senate Judiciary Committee who opposed E complained in their 1970 minority report that E's spokesmen were simply selling the virtues of their reform as against others, and neglecting to demonstrate the need for extensive reform in the first place. As a result, they grumped, the customary perspective had been reversed, saddling the opponents of E with the burden of proof. Their resentment was understandable, their reasoning a bit off the mark. It was not that the proponents of change failed to make a case against EC but that the case was made so easily and was so readily and widely accepted.

The remaining half of a change strategy requires agreement on a specific revision. That attempt would have been foreclosed to E's backers had they been required to meet the stringent standard of proof advanced by the six conservative senators:

> It is not enough to demonstrate that direct election will probably be an improvement. It must be shown beyond all reasonable doubt that the adverse consequences which are predicted by many . . . will not occur.

Few legislators subscribed to so rigorous a view, except perhaps to apply it to plans they opposed while exempting their own proposals from its reach. Not many more were willing to accept the challenge of conducting the widest possible analysis of impact implicit in Professor Charles Black's sobering judgment that

> . . . a case can be made for the proposition that direct election, if it passes, will be the most deeply radical amendment which has ever entered the Constitution of the United States.

Congress's scope of debate on electoral reform in 1969–70 went well beyond the mechanics of vote-counting alternatives to deal with important implications for the political system. But the quality of its debate varied greatly and, overall, it fell notably short of the thorough examination called for by Black's proposition. This was partly due to the ambiguities inherent in the subject matter, which made impossible any strict application of agreed-on rules of analysis, evidence, or proof. Most of the arguments turned not on the

*Allan P. Sindler*

actual record of performance of EC — which was not at all bad — but on the more speculative matters of what else could have happened in past elections and what could happen in future elections. Then, too, some of the key causal relationships, such as the effects of election method on party system and vice versa, remained in dispute among political scientists and other analysts, permitting or compelling legislators to rely on their own estimates.

Readers of this study are not likely to be different from legislators in this regard; each person must judge the relevance and persuasiveness of the varied arguments to his or her own satisfaction. A few broad guidelines can be suggested, on the understanding that they, like any other position advanced by the writer here, are not exempt from evaluation by the reader.

*Guideline 1.* Heavy but not controlling weight should be given to EC's actual record of performance.

*Guideline 2.* There is no way to demonstrate whether and how past elections would have been changed had different counting formulas been used. Such an attempt typically takes the votes as cast under EC and refigures them by another formula. The implicit assumption that "all other things would have remained the same" is grossly inappropriate for the study of alternative presidential election methods. The "evidence" obtained by this procedure is suggestive and far better than nothing, but it does not "demonstrate" anything.

*Guideline 3.* Little to no reliance should be placed on do-it-yourself constructions which purport to show the maximum distortions an election method could theoretically permit. One example, for EC, could construct an electoral majority from a slim minority vote by having a candidate carry a dozen large states by plurality and gaining virtually no votes in the rest of the nation. Another example, for E, could construct a sectionalized popular plurality by having a candidate win 90 percent of the votes of some areas but tiny proportions of the vote elsewhere.

Such constructions are not only sterile in their neglect of the realities of political behavior but they also miss the key point that any electoral system which often operated in those ways would not have been tolerated for long. Consider, by analogy, our election of U.S. Congressmen by the method of single-member districts and plurality votes. That method could result in one party capturing all the seats in the House on the basis of a bare majority or even plurality of the popular vote in each district, leaving the rest of the nation (ranging from 49 percent-plus to a large majority) completely unrepresented. There is not much clamor, however, to junk a method capable of producing such unpalatable results precisely because those results have not occurred. And if they were to occur, can there be much doubt that the method would be abandoned? It seems only fair and sensible to apply the same perspective to analysis of EC and its alternative reforms.

## Choosing Among Relevant Criteria

The quarrel over electoral reform often turned on the disputants' use of different criteria or of shared criteria weighted differently. Disagreement derived from the inability of any one election device to satisfy uniformly all criteria, some of which are competitive. Other conflict involved participants who agreed on the importance of a particular criterion, but not on the conclusions to be drawn from its application to the same data. Hence this study's early and careful review of some relevant criteria seems appropriate.

*The Winning Candidate Should Have the Most Popular Votes.* This core democratic standard is intimately associated with the norms of vote equality and majority/plurality rule, and with public acceptance of the election's legitimacy and the winner's mandate to govern. Popular attachment to this standard lies at the heart of the disaffection from EC and the appeal of E. No indirect election method can guarantee meeting this standard; only E can.

The wide effects of an election method on the political system argue against sanctifying this or any other single standard as the sole commandment. Its importance merits giving it a preferred spot, but as the first commandment in the company of others. An indirect election method should not be automatically rejected, but initially reviewed to determine how seriously it violates the criterion under discussion. If the popular-vote decision has been frequently overturned in all categories of elections, including lopsided contests, the election method should be promptly disapproved. However, if the popular verdict was almost always confirmed and the exceptions were very close elections, that should satisfy the key criterion enough to justify a full analysis involving many other criteria. Acceptance of this position involves substantial agreement with Professor Alexander Bickel's argument, with respect to presidential elections closely divided in popular vote, that

> . . . only an immensely dogmatic majoritarianism would insist that the so-called winner has *the sole legitimate claim to office.* In truth, there is a stand-off, and the question is merely of a convenient device — any convenient device previously agreed on — for letting one of two men govern. [Emphasis added.]

The ultimate assessment made of an election method, based on application of diverse criteria, should continue to recognize the special, though not exclusive, standing of the key criterion. Thus E's satisfaction of the first commandment gives it an important edge over indirect election methods, requiring a finding of other grave defects for E or of markedly superior other advantages for an indirect method to permit final rejection of E.

*Allan P. Sindler*

*The Winning Candidate Should Have a Minimum Level of Vote Support.* The preceding key criterion sanctions simple plurality victory. But many legislators were uneasy about accepting so slack a standard for the highest office in the land, even though it was used for the election of most public officials, congressmen and senators included. Should a three-party contest develop, the leading candidate might have as little as 35 percent of the vote, or less than 30 percent in a four-way race. Would not such low support jeopardize the legitimacy of the outcome and the president's capacity to govern? Yet remedying that difficulty inescapably raised other serious problems.

Once a candidate was required to have a minimum percentage of the total vote to win, contingency procedures had to be devised and might come into play. This raised the possibility of a complicated two-stage election sequence which might leave the nation in doubt for weeks as to the final result. And what kind of contingency procedure should be used? A runoff election between the two top contenders might encourage a multiplicity of parties or candidates to enter the initial contest. Selection by the Congress, on the other hand, hardly squared with the key criterion. Conflict on this point, indexing concern for criteria other than the key principle of E, contributed to the defeat of E in the Senate.

*Protecting and Promoting Two-Partyism.* To many legislators the preservation and enhancement of the two-party system constituted a criterion as or more compelling than the standard of a popular-vote plurality just discussed. Acknowledging the depth of that concern, E's spokesmen took pains to give the two criteria equal weight. Senator Howard Baker (R., Tenn.) asserted:

> . . . if I thought for one moment that such a proposal [E] would disrupt the basic tenets of the two-party system, I would not propose it, because I believe the two-party system in the American format is one of the things that has made our great experiment in democracy what it amounts to today.

Senator Birch Bayh (D., Ind.) went a step further:

> . . . it was not until I had become convinced that the two-party system would not only not be destroyed, but rather strengthened, . . . that I changed my mind to [support] popular vote.

Most legislators gave a somewhat elastic meaning to "a two-party system." Senator James Eastland (D., Miss.), no foe of southern-based third parties, candidly urged:

> I do not see anything holy in the two-party system. Now, three parties,

yes. I would say that what we have to keep away from is a multitude of small parties.

Eastland expressed a view widely held; most congressmen as a matter of sound public policy preferred that the system remain open to occasional serious third-party movements. (Did not the Republican party itself originate as a third party?) Besides, there were constitutional constraints precluding the granting of a statutory monopoly of presidential politics to the two major parties and freezing all others out.* What Congress wished to avoid, therefore, was an election structure which would give strong incentives to persistent multipartyism.

A number of senators did not share the conviction of Bayh and Baker that E safeguarded the two-party system. Some who were friends of E proposed ways to decrease what they believed was its undue encouragement of multipartyism. Others, opponents of E in any event, applied the same argument to demonstrate that E had special disadvantageous effects. The Senate filibuster precludes knowing how the Senate would have handled E substantively, but it is a good bet that E would have been modified to satisfy better the criterion under discussion.

The two-party criterion generates related important standards which, though frequently applied in the debates, were somewhat lower in priority for most legislators. For example, it was deemed desirable that an election system promote party competition both at national and state levels, in association with geographically widespread campaigning and high voter turnout. The election method, most believed, should move candidates to seek broadly based vote support cutting across regions and classes rather than consolidating them into separate and opposed blocs.

*Maintaining Checks and Balances.* In spite of the closeness of the subject of presidential election methods to that of the separation of powers and of the checks and balances among political institutions which implement that separation, Congress never really came to grips with the connection. Of the two linkages that were made, one was pressed but feebly and the other was converted into an entirely different issue of fairness and equity.

The maintenance of different and independent electoral bases for president and Congress is usually considered indispensable to the separation of powers. Of the options before Congress, only DP was open to serious doubt on this score. (Under DP, the electoral districts and the House districts were virtually certain to be identical.) Yet though DP emerged as the major reform alternative to E, no emphasis was given to this concern.

---

* These limits include the First Amendment guarantee of the right of effective political association and the prohibition of unreasonable discrimination among voters or candidates under the equal protection clause of the Fourteenth Amendment. State regulation of party often discriminates against third parties, whether intentionally or otherwise; some of these biases may become vulnerable to litigation.

*Allan P. Sindler*

The other linkage, which led some liberals to support retention of EC, updated an argument liberals had unapologetically and successfully used in 1956 to oppose the displacement of EC by PP. Its touchstone was Senator John F. Kennedy's speech in that year which insisted that EC should not be evaluated in isolation but as part of the "whole solar system," i.e., as part of the larger political system. "If it is proposed to change the balance of power of one of the elements of the solar system," he stated, "it is necessary to consider the others." Applying the point, Kennedy urged that EC's biases favoring populous and industrialized states were justified as a counterweight to the inflation of nonurban and conservative influence through legislative malapportionment, state equality in the Senate, the seniority rule in legislative operations, etc. Called by some a "doctrine of countervailing inequity," this position sought to maintain checks and balances among diverse and often divergent constituencies and interests.

The willingness of liberals to endorse the argument anew plummeted in the late 1960s. The position taken in 1969 by three liberal organizations, each of which experienced severe internal disagreement on endorsing EC or E, was instructive. The American Civil Liberties Union came out strongly for E. The NAACP endorsed E in principle, but held out for effective protection for blacks to register and vote: ". . . we would be better off with the present system until we can be sure that everybody can vote."* Only the American Jewish Congress (AJC) supported EC, and on the "countervailing inequity" thesis that "megalopolis will be hurt . . . by direct popular election." But when the AJC spokesman testified before the Senate subcommittee, he admitted his embarrassment as a liberal in opposing E and readily agreed that E was the "most democratic method of electing the president." However, until the presently imperfect political system implemented the "one man, one vote" principle throughout, the AJC was opposed to applying that desirable norm just to the election of the president.

The shift of liberal outlook was explainable by the transformation of context. The E plan was not politically feasible in 1956, but it was the leading reform in 1969. And the argument in question, as our later analysis will show, was better directed against PP, which would favor nonurban interests more than E would. Since 1956 the civil rights movement, the pursuit of political equality and public concern with the representativeness of the political process, had flourished. Liberal organizations were among the leaders in securing national civil rights legislation and landmark court rulings on race and legislative apportionment and in endorsing the "one man, one vote" standard. The discomfiture of urban liberals at the thought of opposing E was thus understandable; it would surely be taken as a crassly opportunistic stand. Congressman Allard Lowenstein (D., N.Y.), a "new politics" leader who had initiated the "dump Johnson" movement in the last year of LBJ's term and

---

* Two of the nine black Congressmen opposed E's passage in 1969.

who was a strong backer of E, laced into his fellow liberals on just that point:

> . . . many of those who oppose the direct election of the President place themselves in an extraordinary posture. The most sophisticated of them continue to try to cloak their opposition in democratic rhetoric, to base their support for the electoral college on an elaborate hypothesis about delicate balances and countervailing powers. But if they are really concerned about the strengthening and extension of the democratic process — perhaps even in the halls of Congress itself — they can hardly add to their credentials or the force of their argument by seeking to preserve archaic subterfuges when it comes to filling the most important office of all. The sacrifice of the basic principles exemplified in, and best served by, popular election is ill balanced by speculative conjectures about which group, or bloc, or point of view might profit the most from such a denial.

Yet what were the chances, after all, that effort to correct all inequities (as defined by liberals) throughout the system would succeed? Professor James M. Burns has forcefully argued that even if all political mechanisms were reformed as liberals desired and all interests attained equal influence as veto groups, "a fundamental bias against egalitarian government would remain." "In politics," Burns urges, "the sum of the [localistic] parts does not necessarily equal the whole [a national outlook]." The moral for Burns is that "to fragmentize is to conservatize." Since the American commitment to the values of localism and fragmented authority shows little sign of abating, an attempt to sustain offsetting inequities may well be — contrary to Lowenstein's strictures — both practically sound and morally justified.

Whatever the judgment of the position under discussion, its unpopularity with Congress in 1969–70 was all too evident. The reluctance of populous states to push this self-defensive argument reflected and contributed to their willingness to support E. With the large states behind E, the concern of E's backers was to attract enough support among small states and the South in the Senate to assure passage by two-thirds vote.

*Reflecting Federalism?* An election method reflecting federalism must incorporate states as essential voting units, and hence violation of the criterion that "the candidate with the most popular votes should win" may occur. Because the logic of E could not accommodate federalism (and vice versa), E's spokesmen rejected the relevance of federalistic criteria. E's opponents, on the other hand, naturally emphasized their relevance, hoping thereby to gain support for a standard which E by definition could not satisfy. More accurately, it was anti-E conservatives who played this strategy; the relatively few liberals who preferred EC to E had no interest in E's indifference to federalism. The AJC spokesman earlier cited, for example, explicitly disavowed concern with federalism on this issue, even though his large-state

*Allan P. Sindler*

argument logically had to rest ultimately on a federalistic rationale. Conservatives, by contrast, harped on the need for a federal structure of presidential elections and then promoted those kinds of indirect methods favoring the small states and the South (DP and PP). None went so far, however, as the representative of a World War I veterans' organization who urged the House Judiciary Committee to adopt a "one state, one vote" formula!

Denying that the original EC was an integral part of the overall federal compromise, E's supporters characterized it as an "afterthought" late in the Constitutional Convention which, anyway, had never worked as the Framers intended. Federalism's viability was held to relate to the Senate and to many other political and constitutional protections, not to the convoluted procedures of EC. The president and vice president had become the only truly national officials; their constituency was the people of the nation and not the aggregate of state electorates. It followed, according to this thesis, that those officials should be elected by direct popular vote of the people.

E's conservative critics read constitutional history differently and assigned EC to a prominent place in the pantheon of federalism. The presidency, properly understood, was a federal official: ". . . from the standpoint of just using a little English language," asserted Senator Sam Ervin (D., N.C.), "the President is the President of the United States, not of the people." The EC, according to the conservatives, obviously contributed to the viability of federalism. Equally obviously, the E reform would eliminate the federal aspect of presidential elections, and they opposed that transformation.

E was seen by conservatives as expressing an unqualified majoritarianism detrimental to the values of sectional balance, policy moderation and interest diversity. Insisted Senator Strom Thurmond (R., S.C.):

> . . . I had rather see a President who has received a good vote from a lot of the States than to see a President who received a large vote in a few States elected as President of the United States.

Further, urged the conservatives, the professed support of the principle of federalism by E's backers held no reassurance because the logic of their position was profoundly hostile to federalism. The 1970 minority report of the Senate Judiciary Committee, referred to earlier, pointedly asserted:

> If one day, someone comes forward to say that it is surely an absurdity to give New York and Hawaii equal representation in the Senate, that a recent computer study has conclusively demonstrated that a citizen of New York is disfranchised 33 times relative to a citizen of Hawaii, and that, in so important a matter as the passage of national legislation this is tantamount to a denial of equal protection of the laws — when that day comes, what argument can the proponents of direct election make to defend State equality in the Senate?

The conservatives sensed that direct election of the president would promote his moral and political leadership role, doubtless at the expense of the influence of Congress. One likely result would be the strengthening of national government policy initiatives, an outcome hardly pleasing to conservatives. As Roger Fleming of the American Farm Bureau Federation commented in testimony before the Senate subcommittee in 1969:

> . . . we [AFBF] have a conviction that a direct presidential election is more consistent with the idea of centralization than with the idea of diffusion of power and decentralization, and therefore we are for an alternative to that.

Whatever the validity of their other fears, conservatives were justifiably sure that the adoption of E implied a larger if not exclusive role for the national government in the whole process of voter registration requirements, access to the ballot by candidates, voting procedures, honest elections, recount procedures, etc. An outright nationalization of the registration and voting process might occur or, at the least, the national government would have to standardize and monitor state performance on these matters. Indeed, some liberal backers of E had already proposed and spoken for increasing Congress's authority in this area; only the concern of E's managers not to alienate moderates explained its exclusion from the terms of E. The South was especially smarting and resentful on the topic because of national civil rights legislation which had fallen with special force on that region. The debates in the *Congressional Record* include several comments by southerners that illiterates were allowed by national law to register to vote in Mississippi while the authority of New York and other nonsouthern states to bar that category from registering remained unimpaired.

*Political Feasibility.*   A pronounced concern with "what could be passed" pervaded Congress's handling of electoral reform, especially in light of the hundreds of failures over the past century to amend or displace EC. Senator Bayh, chairman of the Subcommittee on Constitutional Amendments of the Judiciary Committee, put this reality principle well at the outset of his subcommittee's hearings in 1969:

> Our responsibility in this committee, and particularly mine as chairman, is really twofold. One is to try to determine, after sorting out all the evidence, which plan we believe would do the best job of electing our President, and two, to try to see if we can pass this. If we cannot pass the best, then what is our fallback position, our second best? Hopefully we will be able to get the best.

For reasons to be discussed later in this study, E's prospects had never been brighter than in 1969–70. Championed by Emanuel Celler (D., N.Y.)

in the House and by Bayh in the Senate, it was the front-runner reform throughout the two-year period of congressional consideration. The feasibility of its passage by Congress was greater than that of any other plan, though still very much a gamble. Opinion polls showed lopsided public support for E, surveys of state legislators indicated its chances of state ratification were excellent, and an unusually diverse and strong combination of interest groups backed its enactment. If it failed, likely no reform would occur, except perhaps a considerably modified E or PP.

Initially more congressmen preferred E than were willing to vote for it because of fear that E could not survive the ratification gauntlet in the state legislatures. President Nixon gave credence to that estimate in an early 1969 statement indicating that he preferred E but, on grounds of political feasibility, he would be willing to settle for some variation of PP. The margin of House support for E, which was passed 338–70, convinced many, including the president, that E was politically feasible. By the time of the Senate filibuster there remained few legislators who, though preferring E, supported something else on the grounds that E had little chance to pass the Senate or the state ratification process. The failing vote on cloture rested basically, then, on substantive opposition to E in whole or in serious part by a sizable minority.

### Evaluating the Present System

*Why the Electoral Vote Distorts the Popular Vote.* As an indirect election, EC distorts the counting of the popular vote. Like PP and part of DP, it counts the vote as a synthesis of separate and final state choices between competing candidates, and translates those results into 538 electoral votes by some formula. Several distinct features give rise to significant distortion of the popular vote.*

1.  102 electoral votes (19 percent) are allocated to the states to reflect equal Senate representation, without regard to population. Almost two-thirds of the states deviate by more than 10 percent from the national average ratio of electoral votes to population of 1:333,000. Twenty-four less-populated states have better ratios by this measure, ranging from Alaska's 1:75,000 to Arkansas' 1:298,000. Only eight states, all with large populations, have clearly worse ratios than the average, ranging from Massachusetts' 1:368,000 to California's 1:393,000.
2.  By the state-unit procedure, the totality of a state's electoral vote is cast for the candidate with a plurality of its popular vote, i.e., as if the state

* Since Congress handled electoral reform in 1969–70, this study makes use of 1960 census data. The District of Columbia, with three electoral votes, began voting in presidential elections in 1964; when included in the analysis it is treated as a state, making a total of 51.

were unanimous in its choice. The distortion thus is greatest for states with close election outcomes and with large numbers of electoral votes.

3.  Each state casts its full quota of electoral votes without regard to its voter turnout rate. In the 1964 election, with a national turnout rate of 62 percent, forty-one states deviated by more than 10 percent. By this measure, eighteen states (including all eleven southern states) had low turnout and twenty-three states had high turnout. The range of turnout varied from Utah's 79 percent to Mississippi's 33 percent.

*Relative Advantage.* The first distortion favors low-population states; the second favors populous states with competitive elections. Thus, altogether different sets of states profit from each bias. While low-turnout states are benefited by the third distortion, turnout rate is not consistently related to population size: seven of the ten least-populated states and four of the eight most-populous states were in the top half of turnout rate in 1964. The location of southern states at the low end of the turnout scale provides the most politically significant datum. Our analysis may conveniently concentrate on distortions 1 and 2 which, unlike the turnout factor, deal centrally with relative state power, with the allocation of electoral votes to, and the casting of them by, the states. Further, when the states are ranked by population per electoral vote (distortion 1) the addition of the variable state turnout factor produces only minor modification, giving assurance that our relative neglect of distortion 3 will not unduly skew the analysis.

That distortion 1 enhanced the relative power of small-population states was obvious; that was, after all, part of the Framers' purpose in designing the cumbersome EC. Moreover, it was easy to manipulate the arithmetic on paper to illustrate how extreme the bias could be. For example, a dozen of the least-populated states, taken together, might cast only 40 percent of New York's popular vote, but they collectively disposed of the same number of electoral votes as New York (43). From arguments like these, advanced by many, some indeed concluded that the EC built in important special protection for small states.

But the prevailing practices of presidential nominations and campaigns suggested opposite conclusions. Disproportionate attention was given to "pivotal" states with respect to the state residence of nominees, policies, pressure group interests, the sites of campaign efforts and candidate visits, etc. "Pivotal" meant states characterized by large populations, many electoral votes, and competitive election outcomes, i.e., the beneficiaries of distortion 2.* The thesis of large-state dominance of presidential elections should not be overdrawn; candidates sought support in more than a handful of key states and those states were seldom unified in their presidential preference in close

---

* In the summer and early fall of 1972, the mass media emphasized that the campaign strategy of Democratic presidential candidate George McGovern, who lagged well behind Nixon in the national opinion polls, was to try for an electoral vote majority by concentrating on carrying the "pivotal" states.

*Allan P. Sindler*

elections. But it seems fair to conclude that distortion 2 — the state-unit rule — partially explained such diverse phenomena as:

1. The declining influence of the Democratic South within the national Democratic party. The region's delivery of 120-plus electoral votes was no longer critical to national Democratic victory, which could rest on nonsouthern support. Franklin Roosevelt would have won each of his four elections even if every southern electoral vote had gone to the Republicans in the 1932–44 elections.
2. The increasing attention paid by both parties to the aspirations of blacks, especially as they shifted residence from rural South to urban North.
3. The Republican tendency to choose a presidential nominee more "liberal" than the policy outlook characteristic of that party's congressional wing (Goldwater and 1964 excepted, but as the kind of exception that proves the rule).
4. The disproportion of twentieth-century presidential candidates, when governorships were the typical recruitment source, from the states of New York and Ohio.

All these patterns, to reemphasize, were bottomed at least partly on the state-unit rule of EC.

Which of EC's two divergent biases was predominant? Debates over electoral reform typically disputed the matter, and often somewhat inconsistently.* At the congressional hearings in 1969–70, the research of a young reform-minded lawyer, John F. Banzhaf, offered systematic theoretical evidence on the issue for the first time. Although based on mathematical formulations applied through computer simulation, which doubtless reduced its comprehendability and persuasiveness for many, it proved an influential new addition to the debate and helped promote the cause of E. The mathematical analysis purportedly demonstrated that the disadvantage to politically uncertain states of large population of having less electoral votes per unit of population was more than offset by their ability to affect the disposition of a large block of electoral votes. To be sure, a voting bloc had a lesser chance of casting a decisive vote in a large than a small state. But if it did cast the decisive vote, its impact — in terms of the large number of electoral votes affected and of the possible effect of that large number on the national outcome — would be exponentially greater in the populous state. In sum, asserted this theory, politically competitive populous states were the chief beneficiaries of the EC's biases. This conclusion was of high use, for obvious reasons, to E's managers who were anxious to persuade small states that a shift from EC to E would be to their advantage.

---

* A not uncommon argument combined the assertions that EC unduly favored populous states and that small states would oppose abandoning EC for E.

*The Politics of Relative Advantage.* EC's sharply divergent distortions provide a major key to understanding the strategy and politics of the electoral reform controversy of 1969–70. By favoring and disadvantaging different interests, the distortions logically opened up three broad options. Two of them involved retention of an indirect election, with one inflating large-state influence and the other of benefit to small states. The third option sought to eliminate both biases by substituting direct popular election — a solution which had its own biases.

Had each legislator decided among the options on the basis of parochial constituency interests, congressional deadlock would surely have resulted. The hope of securing two-thirds support derived from E's appeal to many congressmen on grounds other than narrow constituency advantage. Large-state legislators thus tended to support E rather than EC, and many small-state legislators endorsed E rather than EC, DP, or PP. Still, however muted, the force of constituency interests was not eliminated. Ultimately, enough senators who saw their state's interests as opposed to E acted on that perception and brought electoral reform to a halt.

EC had few public friends because southern and small-state spokesmen attacked the state-unit rule, E's proponents repudiated on principle all distortions of the popular vote, and large-state legislators found it too awkward to defend the state-unit bias, at least against E. The condemnation of EC's distortion favoring small states was subdued and infrequent as compared to that of the state-unit device, a difference of treatment which reflected political feasibility concerns, i.e., the need for small-state support for E's enactment by Congress and ratification by the states. Though dovetailing in their common discrediting of EC, the different indictments provoked incompatible remedies. Southern and small-state interests, for example, could see great advantage to knocking out the state-unit rule and keeping distortion 1 — which is precisely what DP and PP proposed to do. J. Banks Young of the National Cotton Council put this line of argument well:

> . . . we do not favor the district plan exclusively over the proportional plan. We would take either one. We think it is extremely important that we have a maintenance of the electoral vote system, the union of States concept, and eliminate as much as possible the winner-take-all influence, and avoid the concept of the direct election, the national, no union of States, elimination of the small State ballots that we have in counting the electoral vote and counting the two Senators.

Given its low turnout rate, the South feared for its relative influence under E, in which turnout counted. And the small states, with their tiny populations, wondered whether they would fare any better under E. Maybe the EC also worked to the relative neglect of small states, but what about the following unsettling "hard data" comparison? Each of the fifteen small states with three or four electoral votes cast 0.006 or 0.007 of the total electoral vote, but had only from 0.001 to 0.005 of the total population.

The broad strategy of E's advocates was to play the biases of EC against each other in such a way as to promote E. Thus they urged that basic electoral reform should derive from democratic norms free from calculations of advantageous bias. It was stressed to small states that large states dominated EC and that E would result in greater attention by presidential candidates to more diverse populations. Large states were reminded of the small-state bias of distortion 1 and were assured that their concentrations of population guaranteed their importance under E.

E's backers were not talking out of both sides of their mouths but rather adjusting to a situation which required the shading of themes neither fully consistent nor clearly inconsistent. Just as EC was the common target for attack by different interests and criteria, so E was promoted by linking clusters of different arguments to sets of different interests. Just as that strategy had succeeded in discrediting EC, so it was hoped it would succeed in amassing the two-thirds support to enact E.

Central to the strategy of E's backers was the overstated or insufficiently qualified argument that EC sustained large-state domination of presidential elections, implying the exaggeration of liberal influences resident in those states. Important caveats could easily be offered to that thesis: suburban no less than central-city interests were favored; many Democratic urban groups were less than reliably liberal; Nixon's pattern of victory in 1968; etc. But the more the flat assertion of large-state advantage under EC was deemed questionable, the more unlikely the aggregation of two-thirds support for E. Small states needed the assurance that their low influence under E nonetheless bettered their position when compared to the present system. The particular tightrope walked by E's proponents in 1969–70 thus would appear to be the most sensible political strategy generally to pursue on behalf of E.

*Majority, Plurality, and Nonplurality Presidents.* The EC awards victory to the candidate with a majority of electoral votes; presidential winners, therefore, could have a popular majority or plurality or could trail in popular vote. What has been EC's record on relating electoral to popular votes, and especially on nonplurality winners? The twenty-four elections of the last 100 years (1872–1968, excluding the disputed election of 1876) provide the data for the examination that follows.

The record reveals that the electoral-vote distribution between the major-party candidates was typically more lopsided than the popular-vote distribution. Whereas the popular-vote division fell within the 60/40 range in 80 percent of the cases, the electoral-vote division fell outside that range in 72 percent of the cases. On the average, the winner received 52 percent of the popular vote and 71 percent of the electoral vote. By giving the winner the appearance of greater backing, this bias may well strengthen public belief in the president's standing to govern, especially in those instances when he is elected without a popular majority (nine of the twenty-four elections). The same bias also helps assure than the election itself will produce an electoral-vote majority and a president, without need to involve contingency selection procedures.

In fifteen of the twenty-four elections, a candidate got a popular majority; in every case he won the election and with a substantially larger proportion of the electoral vote (79 percent compared to 56.5 percent, averaged, and with more than 60 percent of the electoral vote in every instance). In eight of the remaining nine elections, the candidate with a popular plurality won, averaging 47 percent of the popular vote and getting from 52 to 62 percent of the electoral vote in seven cases, 82 percent in the other (1912). In only one election — 1888 — did a nonplurality candidate gain an electoral major-ity. (Cleveland, with 48.7 percent to Harrison's 47.9 percent, a margin of less than 100,000 votes, got only 42 percent of the electoral vote.) That single exception illustrated the effects of an "inefficient" distribution of the plur-ality candidate's popular votes. Cleveland carried the southern states by large majorities ("wasting" many votes thereby) and lost many key non-southern states narrowly. The EC penalizes such sectionally overconcentrated backing and favors geographically more widespread patterns of support. In-structively, Cleveland made no protest about the legitimacy of the 1888 results and, given the source of Cleveland's national popular vote lead, Har-rison's mandate to govern appeared just as valid.

While the degree of closeness of the winner's popular vote margin was not linked precisely to specific percentages of electoral vote, a gross relationship was persistently evident. The eight elections (excluding 1888) with the closest popular-vote margin of the winner (from 0.1 to 4.5 percent) were also the eight elections with the closest division of electoral vote (from 52 to 62 per-cent for the winner). Of the eight most lopsided elections in popular vote (from 15 to 26 percent margin for the winner), five placed among the eight most extreme divisions of the electoral vote (from 82 to 98 percent for the winner). The other three elections involved Republican winners at times (1904, 1920, 1924) when the South, with almost one-fourth the total electoral votes, was solidly Democratic, which put a ceiling on the proportion of elec-toral votes Republicans could win.

Applying the criterion suggested in the preceding section, EC's track record would have to be judged excellent: a nonplurality president won but once, and then only in the context of a very closely divided popular vote. EC's effective performance in this regard, among others, underlay Profes-sor Clinton Rossiter's words of caution on altering EC:

> . . . we should hesitate a long time before replacing a humpty-dumpty system that works with a neat one that may blow up in our faces. All the arguments for the [EC] system are practical; most of those against it are theoretical.

EC's adversaries came to rather different conclusions by stressing what might have happened in contrast to what had happened. In their view EC's potential for producing nonplurality presidents was dangerously high, especially in elections where the leading candidate had only a popular plurality and/or a relatively small popular vote margin. On the former, they noted that candidates with 45 to 49.9 percent of the popular vote (seventeen of the forty-eight major-party candidates) divided about equally into winners and losers. On the latter, they stressed that the outcome of many elections could have been reversed by relatively small shifts in popular vote in a few close states, including even elections with lopsided electoral vote divisions. (To take a hypothetical example, an electoral vote majority of 351–187 (65 to 35 percent) which included eighty-three from New York and California would be reversed if those two states shifted. In actuality, a shift of New York alone would have reversed the outcome in 1880, 1884, 1888, and 1960; of California alone in 1916.) They noted also that winners with a popular plurality or a close popular-vote margin typically got no more than 60 percent of the electoral vote. The nub of their indictment was that the state-unit rule's practice of awarding all the state's electoral votes to its plurality leader, no matter how thin his vote margin, could not help but produce nonplurality presidents at times. That it had not already done so more often was a function of luck, they asserted, and not due to anything foolproof about EC's design.

Past elections were closely reviewed in support of this thesis. In 1948, for example, a shift of less than 25,000 votes in Illinois and Ohio would have deadlocked EC, and a further shift of less than 10,000 votes in California would have given a slim electoral majority to Dewey — despite Truman's popular vote lead of over 2,000,000. In 1960, a shift of less than 9,000 votes from Kennedy in Illinois and Missouri would have denied him an electoral-vote majority. In 1968's close election, Humphrey would have emerged as a nonplurality president had a total of less than 150,000 votes in four states shifted. In elections as close as 1960 and 1968, statistical analysis indicated that there was almost a 50–50 chance of a nonplurality winner. These and other grim conjectures and reworkings of past election data were apparently sufficiently persuasive to most legislators to discredit EC, notwithstanding its impressive record of election outcomes confirming the popular will.* As Senator Estes Kefauver (D., Tenn.) melodramatically expressed it way back in 1961:

> . . . the electoral college is a loaded pistol pointed at our system of government. Its continued existence is a game of Russian roulette.

---

* EC's detractors conveniently neglected the fact that vote shifts, in the real world, would seldom be confined to one or a few states but would be part of a larger regional or national trend, and hence the national popular-vote division between the major candidates would be changed as well. The critics' central point was best applied, then, to elections with an exceedingly close popular vote nationally and in a number of states.

Once its antiquated procedures trigger a loaded cylinder, it may be too late for the needed corrections.

*Two-Partyism and Third Parties.* The term "third parties" is too often applied as a residual to cover everything outside the two major parties. To be analytically useful, at least the following distinction is required. One type of third party refers to ideological parties outside the mainstream of regular politics which do not seriously pursue power, such as the vegetarian, single-taxers, and socialist labor parties. These so-called parties (more akin to interest groups in many ways), if and when they participate formally in presidential elections, do so to satisfy internal group needs and not to affect the election or the policy stands of the major parties. Hence as long as the election system permits their entry to the ballot, changes in the form of the election method are unlikely to affect the habit of some of these parties to run presidential candidates. The effect of such parties on election outcomes is customarily nil, unless by accident the tiny percentage of votes they attract happens to shift the balance between the major parties in a closely divided state. We may safely ignore this category of third parties in our analysis here.

The other type of third party embraces serious, power-seeking parties which attempt to compete directly with the Democratic and Republican parties, to influence election outcomes or to alter the policy positions of the major parties. Examples include parties of economic protest (Populists), "blackmail," "splinter" or "spoiler" parties of defection from a major party (various southern movements from 1948 on), and balance-of-power state parties (Liberals and Conservatives in New York). In the 1969–70 quarrel over electoral reform, arguments about "third parties" referred primarily and often exclusively to this type of third party which, consequently, is the focus of our analysis.

Serious third-party activity in presidential elections under EC has occurred, but at a level and frequency well short of any reasonable definition of persistent multipartyism. The fact that the record was more mixed on third parties than on nonplurality presidents provoked dispute in predictable ways: defenders of EC stressed that the cup was three-fourths full, while critics emphasized it was one-fourth empty. More basically, the disagreement turned on what credit, if any, should be assigned EC for the general pattern of discouragement of third parties in presidential elections. The scoreboard for third parties, using 1872–1968 election data for the most part, reads as follows:

1. *Displacement of a major party.* Occurred but once, with the Republican party in the immediate pre–Civil War period. The two-party system, as distinct from which two parties compose it, has never been under sustained threat from a third party.
2. *Winning a presidential election.* None came within even hailing distance. The largest proportion of popular votes (27 percent) and elec-

toral votes (17 percent) was garnered in 1912 by Theodore Roosevelt's Progressives in their split with the Republican party. (Taft got fewer popular votes than Roosevelt and but 8 electoral votes; Wilson won with 42 percent of the popular vote and 82 percent of the electoral vote.)

3. *Winning electoral votes.* In addition to 1912, occurred four other times: 1892, 1924, 1948, and 1968. In all cases but one (States' Rights in 1948), the proportion of electoral votes gained was lower than that of the popular vote. Under EC, winning electoral votes requires carrying one or more states in popular vote; hence geographically concentrated rather than diffused backing is rewarded. In 1948, for example, both the States' Rights party and the Henry Wallace Progressive party attracted about the same popular vote (2.4 percent); the former, concentrated in the South, got 38 electoral votes (7.3 percent) while the latter, more thinly distributed, got no electoral votes.

4. *Deadlocking the electoral college.* Has not occurred, though the threat to do so was associated with States' Rights party in 1948, George Wallace Independent party in 1968, and so far as congressmen knew and feared in 1969–70, Wallace intended to follow that strategy again for the 1972 election. Actually, according to a December 1971 press interview with Wallace, he did not want to "throw the election in the House" in 1968. "It never would have gotten to the House," Wallace stated, "because our group couldn't have gotten control there." Rather, Wallace's electors would have voted for Nixon if Nixon agreed, in exchange for that support, to commit himself publicly to some of Wallace's policies against school busing, tax inequities favoring the "super-ultra-rich," etc.

Since the EC method awards a state's electoral votes to the plurality leader, no matter how slim his strength, the difficulties of orchestrating a deadlock, as distinct from affecting which major party will win, can scarcely be exaggerated. The third party must have a strong regional base in order to win some E votes for itself. If the major parties are out of balance competitively, the third party must draw more votes from the stronger major party. If the major parties are balanced in strength, then draining too much from one will create a landslide for the other. And so on, on a state-by-state basis.

5. *Affecting which major party wins.* Whether or not a third party wins electoral votes itself, support for it may shift outcomes between the major parties in one or more states and, depending on the overall division of strength between the major parties, may affect the national result. Historian John D. Hicks has suggested that "in possibly six instances the third party vote has snatched victory from one major party ticket to give it to the other"; the six were 1844, 1848, 1880, 1884, 1912, and 1916. In only one of those elections (1912) did the third party gain any electoral votes.

The assessment of the role of third parties is complicated, therefore, by the fact that their impact cannot be measured by number or proportion of electoral votes won. The 1948 election provides an apt case in point. The Henry Wallace Progressives and the States' Righters each represented a punitive flank attack, from opposite ideological directions, on the Democrats. Both failed in their common immediate purpose of bringing about the defeat of Truman. But the Progressives, with no electoral votes, affected the disposition of a much larger number of electoral votes than did the States' Righters, who actually secured 38 electoral votes. The size of the Progressive vote exceeded the Republican lead over the Democrats in New York, Michigan, and Maryland, causing Truman the loss of 74 electoral votes.*

This scoreboard indicates that, overall, EC's record was strongly supportive of two-partyism. But it also indicates that EC could be exploited by transitory, ad hoc third-party activity. On the one hand the state-unit rule seemed to provide occasional encouragement to dissidents to try either to win a state directly or to affect which major party carried a state. On the other hand, that same rule operated in all states and gave comfortable electoral vote majorities to a major party, thereby severely restricting the impact of third parties. The mixed nature of the data and explanation provided opportunities for persistent congressional disagreement over how to interpret EC's record on discouraging third parties and confining their effects.

That disagreement was part of a more fundamental controversy about the causes of American two-partyism, which remained as unresolved in the Congress as in the political science textbooks. Some argued for the primacy of noninstitutional explanatory factors, such as our history, culture, and tendencies to a centrist and nonideological politics. Others stressed the consequences of institutional forms, invariably including the election of legislators and executives by the single-member-district-and-plurality-vote method, and usually including EC. But the latter was slighted by some political scientists who were committed to an institutional explanation of two-partyism. And a few even urged that two-partyism had developed in spite of EC, which was held to be as open to a sectionally based multipartyism or to a lopsided one-partyism as it was to two-partyism. Despite the importance, then, that all attached to the criterion of maintaining a two-party system, the confused accounting for what sustained two-partyism served to discount for many any need to retain EC to meet that criterion.

The same sort of ambiguity about causation operated to deny credit to EC for promoting a moderate, inclusive, heterogeneous and nonideological party system. A requirement for some geographic spread of backing for

---

* The 1948 events suggest yet further complexities in appraising third parties in that the entry of the Progressives, by enhancing the anti-Communist image of the Democrats, intensified support of the Democrats among other groups. The general lesson is that the election effects of many third parties are not simply unidirectional.

winning presidential candidates — implying a broad and diverse base of support — was built into EC as an indirect method and because a majority of electoral votes was needed to win. The force of this argument was somewhat blunted, however, by the fact that EC had coexisted for many post–Civil War decades with a national two-party system based on pronounced sectionalism. Further, many of E's backers argued that the same factors (other than EC) which had nurtured two-partyism also accounted for its particular qualities.

Complementing the unwillingness of E's advocates to acknowledge that EC was an influential institutional factor in preserving moderate two-partyism was their eagerness to overcondemn EC as an institutional depressant of party competition. For states lacking competitive major parties, the state-unit rule provided no incentive for extensive presidential campaigning by either party: an increase in statewide popular-vote strength from, say, 65 to 70 percent for the dominant party or from 35 to 40 percent for the minority party had no electoral-vote payoff for either. And although the shape of presidential and state-office politics in many states was far from identical, perpetuation of predominant one-partyism in the former deprived a state of a significant stimulus to party competition at other levels. This argument, while generally valid, overlooked the fact that party competition in the states was on the increase in recent decades, as dramatically indexed by the demise of the one-partyism of the South and of upper New England. (A Democratic senator from Maine was a serious contender for the presidential nomination in 1972!) The pull of sectionalism, though by no means eliminated, was clearly declining; the election behavior of a larger number of states was becoming highly similar and less sectionally idiosyncratic. EC's critics, in sum, overstated the argument that it weakened party competition and blocked political change, carefully neglecting the highly visible evidence that EC had proved no insuperable barrier to the force of nationalizing political influences.

Similarly, little mention was made in the hearings or floor debate that New York and Ohio had ceased to monopolize the pool of serious contenders for presidential nomination; consider Arizona (1964), Maine (1972), Massachusetts (1960), Minnesota (1960, 1968, 1972), South Dakota (1972), and Texas (1964). True, this development stemmed from the displacement of governors by senators as the prime source of presidential candidacies, but that was itself testimony to the increasing nationalization of politics. Presidential availability no longer was unduly tied to large-state residency.

Finally, the theme of declining sectionalism in national politics was put to use almost exclusively by E's advocates to argue that a nationalized politics, by creating a national constituency for the president, justified adoption of E. However valid that argument, the underlying evidence was not connected to EC to help counter the latter's greatest vulnerability. The chances of EC's distortions producing a nonplurality president were greatest when (as in the pattern of 1888) there were many predominantly one-party states which cast a high proportion of the total popular vote and electoral vote. The trend to increased party competition, which meant that larger number of states would behave similarly in presidential elections in line with the national division of the popular vote, reduced the likelihood of a nonplurality president under EC in all but very close elections. Yet here again, as in virtually all the debate on electoral reform in 1969–70, selective indictments by EC's opponents and the reticence of its few defenders combined to give EC far less than a fair shake in evaluation.

### The District Plan

The DP reform leaves unchanged the formula for assigning electoral votes to the states and mandates each state to cast two electoral votes by the state-unit rule. For the large majority of electoral votes remaining, however, DP substitutes a district-unit system for the state-unit procedure. Electoral districts within each state, which would serve as U.S. House districts as well, would each be assigned one vote, to be cast for the presidential candidate with the highest popular vote in the district. To win, either an absolute majority or at least 40 percent of the total electoral vote (depending on which version of DP) was necessary.

The DP was proposed with some frequency in the nineteenth century, its chief target being the state-unit practice of EC. It enjoyed a revival of interest after World War II, being pushed by Congressman Frederic R. Coudert, Jr. (R., N.Y.) and Senator Karl E. Mundt (R., S. Dak.). In 1956 the Senate (48–37) cojoined DP and PP in a constitutional amendment permitting states to choose either every four years, but, lacking two-thirds support, it subsequently died. In the 1969–70 controversy the DP, backed by a hard core of conservatives, emerged as the major reform alternative to E.

Its flaws are many, but surely its gravest defect is that a precise assessment of its effects turns too much on the particulars of each state's districting pattern, and that pattern is up for state legislative redefinition after each census. To remedy that defect, Senator Mundt had the DP provide that the electoral districts "shall be of compact and contiguous territory containing substantially equal numbers of inhabitants, and shall not be altered until another census of the United States has been taken." Quite apart from the enforceability of such requirements and their invitation to chronic litigation, Mundt's remedy was akin to attempting to block illegal traffic by closing off one lane of a four-lane freeway. Biased districting to maximize party advantage can coexist quite comfortably with adherence to those rules. Indeed, the Supreme Court's denial that such factors as local political boundaries and community of interest can justify departures from the equal-population principle in legislative apportionment works to sanction, however unintentionally, partisan malapportionment which meets the equal-population test.

Since DP vastly increases the stakes involved in districting, it is a sure bet that the controlling partisans in each state legislature would move to rig the political boundaries in their party's favor. (For example, central-city districts tend to vote Democratic by larger majorities than Republican suburban and rural districts do for their favored party. Districting to capitalize on or to counter this Democratic "wastage" of votes would preoccupy the majority party in the state legislature.) In sum, the record permits little confidence that equitable districting would occur on its own, and the proposed safeguards are inadequate and of questionable enforceability.

Because DP's basic election units are subject to manipulation and alteration, analysis of the plan cannot be as precise as that of EC and PP, the other indirect election methods, both of which use the state as the basic unit. Yet the intended effects of DP and the purposes of its sponsors seem clear enough. As against E, it insists on an indirect method and, as against EC, it favors a different set of states and interests. DP seeks a profoundly conservative redistribution of political influence, involving nothing less than a redefinition of the role of the president as national leader.

Of the EC's three major distortions, DP retains the two which give advantage to states of small population and/or low turnout. The third distortion, the state-unit rule, is drained of all benefit to large states by its confinement to the casting of an equal two electoral votes per state. Ostensibly DP recognizes and therefore promotes party competition and turnout within each state by allowing for divided electoral votes, but in practice that would depend entirely on how the districts were laid out: less than one-fourth of the present House districts are regularly competitive. Many states may thus be expected to continue to produce a bloc electoral vote or close to it, and others to cast divided electoral votes as the sum of predominantly Democratic and predominantly Republican districts — which is a far cry from the meaning of heightened party competition. Similarly, the disincentives to turnout alleged of EC are retained by DP, the locus merely being shifted from "safe" states to "safe" districts. Further, the arithmetical complexities of operating by state and district electoral votes would permit a candidate with less popular votes statewide to win a majority of the state's electoral votes by thinly carrying most of the districts and losing heavily in the remaining districts. If this occurred in many states in the same election, a nonplurality president could be the result.

When the DP counting formula is applied to recent elections (a procedure whose shortcomings the reader has been alerted to), the electoral vote is found to be less lopsided than under EC. It corresponds more closely to the division of the national popular vote, though considerable disparities in the same direction as EC's remain. Not a very important advantage in itself, it is overshadowed by the "fact" that the 1960 election would have been reversed under DP: the 56–41 percent of electoral vote in Kennedy's favor under EC would have turned into 52–45 percent in Nixon's favor. Yet another disability is that DP would invite third parties because of the greater ease of gaining a district rather than a state plurality. A direct presidential victory of a third party should be as remote under DP as under EC, but "blackmail" parties seeking to deadlock the electoral vote may be encouraged. (George Wallace in 1968 got forty-six electoral votes under EC, but would have gotten fifty-eight under DP.) The willingness of DP's managers to change the requirement from an electoral majority to 40 percent recognized the potentially greater effect of third parties under DP.

Compared to EC, an altogether different strategy for presidential nominations and elections is called for by DP. States which can deliver all or nearly all their electoral votes to one party rise in political influence at the direct expense of states which tend to produce more divided results. Politically competitive states dissipate their electoral strength while politically homogeneous states solidify theirs. (A small state giving its total of four electoral votes to one party would offset a net of four electoral votes for the other party in a divided New York.) On a district basis, the small minority of competitive districts would receive disproportionate attention, but their interests and policy concerns could differ markedly from those of pivotal states under EC. At bottom, DP's reversal of EC's favoritism seeks to "parochialize" the president by assigning controlling influence over his election to the same configuration of nonmetropolitan interests which collectively dominate the House.

Conservatives who backed DP had little awareness or anxiety that increasing the electoral interdependency of presidential and House candidates infringed the separation of powers. It evidently occurred to few that the opposite of their key assumption might develop, namely that instead of (or in addition to) the presidential leadership role being altered to conform more to House perspectives, House candidacies and elections might become an adjunct of the presidential contest. As Margaret Heckler, a Massachusetts Republican congresswoman and an E supporter, shrewdly noted at the House hearings in 1969:

> The inevitable . . . result of the [DP] would create on the campaign trail . . . an interrelationship between the campaign of the Executive and legislative candidates, which in the long run *could seriously impair the independence of the Congress* as a separate branch of Government. [Emphasis added.]

Yet so intent were conservatives on minimizing metropolitan influence (and all the interests implied by that term) on the president and in transforming his leadership role, that many doubtless would have been willing to pay the price of sacrificing House independency to achieve those goals.


The Proportional Plan

The core of PP is to award each presidential candidate the exact proportion of the state's electoral vote as he has of the state's popular vote,

*Allan P. Sindler*

carried out to three decimal places (thousandths). National victory requires 40 percent of the total electoral vote; the present formula for assigning electoral votes to the states remains unchanged. During the 1930s and '40s this reform was associated with Congressman Clarence Lea (D., Cal.), in 1950 with Senator Henry Cabot Lodge (R., Mass.) and Congressman Ed Gossett (D., Texas), and in 1956 with Senators Estes Kefauver (D., Tenn.) and Price Daniel (D., Texas). It passed the Senate by two-thirds vote (64–27) in 1950, but was then bottled up by the House Rules Committee. (No proposed amendment of EC reached the floor of the House from 1950 until the House passage of E in 1969). In 1956, as noted earlier, it was combined with DP in a single constitutional amendment which lacked two-thirds support in the Senate. Although PP had peaked by 1969–70, it remained a live alternative, especially as a fallback compromise for original DP supporters and for some E backers as well.

PP, like DP, abandons the state-unit rule while retaining the other two distortions of EC. Unlike DP, however, PP provides incentives to turnout because any popular vote is counted in the state's electoral-vote tally, and hence the impact of EC's turnout distortion should be moderated. Many other consequences flow from making the electoral vote reflect, rather than suppress, the intrastate division of the popular vote. Some raise vulnerabilities akin to those of DP; others represent strengths and weaknesses more peculiar to PP.

Inequality of voter power under PP is sharply reduced (especially if the expected high turnout occurs), though not eliminated. On a national basis, the electoral-vote proportions of the major-party candidates would closely approximate their popular-vote proportions. In weakly competitive presidential elections PP theoretically has less chance than EC of producing a nonplurality president. (However, the actual record of EC on this point, as treated earlier, needs no apologies.) Under conditions of a close division of the popular vote, however, a nonplurality president remains a distinct possibility under PP; one computer-based estimate puts the odds at about 1 in 16. EC's outcome in 1888 (its single instance of the "wrong" winner) would have been reversed had PP's formula been in effect, but the elections of 1880, 1896, and 1960 would have been also.

The argument that PP encourages third parties seems convincing at first blush since, unlike EC and DP, all candidates translate their popular votes, no matter how slim, into some share of the electoral vote. (Conversely, PP discourages "balance of power" third parties, like the Liberals and Conservatives of New York, because no longer would a state's entire electoral vote go to one party.) But the problem is more complex and the answer not entirely certain, as a quick look at the 1948 election demonstrates. Having each gotten 2.4 percent of the popular vote, the Henry Wallace Progressives got no electoral votes and the States' Righters got 38 (7.2 percent). Under PP, assuming the same vote, the respective figures would have been 9.4 electoral votes (1.8 percent) and 38.6 (7.3 percent). The difference indexes the persistence of distortion, in this case because the Progressive vote was cast mostly in populous and high turnout states, while the States' Righters concentrated their appeal in states oppositely characterized. It will be recalled from the earlier analysis of EC that the impact of the Progressives on the distribution of electoral votes between the major parties was greater, despite the absence of electoral votes won, than that of the States' Righters. Under certain circumstances, however, the combination of electoral votes secured by both third parties under PP could have had the greatest effect of all by denying Truman victory.

In sum, assessing an election method's incentives to third parties rests in part on gauging the latter's probable impact in a complicated context involving estimates of the size and state-by-state distribution of major-party and third-party popular votes. By producing closer electoral-vote divisions between the major parties and by guaranteeing third parties some electoral votes, PP obviously stimulates third-partyism, perhaps particularly for nationwide minorities unable to secure electoral votes under EC or DP. On the other hand, PP's lowered requirement of 40 percent of the electoral vote to win attempts to contain the effects of greater third-party activity. Perhaps the safest, if inconclusive, overall judgment is that the impact of third parties under PP could vary from high to low depending on the degree to which certain other election factors were present, and there seems no way to predict with confidence the frequency with which those contingent contextual factors are likely to occur.

No comparable ambiguity exists in identifying the critical defect of PP, which it shares with DP. In theory, since a vote gained anywhere becomes an increment of electoral-vote strength, the major parties should campaign broadly and vigorously in every state. In practice, the political power of "safer" states increases at the expense of that of closely divided states; those states regularly providing relatively large net electoral-vote margins for a party will increase their influence within that party and over the outcome of the election. For example, applying the PP formula to the 1960 election, Nixon would have gained a larger net of electoral-vote lead from his 29,000 plurality in Vermont than Kennedy would have had from his 384,000 plurality in New York. In 1968, Nebraska and the District of Columbia each would have supplied a bigger electoral-vote margin to their winners than either California or Pennsylvania.*

For regions with pronounced special interests, such as the South, PP provides a strong incentive to return to or retain predominant one-partyism. If the eleven-state South gave, say, a net of twenty electoral votes to the Democrats (about a 57–43 percent regional popular-vote division), its contribution

---

* In addition to sharing this bias of PP, DP promotes the relative influence of small states, regardless of party competition. Under DP, states with three electoral votes must cast them in a bloc and those with four can divide 3–1 at most (in a two-candidate race). In the 1960s, there were seven states in the first category and nine in the second. After the 1968 election Maine, with four electoral votes, abandoned the state-unit rule as a form of protest, and, instructively, chose DP rather than PP.

*Allan P. Sindler*

to Democratic national victory would likely be crucial because of the difficulty of offsetting that net by thin margins in more closely divided areas. (By contrast, under EC the South's entire electoral vote can be offset by carrying a handful of major states.) Such a development would stack the deck in favor of Democratic presidential victories, but at the high cost of heightened southern influence over the party, the presidential election, and national policy. If, on the other hand, the South became as presidentially competitive as the rest of the country, the Democrats would likely be hurt by PP. Democratic victory often combines the carrying of most pivotal states by thin majorities with the loss by more substantial margins of many other states. Under PP the electoral-vote gains from the first pattern would fall short of the losses from the second. The probability that PP might result either in Democratic/southern ascendancy or Democratic subordinacy suggests its kinship with DP in its complete reversal of the prometropolitan bias of EC.

This analysis underscores how misleading the view, often heard in the 1969–70 controversy, that PP was a "compromise" between EC and E which, if E proved politically unadoptable, E's supporters could flock to in good conscience. President Nixon, among others, pushed that mistaken view prior to House enactment of E. Superficially, PP appeared to be a compromise because it combined the state-based indirect election structure of EC, a more faithful translation of popular votes into electoral votes on a state and national basis, and incentives to turnout everywhere. Conservatives were to be attracted by the first feature, liberals by the latter two features. But the major political effects of PP closely parallel those of DP, and in direction are opposite to those of EC and E.

The possibilities for confused appraisal of PP were reflected in its sources of support. Some who preferred E but doubted its political feasibility opted for PP as a genuine compromise. (This was truer of the 1950s' alignments than of 1969–70s'.) Some who advocated PP as their first choice believed it would hasten and sustain presidential two-partyism in the South, making the major parties nationally competitive. (Senators Lodge and Kefauver were of that persuasion in the 1950s.) But by 1969–70 the bulk of support for PP came from those who backed DP. Most in this camp preferred DP but welcomed PP as an alternative, and many looked on them as equally suitable revisions of EC. For hard-core conservatives in this group, the common tie was the overturning of the state-unit rule without abandonment of an indirect election. The power and policy effects expected from that change were bluntly implied by Congressman Gossett, cosponsor of PP, back in 1951:

> The electoral college [state-unit rule] permits and invites irresponsible control and domination by small organized minority groups, within the large pivotal states. . . . [These] groups, organized along religious or economic or racial lines, by voting together, can and do hold a balance of power within these pivotal states. As a result, the political strategists in both parties make special appeals to these

various groups as such. These groups have become more and more politically conscious. They know their power.

Little wonder, then, that most liberals fought PP in 1956 and rejected it as a viable compromise in 1969–70.

### Direct Popular Election

In form, E is the most radical of the reform options, displacing EC root and branch. It provides for a direct national election in which the plurality leader wins, provided his vote constitutes at least 40 percent of the total vote. If that condition is unmet, a runoff election is held between the two top candidates. Alone or in combination with instituting a national presidential primary, E was crushingly defeated in the Senate in 1947, 1950, and 1956. Those efforts to revise EC focused on DP or PP, with E ruled out as politically unfeasible.

*Congress's Growing Receptivity to Altering EC and to E.* The transformation of E over the 1960s from also-ran to front-runner reflected the increasing receptivity of Congress to reform of EC in general and to the claims of E in particular. In *Baker* v. *Carr* (1962) and later related cases, the Supreme Court compelled legislative reapportionment in accord with a literal "one man, one vote" criterion. This both mirrored and helped stimulate further demands for changed political structures to foster more direct political participation and control. Further, the remedying of legislative malapportionment reduced the attachment of liberals to the "countervailing inequity" defense of EC. One reapportionment case suggested a ready parallel to EC. In *Gray* v. *Sanders* (1963), the Supreme Court invalidated Georgia's "little EC" county-unit system of voting in state and congressional primaries as a denial of equal protection of the laws to nonrural voters. The Court saw EC as promoting political inequality, and implied its constitutional vulnerability were it not itself stipulated in the Constitution. Taking its cue, Delaware and twelve other states filed suit against New York in 1966, charging that the state-unit rule (*not* mandated by the Constitution) unfairly discriminated against less populated states and in effect disfranchised voters on the losing side by converting their popular votes into electoral votes awarded to a candidate for whom they did not vote. (The remedies available within the existing limits of the Constitution presumably were PP or DP on option of each state.) The Supreme Court refused to hear the case, without stating reasons. There the matter currently rests, but it pointed up for Congress the possibility that the core of EC might be repudiated by judicial action.*

---

* The "automatic plan," briefly covered at the outset of this study, also provided for inclusion of the state-unit rule in the Constitution. It was not unreasonable to argue that the

*Allan P. Sindler*

The unusually close elections of 1960 and 1968 rekindled latent congressional anxieties about EC's capacity to "misfire" and produce a nonplurality president. The need to close the loophole surrounding electors was underscored by changes in the laws of five Deep South states to permit the election of unpledged or independent electors, and by a failing attempt in 1960 to manipulate the votes of unpledged and other electors to deny Kennedy victory. In 1968 a Republican elector defected to Wallace. In that election the Wallace movement had made no secret of its intention to deadlock EC, a strategy which nearly succeeded and which most congressmen expected Wallace to repeat for the upcoming 1972 election. A spate of articles on EC and its reform appeared in response to Wallace's "spoiler" candidacy, helping to publicize the cause of electoral reform.

Within this supportive context of a growing sense of urgency on the need to revise EC, E's ascendancy is best explained by its fit with the increasingly populistic temper of the times, as articulated by self-conscious groups dissatisfied with the "old ways" of doing political (and other) business. Whether deemed better or worse than EC or other alternatives, E appeared to be "an idea whose time has come." Opinion polls reported pronounced public preference for E and surveys of state legislators indicated majority backing. Confirming this broad support, an unusual mix of interest groups declared and worked for E: not only liberal groups, as would be expected, such as the ACLU and the ADA, but also the League of Women Voters, the AFL–CIO, the Chamber of Commerce, and the American Bar Association.

*A Redistribution of Relative Advantage.* Candidates, to use a phrase popular with politicians, "hunt ducks [votes] where the ducks are." But some "ducks" are more attractive than others, depending on the election method. In form, E provides for literal vote equality in that all votes, wherever cast, have equal weight. This deprives pivotal populous states and their organized constituent interest groups of their special advantages under EC. However, they would still remain influential because of sheer numbers of voters, assuming no unduly low turnout rates, and because of their "nationalization of strength" under E. Thus the reduced power of black voters in states like New York and Illinois could be partly compensated for by a national pooling of black votes in the South as well as in northern industrial states. Similarly, instead of solicitude for urban interests in key states, the interests of sizable cities everywhere — Omaha, Nebraska, no less than Oakland, California — would come in for attention.

Although less hurt by E than by PP or DP, many metropolitan-based interests would still suffer reduced influence under E as compared to EC,

---

states should operate by a uniform system, which required imbedding it in the Constitution, and that the system should be the prevailing practice, namely the state-unit rule. But such an action presumably would reduce if not eliminate the possibility of judicial invalidation of the rule.

particularly so if, as was often the case, the turnout rate of the group tended to be low. But even disregarding the turnout factor, the share of the national popular vote for most such groups was considerably less than of the electoral vote they might decisively affect under EC. More generally, E favored the influence of states which could supply relatively large popular-vote margins for its favored party. Highly competitive states, especially those with small or medium-sized populations, thus would be less attractive to either party. Large states not persistently close and smaller less competitive states would comprise the major gainers from E's bias. In the close 1968 election, for example, the strong Republican states of Iowa, Kansas, and Nebraska cast some 2.5 million votes and gave their total of twenty-one electoral votes to Nixon. Michigan and Pennsylvania, with 50 electoral votes, went for Humphrey by relatively weaker margins in a vote of some 8 million. But the Republican trio supplied Nixon with a net popular-vote margin of 468,000 compared to 391,000 for Humphrey from the two Democratic states, even though the former cast less than one-third of the total vote of the latter.

E's managers, as indicated earlier, walked a fine line between assuring populous states of high influence under E in spite of the end of EC's state-unit rule and assuring small states of increased influence under E because of elimination of that rule. That analysis of E, shaped by the strategic need of E's sponsors to keep large-state support of E while making inroads on small-state opposition, does not fully square with the writer's assessment. Differences also obtain, though of a different sort, with the analysis stressed by conservative opponents of E. They simply measured the proportion of the total electoral and popular vote cast by each state, emerging with findings reflecting the small-state bias of EC in its allocation of electoral votes. In 1960, for example, the nine most populous states cast 56 percent of the popular vote and but 42 percent of the electoral vote. Overall, the conservatives repeatedly argued, thirty-four states and the District of Columbia would lose power (as defined by this measure) to the populous states if E replaced EC.

*The 40 Percent Minimum Support Level.* On E's merits, as distinct from the strategy of securing its adoption, related problems stubbornly resisted confident solution. They derived from the general unwillingness to settle for a plurality president without regard to how slim his share of the vote might be. E's proponents thus had to set a minimum percentage which would accord legitimacy to the outcome, not encourage third parties and make recourse to contingency procedures unlikely.

A 40 percent support level, strongly endorsed by the American Bar Association, appeared to many to be intuitively satisfactory. It seemed high enough to discourage third parties from attempting to win in their own right or to deadlock the election. In all past elections except Lincoln's sectional victory of 1860, the winner had comfortably met that support level. (Of course the likelihood of greater third-party activity under E rendered suspect the use of popular-vote distributions under EC as a predictor of those under E.)

There being nothing sacrosanct and little proven about the 40 percent figure, other support levels were suggested in the Congress. One urged 35 percent, to make the odds even stronger that the contingency procedure would not have to be used. Another, worried about the legitimacy factor, pushed for 45 percent, noting that since the Civil War only two presidents (Wilson in 1912 and Nixon) had failed to meet that standard. More basic was the argument of E's conservative critics that a 40 percent level contradicted the claim that E was "the only system that guarantees the election of the people's choice." Was that a fair description, they asked, of a winner who could be opposed by as many as three out of every five voters? Accordingly, they pushed for a majority vote requirement, which would have multiplied E's problems with respect to third-partyism and contingency procedures. Another suggestion would have E not include any specific support level and instead empower Congress to determine it. Intended presumably to let actual election experience fix the decision, this proposal constituted a standing invitation to congressional partisan or bipartisan maneuvering which could thoroughly undermine the legitimacy of the election procedure and outcome. The House rejected all these suggestions and kept to the requirement of 40 percent support.

*The Contingency Procedure.* Once an election method sets a condition for winning in addition to simple popular plurality, as E did by the 40 percent rule, contingency procedures are needed. Disagreement on those procedures could imperil support of the overall method itself, though E's spokesmen sought to defuse conflict by arguing that they would seldom, if ever, come into play. However, the procedures preferred by E's managers were believed by many to work against strengthening the probability that the first election would be final and itself produce a winner. Hence the decision on contingency procedures became a significant item of contention concerning E's merits.

PP and DP provided, in the event of electoral deadlock, that a joint session of Congress would choose between the two top candidates, with each legislator having one vote. Initially, E had the same provision, but the ABA's strong endorsement of a runoff election converted Senator Bayh. Had that shift not occurred, E's political acceptability probably would have been enhanced. Greater acceptability, however, is not necessarily greater merit. Whether Congress should be in the business of selecting presidents at all remains quite debatable. Certainly the guidelines for congressional decision desperately need clarification. On what basis should legislators select between the two candidates?

One answer is that Congress should "follow the election returns," defined as confirming as president the candidate with the popular plurality. But common sense, supported by data on gubernatorial runoffs, indicates that the first election's front-runner will lose the runoff in a sizable minority of instances. Hence the plurality candidate has no real claim to automatic endorsement by the Congress. Besides, if that were all that Congress was supposed to do, it could be relieved of that nondiscretionary chore by imbedding a self-enforcing rule in the Constitution. (A parallel to the unneeded-or-dangerous role of electors fits nicely on the point.) "Following one's party label" is yet another conflicting interpretation of the ambiguous directive to "follow the election returns." Since incoming presidents at times have faced a Congress controlled by the opposition, as with Eisenhower in 1956 and Nixon in 1968, the claim that the party gaining a majority of seats is thereby entitled to award the presidency to its candidate is unpersuasive. And what of the impasse likely when each of the two chambers is controlled by a different party?

Lacking a widely accepted rule for congressional choice between presidential candidates, political self-interest would likely be given free play. Consider the 1968 election, when Wallace's third party threatened to deadlock EC and Democratic control of House and Senate was assured. Acting on a political science professor's suggestion, two congressmen sought to persuade House candidates to pledge to vote for the plurality presidential candidate in the event deadlock occurred. Few pledged, the national party conventions did nothing on the matter, and many southern Democrats and Republicans urged House members to vote their districts if the occasion arose. Nixon spoke to the need to assure that the presidential winner was the one with the most popular votes, while Humphrey dwelt on the need to stand by the contingency procedures established in the Constitution.

Although E's advocates were worried about the possibility of congressional wheeling and dealing in any presidential selection situation, their shift from that contingency procedure owed much to their desire to be consistent with E's core principle. If the absolutely essential value is that the popular-vote winner must be the presidential winner, then a runoff popular election is called for. As Birch Bayh, E's Senate manager, put it when grudgingly conceding that provision for a joint session of Congress might be "an acceptable alternative" to the runoff as a contingency procedure,

> But if we are going to have a horse, let us have a horse; let us not have the first half a horse and the back half a camel.

Somewhat ironically, Congress subjected the runoff device to more exacting analysis than the congressional contingency procedure, thereby complicating the chances of E's passage.

*The Runoff and Third Parties.*   Some E supporters who attacked PP for promoting a proliferation of parties illogically professed not to see a similar problem for E. Stated Congressman Bill Burlison (D., Mo.):

> I am concerned . . . that proportional distribution, inasmuch as it would record the electoral vote of every candidate receiving any pop-

ular votes, would breed a rash of splinter parties. . . . I don't buy the argument that we would be engulfed by third parties under direct election. It is true that their votes would be more meaningful than at present, but Americans are too practical and sensible to waste their ballots on fringe groups.

But many backers of E, including the ABA, and most of E's critics agreed that the possibility of a multiplication of parties under E raised a genuine and major problem, however much they disagreed on the answers.

Political science analysis of the effects of the popular runoff device, while less than conclusive, heavily leans to the view that it encourages multiple candidacies. Assured of a possible second round of voting choice, voters are more inclined to back a nonmajor party candidate and to support protesters, dissenters, or extremists. The major parties' organizational control over access to candidacy typically becomes weakened. Geographically concentrated parties likely would have as much incentive under E-with-runoff as under EC, while all other types of nonsectional candidacies usually would have more. "Spoiler" or "blackmail" parties would be particularly encouraged, and their wheeling and dealing with major party candidates would be no more edifying than similar activity by the Congress. Finally, the extraordinarily expensive campaigning required by E, if compounded by the need to conduct another full election weeks after the first, might well require government funding, which in turn might promote publicly subsidized third-partyism.

The temper of our times undoubtedly intensified anxiety about the effects of presidential election methods on third parties. A growing distrust of the legitimacy and effectiveness of established institutions, an increasing independency from party, a heightened self-consciousness and "separatism" of blacks and other groups, a proclivity to moralistic politics which views compromise as tainted — these and other symptoms suggest a rising potential for a "new politics" whose style and substance may be difficult to contain within the traditional frame of two-partyism. Can the two major parties remain inclusive and diverse and yet meet intense segmental demands on specific issues? A proliferation of presidential candidates, rather than of organized parties with full slates, may result, each pushing on a single issue of high controversy, such as school busing, legalized abortion, gun control, and pollution. Whether the major parties would continue as Gullivers amidst an ever-changing cast of Lilliputian one-issue challengers or would themselves become severely fragmented is not clear but, whichever, the effectiveness of the two-party system and of the president would undergo marked alteration.

*Alternatives to the Runoff Election.* As chief sponsor of E, Senator Bayh responded to increasing doubts about the wisdom of the runoff provision by indicating he was open to alternatives not violating the core principles of direct popular election. Several possibilities will be explored in the final section of this study, but two warrant mention now. They were proposed by different pairs of E supporters to protect two-partyism from the threat of multipartyism posed by the runoff device.

One amendment, offered by Senators Robert Griffin (R., Mich.) and Joseph Tydings (D., Md.), provided that when the 40 percent support level was not met the plurality leader would win if he had a majority of electoral votes, computed as under EC. (That EC's record contained but one such instance — Lincoln in 1860 — was not very relevant since the amendment was designed for elections in which at least one if not several serious third parties entered. A state plurality of any size wins all the state's electoral votes.) Failing that condition, a joint session of Congress would choose. By combining core elements of E and EC, the plan superficially seemed vulnerable to the charge of "intellectual schizophrenia" made by conservative critics of E. "It spurns what it embraces," jibed Senator Roman Hruska (R., Neb.), "and embraces what it spurns." The plan was quite consistent, however, in that it sought (1) to depress incentives to third-partyism by substituting congressional selection for a runoff and thereby reducing the incidence of leading candidates failing to pass the 40 percent test, and (2) to provide on those few occasions when no one met the 40 percent rule another way to qualify without having to use the congressional contingency procedure.

The other amendment was proposed by two freshmen senators, Thomas F. Eagleton (D., Mo.) and Robert Dole (R., Kan.). Complex in itself, it was further complicated by intermittent revision by its authors so that which of several versions was "official" remains uncertain. Yet the intent of the plan, dubbed the "Federal System," was quite clear. If a candidate got a popular majority, he was elected. Otherwise, the plurality leader would win if his vote satisfied any one of such conditions as carrying by plurality vote (1) more than half the states; (2) states containing, in sum, more than half the voters; (3) more than half the House districts; or (4) a majority of electoral votes, treated in the manner of EC. (Eagleton testified that every actual presidential winner in this century would have qualified under one or more of these standards.) In the unlikely event none of these conditions was satisfied, a joint session of Congress would decide.

For all of its cumbersomeness the Eagleton-Dole plan was closer to a compromise between E and EC than PP was. Presidents would have either a popular majority or a popular plurality based on relatively widespread geographic support. Additionally pleasing to conservatives was the provision for congressional contingency procedures. Yet there would be slim chance of a deadlocked election, which reduced incentives for third parties and promised little to no use of the contingency procedure. And the alternative qualifying standards further pleased liberals because all but the first of the four conditions favored the same category of populous competitive states as EC did.

Fearing to permit alteration of E's provisions until final political soundings were taken closer to the time of Senate voting on the measure, Bayh retained the runoff provision rather than adopt either of the above two substitutes or any other. Had the Senate permitted itself to vote on the substance of E, it is unlikely that the runoff provision would have emerged intact. What should or would have replaced it are matters raised for the reader's judgment in the final section of this study.

### Congress Disposes

Understanding Congress's disposition of the electoral-reform issue requires, in the manner of this study, the treatment of background, analysis, argument, and strategy before offering an account of House and Senate action. By applying that extensive earlier treatment, the reader can supply context and interpretation to the following chronological account of events.

*Pre-1969 Momentum.* The Johnson Administration in 1966 and again in 1967 passively proposed a minimum reform of EC known as the "automatic plan" (discussed briefly at the outset of this study). Birch Bayh, who as a freshman senator had taken over at Kefauver's death in 1963 as chairman of the Constitutional Amendments Subcommittee of the Senate Judiciary Committee, agreed to be its sponsor. (Bayh developed a high reputation because of his two-year leadership in Congress's enactment in 1968 of the 25th Amendment dealing with presidential disability and succession.) But in mid-1966, with the automatic plan attracting thin support, Bayh abandoned it to endorse E, including the contingency procedure of a joint session of Congress. He acted on his own; the LBJ administration remained quietly adverse to E.

In early 1966 the Chamber of Commerce, tallying a policy referendum of its member organizations, came out for E (about two-thirds support) or DP (about one-third). A year later the ABA endorsed its prestigious study commission report recommending E with the 40 percent rule and popular runoff. That report flatly branded EC as "archaic, undemocratic, complex, ambiguous, indirect and dangerous." (Some months later, Congressman Celler added his own choice adjectives: "barbarous, unsporting . . . and downright uncivilized.") Bayh, who had worked closely with the ABA on the language of the 25th Amendment, subsequently adopted the runoff device. Influential newspapers such as the *New York Times* and the *Washington Post* also urged enactment of E.

The 1968 election, narrowly won by Nixon despite the threat of EC deadlock pursued by Wallace, left a politically exploitable opportunity for those anxious to alter EC. Dr. Lloyd Bailey, a Republican elector from North Carolina and a member of the right-wing John Birch Society, expressed his disenchantment with Nixon's initial appointments by casting his vote for Wallace. Two Democrats, Senator Edmund Muskie (Me.) and Congressman James O'Hara (Mich.) led a bipartisan move in January 1969 in each of the Democratic-controlled chambers to have Congress invalidate Bailey's vote.

The dubious legality of their move persuaded them to settle for a resolution to wipe the controversial vote off the record rather than to allocate it to Nixon. The resolution was defeated, 169–229 in the House and 33–58 in the Senate; both parties split, but Democratic support was relatively stronger. Its sponsors had anticipated defeat, knowing that many who disapproved of Bailey's switch would still view the resolution as an inappropriate intrusion into state affairs. Their real purpose was to spotlight the need to revise EC: Congress's unwillingness to police "faithless" electors implicitly demonstrated why formal change of EC was required. (About one-third of the states had laws binding electors to support the presidential candidate of their party, but their constitutionality had not been tested and was problematic.)

*President Nixon Intervenes.* During the closing campaign months in 1968, Nixon stated several times that if EC deadlock occurred, the plurality leader should be chosen:

> I think that if the man who wins the popular vote is denied the Presidency, the man who gets the Presidency would have very great difficulty in governing.

In his message to Congress of February 20, 1969, he reaffirmed his "personal feeling" that "the candidate who wins the most popular votes should become president," but then on grounds of political feasibility he pushed in directions quite different from E. Repeating President Johnson's view in 1965 that ratification of E would founder on small-state opposition, Nixon urged Congress to "formulate a system that can receive the requisite Congressional and state approval." Acknowledging the diversity of electoral reforms, the president promised to support any plan which abolished the electors, made the electoral-vote division more closely approximate the popular-vote division and made a 40 percent electoral-vote plurality sufficient to win. Nixon also stated his belief that the best contingency procedure was a popular runoff between the two top candidates. Finally, he indicated that he had supported PP in the past, but remained open to other plans which met the conditions he cited.

E's promoters were disheartened by and resentful of what Bayh called Nixon's "retreat to expediency." The *New York Times* labeled his turn from E an "abdication of leadership" and held his own plan to be "tragically bad." How, the *Times* wondered, did the president come by his judgment of political feasibility, when the public opinion polls strongly favored E and Bayh's measure had 40 cosponsors compared to but 10 for PP? Chairman Emanuel Celler of the House Judiciary Committee stubbornly pressed that same question to Attorney General John Mitchell, who testified in mid-March and offered as support only general allusions to the administration's soundings of sentiment in state legislatures. Deputy Attorney General Richard Kleindienst,

*Allan P. Sindler*

in his Senate testimony a week later, termed PP "a good strategic as well as ideological compromise," a statement which revealed the administration's misreadings of both dimensions (as discussed earlier). Shortly afterwards Nixon indicated that he was not wedded to indirect elections but would back E if Congress passed it. But he reiterated that other than the guidelines provided in his February message, he intended to keep hands off the issue. That stance triggered a tart comeback by Congressman Andrew Jacobs (D., Ind.) that "you will help us if we get [E] through Congress, but you won't help us get it through Congress." Provoked by Nixon's insistence that E was politically unfeasible, Chairman Celler of HJC took on as a test of his own leadership skills piloting E to House passage.

*The House Acts.* Celler, a House member since 1922 and chairman of HJC for the past twenty years, proved up to his self-imposed task. After holding extensive hearings as a full committee in February and March, 1969, the House Judiciary Committee late the following month reported E by favorable vote of 28–6. The HJC earlier had decisively rejected amendments to permit election by a simple plurality of popular vote, to require a 45 percent support level, to adopt DP, and to provide minimum reform by abolishing electors. Over two months later, the House Rules Committee cleared E for six hours of floor debate, to be shared equally between proponents and opponents and, in accord with Celler's request, under an open rule permitting amendments. (Judged by hindsight, Celler's strategy appeared to be to invite amendments and substitutes and then secure their defeat, ultimately leaving legislators the polar choice of no reform or E.)

On September 9, the House began what Celler termed an "historic debate," namely the first time since 1826 that the House conducted a full-scale review of revising EC. After an hour's debate on each of six days, E emerged on September 18 unscathed and victorious, passing by a resounding 338–70 vote (almost 83 percent, or sixty-six votes more than the needed two-thirds support). Fifteen proposed changes were beaten back with ease, including those providing for a 35 percent, 45 percent or majority support level and for a contingency procedure involving Congress or a proportional division of electoral votes. The critical tests were two: (1) a 159–192 defeat, by teller vote, of a substitute by Congressman Dowdy (D., Tex.) which provided for DP, an electoral-vote majority to win, and popular runoff as the contingency procedure; and (2) a 162–245 defeat, by record vote, of a last-minute effort to recommit the measure to HJC with instructions to report out a DP plan. Note that the losing vote for DP in both instances comprised well more than one-third of the total vote, easily sufficient to defeat E unless considerable vote shifting occurred — which is precisely what happened. Of some 160 congressmen who preferred DP to E, once DP was defeated about 90 chose E to no reform; the remaining 70 did the reverse.

Responding to the impressive margin of House backing, President Nixon announced his support of E and urged the Senate to do likewise, warning that

. . . unless the Senate follows the lead of the House, all opportunity
for reform will be lost this year and possibly for years to come. . . .
The ultimate goal of electoral reform must prevail over differences as
how best to achieve that goal.

But it remained to be seen whether the president was any more willing to expend political resources on his new position than he had on his previous one.

*Getting E to the Senate Floor.*  Bayh's subcommittee of the
Senate Judiciary Committee completed initial hearings in early 1969. With
a subcommittee majority opposed to E, Bayh's initial goal was to prevent a
turndown of all three major options, which would have ended action on electoral reform then and there. Once the subcommittee reported one of the plans,
Bayh hoped to get a majority of the parent SJC to endorse E in its place. On
May 26 the subcommittee rejected PP 3–8, passed DP 6–5, and then voted 9–0
to report DP without recommendation to the full SJC. But the efforts of the
committee, chaired by James Eastland (D., Miss.), a foe of E, became fixed
on the controversial presidential nomination to the Supreme Court first of
Clement Haynsworth and then of G. Harrold Carswell. As a result, consideration of electoral reform was carried over well into the next year, by which
time the momentum provided by the House's stunning endorsement of E had
dissipated.

In mid-April 1970 SJC held three days of supplementary hearings, with
mostly anti-E witnesses. (Rumor had it that Senators Sam Ervin and Roman
Hruska, with Eastland's consent and without consultation with Bayh, had set
the list.) Recognizing that Bayh had sufficient Senate support to stop DP or
PP, conservatives shifted tactics. Expressing greater satisfaction with EC,
Ervin proposed its minimum reform by requiring pledged electors and changing the contingency procedure to a joint session of Congress. With E's supporters in some disagreement over minimum vote support levels and the
runoff, conservatives hoped their proposal would gain favor as others realized
how slim were the Senate's chances of passing any of the major reform
options.

A week later a bipartisan majority of SJC narrowly defeated PP (8–9)
and Ervin's plan (7–9), rejected Chairman Eastland's hostile amendment
requiring a popular majority to win under E, and then endorsed E by 11–6
vote. It was not until almost four months later, however, that SJC's written
reports were completed and made available. Nine members signed the majority report, which stressed that only E guaranteed a winner by "popular
choice" rather than "political chance." Griffin and Tydings also endorsed E,
but argued for different contingency procedures; they subsequently submitted
an amendment on the point, discussed earlier in this study. The remaining six,
all conservatives, were three southern Democrats, Eastland (Miss.), Ervin
(N.C.), and McClellan (Ark.), and three Republicans, Hruska (Neb.), Fong
(Hawaii), and Thurmond (S.C.). They provided a lengthy minority report

*Allan P. Sindler*

detailing their view that E would "adversely affect the entire institutional and political structure," i.e., including federalism, the separation of powers, two-partyism, consensus politics, etc.

*The Senate Blocks Reform.*  Just prior to Senate debate on E in early September 1970, Bayh's strength was estimated at some eight to thirteen votes short of the sixty-seven needed, assuming a full Senate vote of 100; at least twenty-seven were opposed and about nineteen to twenty-one Senators — the critical sector — were undecided or not fully committed. Bayh called for the president to exert his influence to persuade wavering Republicans to back E. But the tipoff on Nixon's posture was his refusal to see the heads of five organizations which had lobbied hard for E — AFL–CIO, United Automobile Workers, ABA, League of Women Voters and Chamber of Commerce — who wanted to move him to intervene. No presidential moral leadership or muscle on behalf of E could, therefore, be anticipated. (Whether the president's lukewarmness on E derived primarily from substantive or strategic considerations remains unclear. That Bayh was E's major sponsor surely lessened the chances for Nixon's positive intervention; Bayh had been one of the outspoken Senate leaders working against confirmation of two of Nixon's appointments to the Supreme Court and, further, he was a potential candidate for Democratic presidential nominee.)

Four days of debate began on September 9, dominated on the opposition side by the SJC authors of its minority report and on the supporting side by Bayh, Baker (R., Tenn.), and Bellmon (R., Okl.), who had been one of the fifteen members of the ABA· study commission. Three amendments were proposed, including Eastland's plan for majority vote, the Griffin-Tydings proposal, and a new attempt by an E supporter, Edward Brooke (R., Mass.), to replace the runoff provision. (Brooke's plan provided that if the 40 percent level was unmet, the candidate who carried a majority of House districts would win. Failing that, each district carried by the weakest candidates nationally would be credited to the candidate with the next highest vote in the district, a process which eventually would automatically produce a winner without recourse to further contingency procedures.)

When Ervin objected to Bayh's repeated unanimous consent requests to vote on the amendments, including those Ervin himself had proposed, it became clear that E's opponents had opted for a filibustering strategy. Surer of their ability to defeat an unamended E than an E altered to replace the runoff provision, they chose to play it safe by preventing any vote on electoral reform. Southern Democrats were the prime movers in this strategy, which was then tacitly acquiesced in by Republicans hostile to E. With the Senate anxious to adjourn by mid-October (1970 being an election year), Majority Leader Mike Mansfield (D., Mont.), though a supporter of E, was primarily concerned to keep the Senate moving on its varied agenda. At his insistence the pro-E forces submitted a petition for ending debate and fixing a time to vote.

On September 15, 1970, Mansfield moved successfully for a cloture vote to be held two days later, commenting that he thought it unfair for a measure which itself required two-thirds vote to be filibustered and initially subjected to a two-thirds procedural vote on cloture. The cloture vote on September 17 failed 54–36, being six votes shy for the total of ninety votes cast; the thirty-six negative votes, however, assured the defeat of cloture even if the ten absent senators had been present and voted for cloture.

E remained the Senate's pending business but by unanimous consent other business was allowed to proceed. But on September 24 Bayh retaliated and forced resumption of debate on E over another four days by denying Ervin's unanimous consent requests to permit committees to sit during the day while the Senate was in session. Several more amendments were proposed, including one by Ervin for PP (requiring a majority electoral vote and a joint session of Congress as the contingency procedure) and a variant of the Eagleton-Dole plan. Mansfield moved again on September 29 to close debate, but the motion failed by five votes (53–34); the opposition still was sufficient to block cloture even if the full Senate were present and voting.

Agreeing to Mansfield's request that he not object further to unanimous consent requests to take up other Senate business, Bayh feverishly explored what compromises might yet produce two-thirds support. On October 2 Mansfield filed the third cloture petition. Two days later, Bayh reluctantly tested reaction to a substantially altered E plan initially proposed by William Spong (D., Va.): a winning candidate would have to receive both a popular plurality and an electoral-vote majority; otherwise, a joint session of Congress would decide. Ervin, confident of his side's capacity to block E, blandly responded that the new proposal required "more study." Acting on the admission of E's backers that they lacked the votes to impose cloture, Mansfield withdrew his motion on October 5. Technically, E remained pending business, callable at any time, but it was not to be called up for the remainder of the 91st Congress. Electoral reform was dead.

*Analyzing the Votes.* E's sponsors skillfully kept their measure free from excess baggage which might reduce support. Rejecting the addition of a uniform presidential primary system to E, Bayh commented that

> . . . if we were to commingle the nominating process with electoral reform, it would sound the death knell of basic electoral reform.

When the possible inclusion of Guam and other territories within the scope of E was raised, it was quickly pushed off by Celler for later and separate hearings. And, as noted earlier, the same strategic calculations precluded adding provisions to E to strengthen Congress's authority over the registration and voting process. In short, Congress was being asked to determine core electoral reform stripped to its essentials.

The opposition to E in the House and Senate came disproportionately from southern Democrats, Republicans, and legislators from less populous states. On the party factor, 73 percent of the House Democrats opposed recommitting E to the House Judiciary Committee to get DP and 81 percent supported E on final passage; the comparable figures for the House Republicans were 44 and 86 percent. In the Senate, 65 percent of the Democrats but only 54 percent of the Republicans supported the first cloture vote. (The second cloture vote virtually duplicated the first.) Democratic performance is weakened, of course, by inclusion of the predominantly Democratic South in these data. Nonsouthern Democrats were almost unanimous in backing E in the House and for cloture in the Senate.

The South constituted the major center of resistance to E. Almost half the House vote to recommit E came from the eleven former Confederate states, which went 76 percent for the motion. Only 48 percent of the region's legislators endorsed E's enactment while southern opposition accounted for 74 percent of the total of seventy negative votes cast. Interestingly, the twenty-five southern Republicans voting went almost as a bloc for the recommittal motion, but more than half then voted for E. This shift mirrored that of nonsouthern Republicans, whereas no more than 25 percent of southern Democrats initially voting for recommittal later voted for E. In the Senate, 86 percent of the southerners opposed cloture, comprising over half that vote.

The small states outside the South (twenty-three states with eight or less electoral votes) opposed E more than the rest of the non-South, but not nearly as strongly as had been feared by Presidents Johnson and Nixon and hoped for by conservatives. In the House, only 47 percent of small-state legislators supported recommittal in favor of DP and a resounding 85 percent backed E's passage. That small states supplied 42 percent of the anticloture vote was almost entirely a function of party: with an almost equal number of Democratic and Republican Senators from these twenty-three states, thirteen of the fifteen anticloture votes came from Republicans.

Legislative responsibility for E's demise in 1970 can thus be assigned jointly to southerners and to Republicans from small states and/or of a conservative persuasion. Further, the unmodified opposition of the latter group owed much to the unwillingness of the Republican president to assign high priority to his professed goal of electoral reform or to push vigorously for it. In a deeper sense, the political structure had underlying responsibility as well. Two aspects of the inflated power of the fifteen small-state senators who voted against cloture — "inflated" when judged solely by the population principle — are evident. The twenty-three nonsouthern small states had 13 percent of the population but held 46 percent of the Senate seats. And the anticloture votes from these small states, crediting each senator with half the number of his state's residents, represented but 4.4 percent of the nation's population.

The distribution of responsibility for the defeat of E involves multiple ironies, if viewed simply in the frame of small versus large states. Recall that the large-state beneficiaries of EC shunned the "countervailing inequity" theme of justification of EC, and they backed E instead. Enough small states (and the South) were willing, however, to press the advantages given them by a major inequity of political structure in order to block E, which surely confirmed the continuing validity of the "countervailing inequity" thesis. But the success of small-state legislators in helping to defeat E resulted in retention of an unreformed EC, whose operation favored large states!

Most small-state opponents of E doubtless were motivated primarily by conservatism, however, which eliminates the ironies. For committed conservatives the outcome was quite rational. As Senator Carl Curtis (R., Neb.) revealingly asserted, "I would agree to any plan to stop direct election of a President and Vice President." And that is precisely what he and like-minded colleagues did when the choice came down to accepting E or re-embracing EC.


### Concluding Observations

Congressman Chalmers Wylie (R., Ohio), judging that either or both the House and Senate would not enact a plan or the same plan, sought to persuade Congress to pass the issue on to the states. In a proposal which led Celler to observe that his "enthusiasm is a bit misguided," Wylie urged that Congress settle for kicking off the amendment process by offering each state the option of retaining EC or adopting PP, DP, or E. Senator Ralph Yarborough (D., Tex.) similarly argued that Congress should send two amendments to the states, one on E and the other on DP or PP, and let each state choose either or none. But Congress was unwilling, however severe its disagreements on electoral reform, to abdicate its responsibility for constitutional amendments by passing the buck to the states.

Without responsibility on the subject of electoral reform analogous to that of the Congress, this writer now appropriately "passes the buck" to the reader for his or her personal determination of the best way to elect the president. For both writer and reader, it would be tempting to simplify that complicated task by adopting either of two polar positions which apply but a single standard. On the one side, political justice and equity can be held to compel E. As to E's side effects, they can be brushed aside as of little or no concern or as unpredictable. Isn't democracy always a risky venture anyway? On the other side, a federal base for presidential elections can be insisted on, and the biases skewed to favor nonurban and conservative interests. Since when has the structure of American government been based on simple quantitative majoritarianism anyway? Rejection of both positions carries the cost of having to assess mixed schemes but provides the benefit of grappling with the reality of electoral reform, both substantively and strategically.

One overly used standard should be discarded. DP and PP supporters stressed that the electoral vote distributions under their plans would better reflect the popular vote than EC does. President Nixon insisted on a better match of electoral to popular vote divisions as a condition of reform accept-

*Allan P. Sindler*

able to him. But surely the essential feature of the gap is whether the same or a different winner is produced by each measure. The degree of mathematical faithfulness of the translation of popular into electoral votes — on other than the win/lose dimension — is neither of much importance nor of real concern. Whether to accept such marginal refinement would turn entirely on assessment of its other effects, and there seems little reason to search for methods primarily to implement that standard.

In considering electoral reform designs, considerations of political feasibility should not be slighted. It is not difficult, for example, to think up ways to reflect the population or turnout principle more strongly within the present EC. Electoral votes could be allocated only for House representation and/or each state could be limited to casting a proportion of its assigned electoral votes equal to its turnout rate. If, however, either change adversely affected enough states to block congressional endorsement or state ratification, then neither would be of much practical import. One written submission to Bayh's subcommittee, it might be noted, suggested that small states should be "compensated" for their loss of influence if E were adopted. Whatever one's reaction to that advocate's particular suggestion that the fifteen least populous states each should be given an additional House seat, his sensitivity to political feasibility and to the search for "trade-offs" cannot be faulted.

Similarly, a variety of devices come readily to mind to minimize the impact of third parties, a problem central to electoral reform. For indirect methods like EC, PP, and DP, a state's electoral vote could be cast initially in accord with the respective formulas, but if no candidate got the requisite number of electoral votes it could then be recast in confinement to the top two national candidates. For E, election by simple plurality would do the trick. But what of the feasibility (and desirability) of such devices which raise serious questions not merely about the legitimacy factor but about the political rights of voters, candidates and third parties?

Just as what is "best" may not be feasible, so what appears feasible may not be "best." In coming to personal judgment on electoral reform, the reader must work out his or her own estimates of what the political environment will bear and what the "best" system should be, and then develop a design reflecting the interplay of the two. Close attention to a wide range of criteria and impacts is required, in the manner of this study. Identification of relationships serves both to economize effort and to clarify alternatives; this study contains many from which to choose or which could be developed. By way of suggestion, consider the following:

1. The greater the likelihood the initial election will itself produce a winner, the more the contingency procedure can be used to satisfy those displeased by the form of the initial election. (Nixon's endorsement of a popular runoff, in the context of his stated preference for PP with a 40 percent rule, surely was intended to mollify liberals unhappy with PP.)

2. The chances of electoral-vote deadlock are a function in part of how states cast their electoral votes. A state-unit rule comfortably coexists with a requirement that the winning presidential candidate have a majority of the nation's electoral vote. If states cast divided electoral votes, however, the requirement should be eased to provide for a lower proportion of the total electoral vote.

3. The higher the minimum support level required to win, whether for popular or electoral votes, the greater the likelihood of broader geographic backing for the candidate meeting that level, but the greater the incentives to third parties of the "spoiler" type, the risks of deadlock and the importance of the contingency procedures.

4. Under E with the 40 percent level, and assuming it is not met, if any candidate satisfying alternate tests can qualify as president, the possibility of a nonplurality president remains, but the chances of avoiding deadlock are better than if alternative qualification is restricted to the plurality leader.

5. When more than one test can qualify a candidate as president, setting the priority of each test profoundly affects its implications for the political system. Consider the differences, assuming use of the state-unit rule, in awarding the presidency (a) to the candidate with an electoral-vote majority; if none, then to the candidate with the highest popular vote; (b) to the candidate with a popular-vote majority; if none, then to the candidate with the highest electoral vote; and (c) to the candidate with a popular-vote plurality and an electoral-vote majority.

6. Can the effects attributed to a particular method be secured by other and perhaps more modest means? (The assertion of Congressman Jonathan Bingham (D., N.Y.) is worth exploring. Aside from guaranteeing victory to the candidate with the most popular votes, Bingham stated, "every other argument that is raised for [E] can be met by some less drastic change in our system.")

E's defeat in 1970 delays but surely does not end electoral reform in our time. An EC "misfire," a renewal of third-party pursuit of EC deadlock, a president truly committed to revision of EC — for any of these or other reasons the question of electoral reform will be back high on the legislative agenda. Readers accepting this invitation to puzzle through the electoral reform quandary can take heart, therefore, that they are wrestling with an issue both important and alive.

*Allan P. Sindler*

## SOURCES AND READINGS

A large number and variety of books, articles in professional and popular journals, newspaper accounts, congressional documents, and election data and analysis were used in making this study. The selective list that follows, from which the reader is invited to choose to probe the subject further, includes many of the most helpful sources.

The 1969 hearings before the Judiciary Committee of each chamber are an invaluable source, and well worth the reader's dabbling in either volume, each over a thousand pages. Each volume includes formal statements of interest groups, legislators, expert organizations, and individual experts; the text of resolutions and bills on the subject; reprints of some newspaper editorials and journal articles; and considerable data and analysis on presidential elections, state population, turnout rate, etc. Further, and by no means least, the record of the testimony of witnesses and their exchange of views with committee members adds lively and often insightful dimensions to the study of electoral reform. The House hearings are entitled *Electoral College Reform*, the Senate hearings, *Electing the President*; the former were held before the full HJC, the latter before the Subcommittee on Constitutional Amendments of the SJC. Both hearings were held in 1969, 91st Congress, 1st Session; published by the Government Printing Office, Washington, D.C.

The *Congressional Record* for September 1969 and September 1970 covers the debates, amendments, and votes for the handling of electoral reform by the House and Senate respectively. The *New York Times*' coverage of the same subject can be followed easily by use of that newspaper's index. The *Weekly Reports* for the same period published by the *Congressional Quarterly* (CQ) should also be consulted. In some of CQ's other publications, such as *Congress and the Nation, 1945–64*, a sketch of previous attempts at electoral reform can be had.

A recent full account of the subject which influenced Congress is Neil R. Peirce, *The People's President* (New York: Simon and Schuster, 1968). A blend of scholarship and journalism, it argues for direct popular election. Most often cited on behalf of retaining the present system was a set of articles by Alexander M. Bickel which appeared in the *New Republic* (January 28, 1967, and May 10, 1969) and in *Commentary* (December 1968); the gist of his position is set forth in the second chapter of his *The New Age of Political Reform* (New York: Harper and Row, 1968).

Also arguing against the displacement of the present system by direct popular election are Wallace S. Sayre and Judith H. Parris in *Voting for President* (Washington, D.C.: The Brookings Institution, 1970), which appeared too late to affect congressional behavior in the conflict covered by this case study. It is briefer, less historical, and more systematically analytic than the Peirce volume. The most recent study, also brief, is Lawrence D. Longley and Alan G. Braun, *The Politics of Electoral College Reform* (New Haven: Yale University Press, 1972), which helps to understand some of the congressional maneuvering, especially in the Senate, over electoral reform in 1969–70. Otherwise, it covers familiar ground and from the viewpoint of advocates of direct popular election. In a very few pages Nelson W. Polsby and Aaron B. Wildavsky, *Presidential Elections* (New York: Charles Scribner's Sons, 3rd ed., 1971), pp. 258–271, make some cogent observations about electoral reform. Finally, there is my earlier article, "Presidential Election Methods and Urban-Ethnic Interests," *Law and Contemporary Problems* (Spring 1962), pp. 213–233, which treats the political consequences of the present method and of the district and proportional plans.

The influential ABA commission report referred to frequently in this study is published: American Bar Association, *Electing the President: A Report of the Commission on Electoral College Reform* (Chicago: American Bar Association, January 1967). The mathematical study treating relative state voter power under EC is John F. Banzhaf, "One Man, 3.312 Votes: A Mathematical Analysis of the Electoral College," *Villanova Law Review* (Winter 1968), pp. 303–346. My use of James MacGregor Burns' views on the "conservatism of fragmentation" is from his *Uncommon Sense* (New York: Harper and Row, 1972), esp. pp. 118–121. For a brief review and discussion of the diverse arguments on what caused and sustains American two-partyism, see my *Political Parties in the United States* (New York: St. Martin's Press, 1966), esp. pp. 49–71.

# STUDY THREE

## THE COURTS

Policy-making by the courts. The problem of inequitable school financing. *The historical pattern. Local
hegemony. The price of local hegemony. The state as
"equalizer."* Unheeded reform suggestions. The courts
and equal protection of the laws. Does equal protection
require educational equalization? Two unsuccessful
cases. Launching the *Serrano* case. *Rebuff in the lower
courts. Modifying the* Serrano *complaint. Serrano* in
the California Supreme Court. Reaction and overreac-
tion. Prohibited inequity is not compulsory equality.
Will the states comply? How much reform by the
states is likely? *The inertia factor. Education finance
reform: whose priority? Complexity and coalition-
building. A gloomy prognosis?* Will the courts push
into the "educational thicket"? *The equal protection
precedents. Proximate means versus ultimate ends. The
educational thicket. Proximate means and symbolic
consequences.* Intradistrict and interstate fiscal inequities. Will the "no wealth" standard be extended to
other government services? Concluding observations.
Sources and readings.

Judicial Policy-Making:
Inequitable Public School Financing
and the *Serrano* Case (1971)

*David L. Kirp*

Six years ago, John Serrano, Jr., a Los Angeles social worker long active in education affairs, was called by the principal of the East Los Angeles *barrio* elementary school which his two sons attended. "Your sons are very bright," the principal told Serrano. "If you want to give them a decent chance in life, take them out of this school."

The advice was shocking. "What was all that stuff you've been giving us about how good the schools are?" Serrano demanded of the principal. But the wisdom of the principal's suggestion struck home. Within months, Serrano and his family moved ten miles away from the poor, Mexican-American community of East Los Angeles to Whittier, a middle-class suburb (birthplace of Richard Nixon).

The story of John Serrano is not unique. Overcrowded classrooms, poorly qualified teachers, and shabby schoolhouses have long been characteristic of public education in poor communities. But, unlike his counterparts elsewhere, Serrano sought to challenge this pattern. He discussed his problem with Derrick Bell and Charles Jones, two lawyers whom he happened to meet at a dinner party in the *barrio*. Those conversations sparked a chain of events that eventually led to the filing of a lawsuit challenging the constitutionality of the California school financing laws. "That's all I had to do with the case," Serrano says. "After that it was the lawyers' case."

In August 1971, four years after Serrano's suit was initially brought, the California Supreme Court declared that the state's school financing scheme denied Serrano, and other residents of poor school districts in the state, equal protection of the law. In the following six months, state and federal courts in New Jersey, Minnesota, Arizona, Utah, and Texas reached similar conclusions in comparable cases within their respective jurisdictions. The Texas case is, at the time of this writing (October 1972), on appeal to the United States Supreme Court.

Whatever the conclusion of the Supreme Court, a study of *Serrano* and its school finance progeny permits exploration of both the impact of judicial policy intervention and the substantive problem of public school financing.

## Policy-Making by the Courts

Article III of the Constitution, the Judiciary Act of 1789, and the fifty state constitutions, taken together, give both state and federal courts authority to determine the constitutionality of legislative decisions. That grant of power to review legislation renders the American courts the most potent in the world and inexorably involves them in policy-making. It creates a dynamic which encourages increasing reliance on the courts for policy guidance. Alexis de Tocqueville's observation that "scarcely any political question arises in the United States that is not resolved, sooner or later, into a judicial question" remains no less true today.

The courts' policy-making role takes two forms: *legitimating* and *checking* legislative acts. When courts uphold a statute against a challenge to its constitutionality, they explicitly declare it to be consistent with constitutional principles of governance. By legitimating what the lawmakers have done, the courts provide a means of securing the support (or acquiescence) of the minority opposition. As Alexander Bickel notes: "Not only is the Supreme Court capable of generating consent for hotly controversial issues; it has the subtler power of adding a certain impetus to measures that the majority enacts rather tentatively." In conferring legitimacy, the Court supports not only particular policies but also basic patterns of governmental behavior suitable for American democracy.

The power to review implies the authority to set the bounds of permissible policy — to say "no" as well as "yes" — and its exercise has drawn substantial criticism. The anomaly of judicial review in a populistic democracy has frequently been noted. Legal scholars have questioned the courts' capacity to reach reasoned judgments on social issues, and argued that legal analysis, even if conscientiously undertaken, is an imperfect means by which to test the wisdom of social policy. A great many people, most of whom have never read a judicial opinion in their lives, deride the courts for nay-saying decisions which they find personally offensive. Few who displayed "Impeach Earl Warren" bumper stickers knew anything about the Chief Justice other than that "his" court had integrated the schools, protected the rights of criminal suspects, and banned prayer in the classroom. Their unhappiness with those results led them to resent the Court that spawned such decisions.

Both the critics and the supporters of particular policy decisions assume that judicial pronouncements have an impact on individual and institutional behavior. Yet, ten years after the Supreme Court in *Brown* v. *Board of Education* (1954) declared school segregation to be unconstitutional only 2.5 percent of all southern black children attended integrated schools. In Cambridge, Massachusetts (home of "godless Harvard"), and countless communities throughout the nation, the school day still begins with a prayer, in defiance of the Supreme Court's ban on religious exercises in the schools. Police departments regularly employ tactics for gathering evidence and questioning suspects that earlier were held unconstitutional. That court decisions do not necessarily or automatically secure general compliance suggests the utility of a more precise understanding of the relation between court decisions and changes in behavior.

The most obvious measure of judicial impact is the effect on the individual litigant: did X do what the court commanded him to do? For those interested in the relationship between judicial decision and policy impact, however, what happens to a particular individual matters less than what happens to social institutions. A second measure of impact is quantitative: in a lawsuit challenging the actions of a class of individuals, what proportion of the affected population (state legislatures, school teachers, policemen) behaved differently because of a judicial ruling? Determining such a causal relationship is always difficult and often impossible. For example, suppose police department Y stops wiretapping without judicial permission six months after the Supreme Court has struck down the practice. Was the change caused by the courts or were other factors — citizen complaints, the inefficiency of "bugging" — decisive? Quantitative data, which purport to measure how much change has occurred, do not readily reveal why change has (or has not) taken place.

Other and more subtle questions demonstrate the complexities of impact assessment. Did a particular court decision facilitate changes in other policymaking agencies? Did the decision serve an educating function, influencing individual attitudes which might ultimately alter long-run social policies? Did the decision have a symbolic impact, affirming social ideals and norms?

These impact dimensions — facilitative, educative, symbolic — may better be understood by recasting the questions in the context of *Brown* v. *Board of*

*Education.* To what extent did *Brown* help make passage of the 1964 Civil Rights Act, which substantially expanded the rights of racial and ethnic minorities, politically possible? Is *Brown* partly responsible for attitude surveys which show that southern whites have come increasingly to accept desegregation? Did *Brown* symbolize official recognition of a higher status for blacks in the society, thus benefiting the black community even though that official recognition did not yield full and immediate enforcement? What would have been the effect of a court decision reaffirming the constitutionality of "separate but equal" schooling? These questions indicate the difficulties inherent in defining judicial impact.

As the courts are increasingly called on to use their checking power in order to preserve and extend the rights of poor and minority groups, the nature of judicial impact assumes new importance. Lawyers who bring suits challenging education, welfare, and housing policies deliberately bypass the state and federal legislatures, in good part because they believe their views stand a better chance both of winning in the courts, and winning big. Success in the U.S. Supreme Court assures a rule of law which, at least potentially, strikes down similar programs or policies wherever they might be practiced. Its impact is nationwide. Judicial review promises an end run around unresponsive and budget-conscious legislatures, a way to secure just but politically unpalatable outcomes.

Recourse to the courts for relief from inequitable school financing schemes was premised on such strategic calculations by reform-oriented lawyers and scholars, who invested years of research in planning their arguments. How successful were they in persuading the courts to employ their checking function to limit legislative discretion? And what might be the impact of a judicial decision upholding their claims? Before considering these questions, some understanding of the rudiments of school financing is in order.


The Problem of Inequitable School Financing

*The Historical Pattern.* Ever since the Massachusetts Bay Colonies were settled, America has maintained publicly supported primary and secondary schools. The Northwest Ordinance of 1787 made the provision of public education national policy, declaring that "schools and the means of education shall forever be encouraged," and requiring the new territories to set aside land for school construction. Until the nineteenth century, however, education was chiefly financed by individual contribution. The rich went to private academies. The poor generally attended charity and rate-bill schools (the latter charging minimal tuition) whose inadequacy evoked demands for reform from those who, echoing Massachusetts Education Commissioner Horace Mann, saw public education as "the balance-wheel of the social machinery." A general tax, administered by the state, was urged. Instead, all

*David L. Kirp*

states chose to permit (and ultimately to require) local communities to tax their residents, set up and run their own schools.

The minimal state role implicit in such a policy persists. The nation's 21,000 primary and secondary school districts set school tax rates, establish budgets, determine curriculum policy, hire and fire teachers, construct schools, and generally manage the day-to-day affairs of education. The state merely fixes minimum standards. It determines the length of the school year, defines the requisites of teacher competence, and requires that particular courses (in English and state history, for example) be offered. Although states now make substantial contributions to the cost of public instruction, local school districts still foot most of the $43 billion annual bill. In 1970–71, 52 percent of school revenue was provided by local sources, 41 percent came from state sources, and the remaining 7 percent from the federal government.

*Local Hegemony.*   Continued local hegemony over education policy and financing is sustained by pronounced public sentiment that education should be primarily entrusted to the community. Since schooling is the most extended intrusion by government into the lives of its citizens, it is argued that educational decisions are better made by small governmental units which provide parents (those most directly affected by their children's education) greatest influence in policy determination. Local control over education, the argument continues, enables public schools to respond to the asserted needs of parents and communities. It also prevents schools from standardizing children by requiring them to submit to the same educational regime. The mythical boast of the French education minister, that he could tell exactly what was happening in every classroom in the Republic merely by consulting his watch, evokes shudders among American parents long committed to diversity. Local control also permits those communities who care a great deal about the quality of their schools to tax themselves heavily, putting their money where their concerns are.

These asserted virtues of leaving educational policy-making to the community appear to be more a claim than a reality. Parental involvement in educational decision-making, for example, is often no greater in small districts than in mammoth ones like New York City. Nor does the extent of parental participation in school policies appear to affect pupil performance. While local control should promote diversity, American schools are remarkable not for their differences but for their sameness. Whether or not more myth than fact, the argument for local control retains its political potency. It was successfully utilized to stall substantial federal aid to public education until the mid-sixties and, when couched as a defense of the neighborhood school, to discourage school integration efforts.

*The Price of Local Hegemony.*   Because school districts raise the bulk of educational revenues from their own taxable resources, local control also creates great fiscal disparities among districts. By any measure of wealth, some communities are richer than others: they contain more wealthy people or fancier homes or bigger industries. Since school districts raise 98 percent of their revenues through the property tax, a district's real property (the value of its buildings and land) effectively defines its wealth. Thus, the presence of valuable real property, or, more accurately, a high ratio of valuable property to the number of schoolchildren, makes a community "wealthy," in educational finance terms.

Consider, for example, districts A and B. Both have 1,000 schoolchildren. District A, with $10 million of taxable property, has a $100,000 tax base for each child; district B, with $1 million of taxable property, has only $10,000. District A is ten times wealthier — has ten times more taxable resources per child to draw upon — than district B.

In theory, a school district determines the number of dollars that it needs to educate its children. From this budget it subtracts the money provided by the state and federal governments, and then fixes a tax rate which will yield the desired amount. Suppose, for example, that both districts A and B wish to raise $500 for each schoolchild. If district A taxes its property at one-half percent, it will accomplish this goal. District B, however, would have to tax itself ten times more heavily — 5 percent — to reach the same end.*

The ten-fold wealth difference between districts A and B is not just hypothetical. In California, the richest school district (the district with the highest property valuation per pupil) is twenty-five times wealthier than the poorest. In Michigan, the ratio is 30 : 1, in Illinois 20 : 1.† For that reason, the poorest California school district would have to fix a tax rate twenty-five times higher than the richest — in economists' terms, would have to make twenty-five times greater tax effort — in order to raise an equal number of dollars. Not surprisingly, poor districts have not made such Sisyphean demands on their residents. Rich districts consistently raise more money for schools than poor ones, even though poor districts typically set higher tax rates than rich ones. California school finance data, set out in Table One, illustrate these two points. The disparities are so pronounced that no lengthy inspection of the data is required. The richest ten districts spend more than

---

* One complicating factor, which this analysis does not treat, is the typical practice of assessing property at a fraction of its real or market value, and applying tax rates to this assessed valuation. If assessment practices differ from district to district, relative wealth may be difficult to determine, since an apparently poor district may simply be under-assessing its real property relative to other districts. In considering district wealth, this analysis assumes that assessment variations do not explain district wealth discrepancies; available data are consistent with that assumption.

† The data on wealth disparities, presented in the text, based on data gathered by the President's Commission on School Finance, includes only consolidated districts (which have both elementary and high schools). When one considers all California districts, property valuation per child ranges from $952,156 to $103, a ratio of nearly 10,000 : 1. The range diminishes considerably if one compares not the wealthiest and poorest districts, but districts at the 95th and 5th wealth percentile. In California, that wealth ratio is 5.9 : 1; in Michigan, 3.4 : 1; in Illinois 2.4 : 1.

*David L. Kirp*

California's Rich School Districts Raise More Money Through Less Tax Effort Than Poor School Districts (1968–69)

| Of All Unified School Districts Above 1,000 Average Daily Attendance (ADA) | Modified Assured Valuation per ADA (All Students) | Current Expenditure per Pupil (ADA) | Tax Rate per $100 |
|---|---|---|---|
| *Ten Richest Districts* | | | |
| Average | $34,542 | $929.94 | $2.82 |
| Range | $28,170–$50,885 | $781–$1,232 | $2.17–$3.70 |
| *Ten Poorest Districts* | | | |
| Average | $4,144 | $609.54 | $4.61 |
| Range | $1,883–$4,963 | $563–$682 | $3.46–$6.10 |

any of the poorest ten, while the poorest ten have higher tax rates than all but one of the richest ten districts.

Because school district wealth is defined in terms of property, and not the aggregate income of its residents, the fact that *poor districts* spend more money on schooling than rich ones does not necessarily mean that *poor children* are shortchanged. Scant evidence correlating district and personal wealth exists. In Texas, the very wealthiest school districts have the highest family incomes in the state, the very poorest districts include the poorest families. But for the 85 percent of Texas' districts which lie between these extremes, no such correlation exists. The relationship between personal and school district wealth is likely to vary from state to state, and between rural and urban areas of a given state. In short, school finance inequity, while real, may not correspond with wealth variation among families or individuals. The California Supreme Court, when confronted with the fact that district wealth is at best an imperfect proxy for personal wealth, proved willing to base its analysis and decision on district resource disparities alone.

*The State as "Equalizer."* During the past seventy years, states have markedly increased their financial contribution to education. The intent of these grants, as Ellwood Cubberley, the most influential of the early school finance reformers noted, is "to secure for all as high a minimum of good instruction as possible . . . to equalize the advantages to all as nearly as can be done with the resources at hand." Yet in fact, state aid policies only slightly mitigate the consequences of community wealth variations.

Most states provide basic and/or "flat grants" — a fixed number of dollars per schoolchild — to all school districts, rich and poor. California, for example, provides $125 for each pupil. But because these grants are both relatively small and are distributed to all districts, they do nothing to reduce the wealth disparities among districts.

State "equalizing grants" are ostensibly designed to satisfy Cubberley's goal of "equalizing the advantages to all. . . ." In calculating a district's equalizing aid, the state first determines how much local property tax revenue would be generated if the district levied a hypothetical property tax (in California, the tax rate used in the calculation is $1 per $100 assessed valuation for elementary school districts). To that figure, the state adds the flat grant. If the sum of these two figures is less than a minimum per student "foundation," the state contributes the difference. In California, the foundation guarantee per child is $355 for elementary school districts and $488 for high school districts.

The workings of this formula may be better understood by considering its effect on our hypothetical districts A and B. District A, with $100,000 tax base per child, receives a flat grant of $125. If it taxes itself at $1 per $100 assessed valuation (i.e., at 1 percent), it will raise $1,000. Since $1,125 is greater than the equalizing grant of $355, district A receives no foundation aid money. District B also receives the $125 flat grant. The 1 percent tax on its $10,000 tax base per child yields only $100. Thus, district B is entitled to $130 for each elementary school child ($355 foundation grant minus both $125 flat grant and the $100 which its taxes raise) and $263 for each high school student.

While combining flat and equalizing grants could equalize schooling resources among rich and poor districts, it has not done so. In many states flat grant funds are subtracted from the foundation guarantee, and hence aid only the rich districts which would not receive foundation grant support in any case. The equalizing grant has almost invariably been set at a level lower than what politicians and schoolmen recognize as necessary to maintain an educational system. As Table One indicates, the ten *poorest* California school districts spent an average of $609 for each school-age child, $254 more than the elementary school foundation grant and $121 more than the high school foundation grant. While the formula by which foundation support is calculated varies from state to state, the inadequacy of state assistance to poor school districts is universally true. In Cubberley's terms, the "resources at hand" have never been sufficient.

"Categorical" state grants provide additional dollars for the education of children whom the state deems particularly needy: the physically handicapped, the retarded, and, in a few states, poor and "educationally disadvantaged" children. But these programs account for only a small proportion of state aid and their impact on the problem of fiscal inequity has been minimal; they are not designed to address that problem.

The consolidation of school districts, reducing their number from 150,000 to 21,000 during the past fifty years, has succeeded in eliminating some of the most glaring inequities by combining rich and poor districts. But the legal and political feasibility of district consolidation varies from state to state. And while the broad effect of consolidation has been to reduce resource disparities, it cannot eliminate them. Many poor districts simply do not have rich neighbors with whom they can merge.

Federal educational monies have had a marginal equalizing effect. The largest federal program, Title I of the Elementary and Secondary Education Act, initiated in 1965, annually provides $1.6 billion for the schooling of poor and educationally disadvantaged children. But the federal contribution is simply too small — about 6 percent of school expenditures — seriously to upset the pattern of inequity. Throughout the nation, inequities similar to those in California prevail. They call to mind Matthew's biblical prophecy, "To everyone who has will more be given, and he will have abundance; but from him who has not, even what he has will be taken away," and its contemporary rendering, "The more, the more."

### Unheeded Reform Suggestions

The problem of inequitable school financing has not gone unnoticed, at least by educational experts. A decade ago, James Allen, then New York State Commissioner of Education, called upon states to assume a greater proportion of the burden of education support, in order to reduce disparities among school districts. Charles Benson, the acknowledged dean of education economists, discussed the inadequacies of foundation plan support in his influential book, *The Economics of Public Education*, first published in 1961.

During the late '60s, taxpayers began to rebel in the face of ever-mounting property tax increases to support public schools. In Youngstown, Ohio, repeated taxpayer rejection of proposed tax hikes forced the city to shut down its public schools for more than a month. Schoolmen in Chicago and Philadelphia have had to sustain substantial budget deficits to keep schools running. Elsewhere, school boards trimmed bus and maintenance services, extracurricular activities, art and music classes, in an effort to keep school costs and the property tax burden within politically acceptable bounds. The taxpayers' rebellion continues: in 1971, voters turned down roughly half of all school bond and tax hike proposals; more than 70 percent had been approved between 1958 and 1966.

The heightened political consciousness of black and poor parents gave the school finance issue increasing impetus. In the late '50s, several black parents in New York City, objecting to the run-down, understaffed schools to which their children were assigned, sought to keep them home. A state judge upheld their right to do so, until the Board of Education improved those schools. During the '60s, these groups changed their tactics and pushed directly for legislative and administrative reforms which would improve the condition of the benighted urban schools. They argued, quite correctly, that because of the finance system's built-in bias favoring wealthy communities, the very children who might benefit most from education — poor and minority students — often received the least.

Faced with these demands from strapped taxpayers and poor parents, the state declined to do more than make miniscule adjustments in foundation plan formulas. Flat grants were popular with wealthy districts, and for that reason proved politically unassailable. And proposals to increase the state's share of the educational budget substantially were resisted by legislatures, unwilling to impose the unpopular tax hikes which those proposals would have required. Nor did Congress intervene with massive infusions of federal funds.

Rebellious taxpayers and newly aroused organizations of poor and minority parents viewed the political system as unresponsive to their demands for reform. But the increasing willingness of federal courts (and some venturesome state tribunals like the California Supreme Court) to exercise their checking function, to limit legislative actions which deny the poor the equal protection of the laws, rendered an appeal to the judiciary a plausible alternative.

### The Courts and Equal Protection of the Laws

The equal protection clause of the Fourteenth Amendment is phrased as a command to the states. "No state shall . . . deny to any person within its jurisdiction the equal protection of the laws." But what governmental action is prohibited by that command? The resolution of that question, largely undiscussed when the amendment was ratified a century ago, has been left to the courts. The courts have not proferred a simple and unalterable definition. Instead, as for other broad constitutional provisions subject to judicial interpretation, the views of the courts (and the society) as to the scope of government's obligation to treat its citizens fairly have changed over time.

Courts have long recognized that the equal protection clause could not be read literally to compel all legislation to have equal and universal impact. "From the very necessities of society," the U.S. Supreme Court noted almost a century ago, "legislation of a special character . . . must often be had in certain districts. . . . Special burdens are often necessary for general benefits." The judicial wisdom has usually deferred to legislative expertise in discriminating between — classifying — persons affected. Courts have been satisfied if some rational relationship between a legitimate legislative purpose and the classifying principle could be established. They have not required a showing that the relationship be the *most* rational that could be conceived, that the alternative chosen be somehow the wisest. Such questions, it has been felt, are "political," and thus inappropriate for judicial examination.

Only infrequently has legislation run afoul of the equal protection clause. Statutes have been struck down where the classification appears to be based on pure hazard or caprice, where *no* reasonable classification relates the legislation to the persons affected. "The equal protection clause prevents States from *arbitrarily* treating people differently under their laws," the Supreme Court declared nearly a century ago.

When the legislature relies on certain traits, notably race and creed, in making classifications, courts historically abandoned their posture of deference to the legislature, erecting a presumption of unreasonableness. "All legal restrictions which curb the civil rights of a single racial group are immediately suspect. That is not to say that all such restrictions are unconstitutional. It is to say that the courts must subject them to the most rigid scrutiny."

The reasons for this judicial presumption are both historical and ethical. The Fourteenth Amendment was a Civil War Amendment, whose "clear and central purpose," the U.S. Supreme Court declared, "was to eliminate all state sources of invidious racial discrimination." The political powerlessness of racial minorities, their vulnerability to adverse treatment by political majorities, justified a more expansive judicial role. Discrimination against minorities also raised serious ethical issues. In a society which proclaims the equality of all men, race and lineage, traits over which an individual has no control, presumptively provide no basis for an inference of differing worth.

During the past fifteen years, the scope of equal protection has broadened. The Supreme Court has struck down legislation which, while "rational" in purpose and "reasonable" in application, either affected fundamental interests or created suspect classifications, a category broadened to include the poor as well as racial minorities. Thus, in the '50s and '60s, states were required to make available free court transcripts and appellate counsel to criminal suspects too poor to afford them; the poll tax was invalidated because it denied indigents the opportunity of voting; welfare residency requirements were found to impose an unconstitutional impediment on the right of the poor to travel from state to state. Each of these interests was viewed as fundamental; in each case, state law also had a profound effect on the poor.

What Archibald Cox terms "the relative invidiousness of the particular differentiation" and "the relative importance of the subject with respect to which equality is sought" interact with each other in these cases. The interaction can be conceptualized by imagining a hierarchy of classification ranging from the presumptively rational (age-grading in schools, for example) to the suspect or invidious (laws which discriminate against racial minorities), and a hierarchy of interests, ranging from the trivial (parking meter pricing) to the fundamental (voting and criminal process). When the classification appears invidious, courts will carefully appraise it even if the interest affected is relatively unimportant. Where the classification is less obviously suspect, courts will closely scrutinize the legislation only if it affects basic interests.

When courts apply this strict review standard, the government must demonstrate both that the challenged legislation serves a compelling purpose and that the mode chosen to effectuate that purpose is least likely to cause inequality. This stricter standard of review has more than semantic implication. When invoked, it poses for the state a burden of justification that has almost invariably proved impossible to satisfy. Only in wartime emergency has a statute singling out a racial or ethnic group been upheld; and in almost all cases in which the Supreme Court has regarded an interest as fundamental, government action restricting exercise of that interest has been overturned.

At no point has the Supreme Court ever clearly defined fundamentality or invidiousness. Without doubt, the interests the courts have deemed "fundamental" — effective participation in the political process, adequate defense against criminal charges, freedom to travel — are important to the individual. Unequal treatment of these interests clearly causes severe injury to those disadvantaged, and may affect freedoms guaranteed by the Constitution. Yet assertions of importance and injury do not yield a cogent limiting principle. The very open-endedness of the constitutional standard led lawyers to speculate whether other important governmental services — provision of welfare, health, police, and fire protection; most notably education — could be characterized as affecting fundamental interests or injuring the poor (or both). If so, disparities in the provision of those services might well be unconstitutional.

## Does Equal Protection Require Educational Equalization?

The appropriateness of treating public education as a "fundamental interest" is premised on comparisons between schooling and other interests which the Supreme Court has assigned to that category. Advocates of such treatment, and the meticulous judicial examination of inequalities that it implies, argue that education represents the state's longest and most extensive involvement in the lives of citizens, designed to shape attitudes and develop intellectual and social skills to an extent undreamt of by any other government action. Education also seeks to prepare children for effective participation in the political process. It nurtures their capacity to understand and use their constitutionally secured rights of speech and action, and to defend themselves when accused of crimes. To that extent, the advocates argue, schooling underlies the effective exercise of all other constitutional rights — including those which the Warren Court had found to be fundamental. Furthermore, lawyers began wondering, if access to a trial transcript of legal counsel in a criminal appeal, or to the ballot box in state elections could not be conditioned on wealth, why should the allocation of education dollars based on the wealth of the school district in which a child's family lived be treated differently?

Yet even if a credible constitutional argument requiring some measure of equalization could be fashioned, there was little agreement on what that measure should be. The range of alternatives is broad. Resources — what economists term "educational inputs" — can be equalized; for example, by setting uniform student-teacher ratios, or spending an equal number of dollars on all children. Alternatively, resources can be distributed unequally, with additional dollars used to compensate for differences in children's background and ability; for example, by providing extra assistance to slow learners or children whose native language is not English. Finally, success in schooling — "educational outcomes," in economists' terms — can be equalized, to assure either that all children graduate from school with the same skills or that educational success is randomly distributed among racial and class groups so that (as James Guthrie proposed) "a representative individual of any racial or social grouping has the same probability of succeeding as does a representative individual of any other racial or social grouping."

Each standard — input equality, compensatory input equality, and outcomes equality — poses troubling questions. What resources, for example, would have to be equalized to satisfy the first approach? What resource allocation formula would enable all children to begin school with an equal chance? What are the social consequences — changes in budgetary and goal priorities, in the role of the state vis à vis the individual — of each alternative? How might the equality standards be implemented, given the present limited knowledge about the effects of schooling? While critics scored these egalitarian visions as unfeasible or undesirable (or both), those who initiated legal attacks on existing school finance arrangements defined "equality" in input or outcome terms.

### Two Unsuccessful Cases

In 1967, the Detroit, Michigan, school board was, like so many other city boards throughout the nation, desperate for funds. Although Detroit is not a poor school district, its municipal expenses far exceeded those of any other Michigan community and drained locally raised dollars that might otherwise have been available for schools. Many of Detroit's children were doing badly in school, scoring two to four grade levels below their counterparts in the surrounding suburbs. The school board, which had unsuccessfully sought financial relief from the state legislature, requested that its attorneys puzzle out an escape from the schools' fiscal crisis. In 1967, Detroit brought suit against the state of Michigan, charging that the state's school finance system did not equally meet the "educational needs" of all children, and thus denied those children equal protection of the laws. (The Michigan system, like the typical state scheme described earlier, provides limited state funds in the form of flat grants and equalizing aid, while requiring local districts to raise the balance of their revenue through property taxes.)

While the case never went to trial, the Michigan suit made headlines in newspapers all over the country, and it spurred the Chicago Community Legal Services Program to imitation. That office, part of the Office of Economic Opportunity Legal Services Program, was founded to serve the legal problems of those too poor to afford an attorney. Like most other legal services offices, much of its time was spent on individual complaints: divorce actions, consumer squabbles, and landlord-tenant problems. But the Chicago program was interested in more than what it termed "band-aid" solutions to the problems of the poor. By bringing major and politically controversial law-reform suits on behalf of the *class* of poor people, it also sought systemic change which would improve the basic conditions of their lives.\* School finance reform afforded what appeared a superb opportunity to secure significant benefits. In 1967, the Community Legal Services Program, on behalf of all the poor people of Chicago, filed a carbon copy of the Michigan complaint in the United States District Court.

The Legal Services complaint in *McInnis* v. *Shapiro* sought a court order requiring Illinois officials legally responsible for administering the school finance laws "to submit . . . a plan to raise and apportion all monies . . . in such a manner that such funds available to the school districts wherein the class of plaintiffs attend school will . . . assure that plaintiff children receive the same educational opportunity as the children in any other district," a plan which met the "educational needs" of all children. As an alternative remedy, plaintiffs proposed that per-pupil expenditures be equalized throughout the state. In short, the Chicago attorneys argued, either input equality or compensatory input equality was constitutionally required.

The District Court rejected both suggestions. An educational-needs standard, it declared, was too "nebulous" to afford a "judicially manageable remedy." An equal-dollars standard, while readily defined, promised only "uniform, mediocre instruction." The voting rights, criminal procedure and school desegregation cases, which plaintiffs had relied upon in making their argument, were distinguished by the court, which noted that "the decided cases established significant, but limited principles" inapplicable to the realm of school finance. The court concluded: "There is no constitutional requirement that public school expenditures be made only on the basis of pupils' educational needs without regard for the financial strength of local school districts. Nor does the Constitution establish the rigid guidelines of equal-dollar expenditures for each student." If the Illinois financing scheme distressed Chicagoans, change "should be sought in the legislature and not in the courts."

Most district court decisions may be appealed to the Court of Appeals, an intermediate federal court. The party who loses at that level may request the

---

\* Class action suits are brought by individuals whose interests allegedly are similar to those of a larger group; the named individuals "represent" the class in court. A class might consist of all those allegedly defrauded by the credit policy of a particular company; or, as in this case, those who are injured by a governmental policy. The court does not undertake to poll the class, to determine whether the individual litigants do in fact represent its interests. Rather, it invites other members of the class to intervene in the lawsuit if they wish to challenge the existence of a class, or press a viewpoint contrary to that advanced by the individual litigants. A decision in a class action suit potentially binds all members of the class, and for that reason such suits are the primary vehicle for "law reform" litigation.

*David L. Kirp*

Supreme Court to review the case, but in most instances the Court has discretion to deny the request. *McInnis* had challenged the constitutionality of a state statute. Federal law requires that such a challenge be heard initially by a three-judge district court, whose decisions are directly appealable to the Supreme Court. In those instances, the Supreme Court cannot refuse to hear the case and must decide, one way or the other.

In 1969, the Supreme Court affirmed *McInnis*, without opinion. Although the Court did not say that school finance inequities were free from constitutional infirmities, its action effectively foreclosed judicial reconsideration of the matter until the August 1971 decision of the California Supreme Court in *Serrano* v. *Priest*.

### Launching the *Serrano* Case

*Rebuff in the Lower Courts.*   Linda McInnis's challenge to the Illinois school financing scheme failed, while John Serrano's attack on the California system succeeded. What differentiates the two cases is not the fact of inequality — in both California and Illinois, wealthy districts are able to raise more education dollars with less tax effort than poor districts — but the constitutional arguments advanced and judicial remedies proposed. The *McInnis* suit, which insisted on the imposition of an educational-needs standard, threatened to diminish local autonomy and to bankrupt the state treasury. *Serrano* proposed a more modest and manageable constitutional formulation, one which the California Supreme Court ultimately concluded could be implemented without incurring undue political or economic costs.

While the origins of *Serrano* date to that fateful dinner party at which John Serrano discussed his plight with two attorneys from the O.E.O.-sponsored Western Center for Law and Poverty, the constitutional arguments initially bottoming the case were largely developed by Harold Horowitz, a U.C.L.A. law professor; Sidney Wolinsky, then a partner in a prestigious Beverly Hills law firm; and Derrick Bell, who had just been appointed director of the Western Center. Horowitz had been interested in the school finance problem for a number of years. In 1966, he published an article which groped for a constitutional handle on the issue. The U.S. Civil Rights Commission asked him to prepare a paper on equality of educational opportunity for a 1967 conference. That paper, later revised and published in the *U.C.L.A. Law Review*, concluded: "territorial variations within a state in public education . . . create especially significant inequities that, it seems clear, must now come under careful judicial scrutiny." Horowitz's article provided the basis for the *Serrano* complaint which, after 20 drafts and countless revisions, was filed in August, 1968, in Los Angeles Superior Court.

The litigants had two initial decisions to make: whom should they sue, and in what court should the case be filed? While the lawyers first considered suing all districts except the poorest in the state, the logistical difficulties with that approach proved overwhelming, and they decided instead to sue the three state officials responsible for disbursing education funds, and school officials in Los Angeles County, where the plaintiffs lived. In order to keep the case as politically noncontroversial as possible, the attorneys did not include Governor Reagan among the defendants.

The decision to file in state rather than federal court was exhaustively discussed by the coalition of lawyers. Since both federal and state courts could hear challenges to the constitutionality of California's laws, the lawyers had their choice. They ultimately opted to proceed in the state court system because of the progressive and innovative reputation of the California Supreme Court, the state's highest tribunal, which had demonstrated its willingness to apply the equal protection clause boldly and expansively. Several years earlier, in a school desegregation case, the California court had declared: "In view of the importance of education to a society and to the individual child, the opportunity to receive schooling furnished by the state must be made available to all on an equal basis." Serrano's attorneys hoped that the California court would reach the same conclusion with respect to education finance. Filing in state court afforded another advantage: it shielded the case from quick review by the U.S. Supreme Court. Serrano's attorneys hoped to build up a series of successes in lower courts before confronting the Supreme Court with the novel constitutional claim they were pressing.

The original *Serrano* complaint was, as Horowitz remarked, a "kitchen sink" challenge to California's school finance laws, proposing a host of constitutional issues and suggesting a variety of plausible remedies, including those which had been proferred in *McInnis*. It sought a declaration that the system of financing public schools violated the equal protection clause, an order directing state officials to restructure the financing system to undo these violations, and an adjudication that the court retain jurisdiction to impose its own plan, should the state fail to do so within a reasonable time.

*Serrano* did not fare well in California's lower courts. The Superior Court dismissed the case without writing an opinion in January 1969, three days after the U.S. Supreme Court decision in *McInnis* was announced. Wolinsky commented ruefully: "We drew the wrong judge, and the case is thrown out of court." In September 1970, the state's intermediate court affirmed the trial court's action. In a brief opinion, the court cited *McInnis*, concluding that "even if we are not bound by the *McInnis* holding, it is certainly of persuasive character and entitled to great weight. . . . And irrespective of its effect, as legally binding or not, its reasoning and logic are unquestioned." A petition for rehearing was denied the same month. In October 1970, one month after the appellate court's final action, Serrano's lawyers sought review by the California Supreme Court. The supreme court responded with a plain white postcard that said, "Serrano v. Priest/Hearing Granted," and called for oral argument in May 1971.

*David L. Kirp*

*Modifying the* Serrano *Complaint.* During the time between the filing of the *Serrano* complaint in 1967 and preparation of briefs for the California Supreme Court three years later, the suit was gradually modified to accommodate developing constitutional approaches. The complaint had originally demanded "geographical uniformity" in educational expenditure, and responsiveness to children's "special needs." These claims were initially coupled with and ultimately replaced by a quite different approach developed by Berkeley law professor John Coons, who had been pondering the problem of school finance inequities for almost a decade. He had been asked by the U.S. Civil Rights Commission to document discrimination in school spending in Chicago, and noted in his report that the discrepancies between Chicago and its wealthy suburbs were far greater than those among schools in the city. In 1966, Coons and two colleagues, Steven Sugarman and William Clune, began considering the issue of intradistrict finance disparities in earnest; by 1969, a bulky draft manuscript, *Private Wealth and Public Education,* outlining their constitutional argument, had emerged.

The argument advanced by Coons and his colleagues differed notably from *McInnis.* It did not insist that any particular measure of resource or "needs" equality was constitutionally required, but focused instead on the unequal capacity of school districts to provide financial support for schooling. The constitutional standard proposed by the triumvirate, and incorporated in the *Serrano* complaint, asserted that "the quality of public education [defined in terms of dollars spent] may not be a function of wealth, other than the wealth of the state as a whole." The prevailing system did just that, the *Serrano* suit argued, by creating wealth disparities among districts and making the amount of education a child received a function of where he lived.

The differences between the legal remedies sought by the litigant in *McInnis* and *Serrano* reflected differing views of the appropriate judicial role in addressing the school finance issue. *McInnis* attempted to substitute its own particular remedy (equal attention to student needs) for the existing formula, thus directly involving the courts in choosing among competing notions of good policy. Had the *McInnis* approach been adopted, the state would have been denied the opportunity to make its own judgments as to the importance of local control over schooling, equality, compensatory support, and the like.

*Serrano's* modesty suggested a more limited judicial role. The court was asked only to reject the existing scheme as arbitrary and unfair, to declare not that "the state must do this" but that "the state may not continue to do what it is presently doing," to insist upon fiscal neutrality as constitutionally required. That approach left the legislature free to adopt any of a variety of alternative schemes in accord with its calculation of what was educationally desirable and politically possible. As John Coons said, "we hoped that *Serrano* would break the legislative logjam that has blocked consideration of *any* rational policy for the distribution of educational dollars."

In conversations with the Detroit school board council, Coons had sought unsuccessfully to persuade them to alter their approach. Coons recalls: "We had a friendly disagreement. They were determined to proceed with the needs argument. We felt it was a loser." The distinctiveness of Coons' approach from that of *McInnis* enabled the California Supreme Court preliminarily to distinguish the two, and to agree to hear the *Serrano* case.

### *Serrano* in the California Supreme Court

In the winter of 1970–71, *Serrano's* prospects looked bleak. While the California Supreme Court had decided to hear the case, it seemed doubtful that a majority of the court could be persuaded that *Serrano* was sufficiently different from *McInnis* to warrant a different judicial conclusion.

What happened in the intervening months to reverse this gloomy prediction? *Private Wealth and Public Education*, published the previous year, was quickly recognized as a landmark work in constitutional law. The authors wrote as articulate advocates and scholars, willing both to criticize and to qualify their arguments. One commentator observed that "while *Private Wealth and Public Education* may not be the last word on the relation of education finance, law and public policy, it is without doubt the best word on the subject to date. It is one of the most ambitious, eclectic, and intelligently argued forays by lawyers into any educational policy realm." The three coauthors of *Private Wealth and Public Education* also filed a "friend of the court" brief on behalf of the Urban Coalition and the National Committee for the Support of the Public Schools, two national groups concerned with educational policy.* That brief, and a law review article written by Coons and his colleagues, doubtless influenced the decision. The court adopted the fiscal neutrality standard as its own, closely tracked the constitutional arguments advanced by Coons and his colleagues, and cited the law review piece eight times in its opinion.

The efforts of California's legislative analyst, Alan Post, were also significant in shaping the court's view. The legislative analyst serves the state legislature, reporting on the operation of state-mandated programs and assessing the consequences of proposed legislation. It is a nonpartisan office, meant to embody the concerns of "good government." During the two decades Post has held the job, he has acquired enormous respect among legislators and judges for the competence and fairness of his office's work.

---

* In most cases, briefs (written factual presentations and legal argument) are filed only by the parties to the action. Others who, while not parties to the lawsuit nonetheless have an interest in its outcome, may seek permission of the court to file what are termed "friend of the court" briefs. These briefs either adopt a point of view somewhat different from that espoused by either of the parties in the case, or attempt to bolster one side in the case by demonstrating that the position has broad organizational support.

*David L. Kirp*

The legislative analyst's suggestions for reforming the existing school finance scheme, while prepared entirely independent of the *Serrano* litigation, supported many of the contentions of the suit. The *Serrano* opinion relied heavily on those reports in demonstrating the inequities of California school finance. It cited, for example, the legislative analyst's findings that "poorer districts are financially unable to raise their taxes high enough to match the educational offerings of wealthier districts."

The quite different roles played by John Coons and Alan Post in *Serrano* suggest something about the importance of expertise in affecting judicial decisions. Coons was an articulate advocate, able through his writings to dispel many of the court's concerns and to provide a legal framework upon which to base the *Serrano* decision. Post had, over many years, acquired a reputation for accurate and unbiased work. That many of the same features of California's finance laws challenged in *Serrano* also had been critized by Post provided some assurance to the Court that the "no wealth" principle was politically feasible as well as constitutionally appropriate.

If Coons and Post suggested the real, if unstated, power of expertise, the "friend of the court" brief filed by the San Francisco Board of Education indicated the importance of subtle political persuasion. What was unusual was not the substance of the brief, which was relatively familiar, but that San Francisco supported the contentions of poor districts. As the brief noted, "the San Francisco Board of Education administers the richest urban district in California," a district that might well suffer if *Serrano* were successful. Yet, declared the board, "the system worsens the plight of our cities, and encourages the growing exodus of more affluent residents to the suburbs which offer them both tax haven and better-supported education. . . . We believe in a rational distribution of public resources for public education." Most surprisingly, the brief was cosigned by the six state senators and assemblymen who represented San Francisco. The political implications of that fact could not have been lost on the court.

During the May 1971 oral arguments, sharp and frequent questions posed by the judges indicated that they still were troubled by the issues which had defeated the *McInnis* suit. Sidney Wolinsky, who handled much of the plaintiffs' arguments, had barely begun speaking when Judge Raymond Peters interrupted to inquire: "What will happen if you win the suit? Will the schools go out of business?" "No," Wolinsky replied, "the state legislature may adopt any of a wide variety of alternatives." "And what about other governmental services — streets, libraries, sewers — are they fundamental too? Do they have to be equalized as well?" Judge Mathew Tobriner asked. Wolinsky responded that *Serrano* did not demand equalization of all public services, that it focused on education because of its importance to the exercise of the individual's political and economic rights.

Judge Louis Burke wondered whether dollars constituted a true standard of education, and Wolinsky replied: "Where dollar disparities are so gross, dollars do reflect educational inequality." Judge Burke was also troubled by what the court was being asked to do. "Can a court determine the quality of education in different school districts, or should the legislature determine what standards there should be?" Wolinsky's reply underscored the modesty of the *Serrano* approach. "We ask only that the court set the outer constitutional parameters in which the legislature should be left free to act — so long as it does not discriminate against the poor."

Chief Justice Donald Wright was worried about across-the-board equalization. "Surely you wouldn't apply the same standard in Quincy [an area of low living costs] and San Francisco?" "Equalization is not required," Wolinsky responded. "The state can take account of a wide variety of differentials in distributing resources."

John Coons, whose argument followed Wolinsky's, briefly described the variety of remedies that a legislature could adopt. Forced to set out a number of alternatives in a very few minutes, Coons initially puzzled the judges. "Does *Serrano* foreclose all local automony? Does it require dollar equality?" Judge Burke inquired. "Aren't you placing an intolerable burden on poor districts?" asked the Chief Justice. "These arguments should be made to the legislature," said Judge Peters. Ultimately, Coons convinced the court that it did not have to choose among remedies, and that legislative alternatives were available.

Serrano's lawyers proved remarkably adept at fielding complicated questions. The attorneys who represented the state of California were far less successful. Throughout their argument, they continually sought refuge in the *McInnis* precedent, declaring that it was determinative. That stance made the court impatient, and it repeatedly sought to fathom the state's position on the merits of the issue at hand. "Don't disparities exist? Don't they affect the educational opportunities of children?" the judges asked. Judge Peters put the same point in more homespun fashion: "I've been brought up to believe that you pay for what you get." Counsel for the state offered no response.

In August 1971, the California Supreme Court handed down a 35-page opinion. Technically, the decision (in which six of the seven justices concurred) reversed the trial court's dismissal and remanded the case for trial. But the opinion left no doubt as to the court's ultimate views on the dispute. The California court concluded that the arguments advanced in *McInnis* were "significantly different" from those pressed by Serrano's attorneys; the U.S. Supreme Court's summary affirmance in *McInnis* did not foreclose judicial review.

In undertaking that review, the court adopted almost all the plaintiffs' arguments. It described the state financing scheme as one which affected a "fundamental interest" and discriminated against the "constitutionally suspect classification" of poor districts. "Plaintiffs contend that the school financing system classifies on the basis of wealth. We find this proposition irrefutable." The court considered irrelevant the fact that poor people might not live in poor districts; discrimination among districts was constitutionally suspect.

We think that discrimination on the basis of district wealth is equally invalid [as discrimination based on personal wealth]. . . . To allot more educational dollars to the children of one district than to those of another merely because of the fortuitous presence of [valuable] property is to make the quality of a child's education depend upon the location of private commercial and industrial establishments. Surely this is to rely on the most irrelevant of factors as the base for educational financing.

The court concluded:

The California public school financing system . . . conditions the full entitlement to [education] on wealth, classifies its recipients on the basis of their collective affluence and makes the quality of a child's education depend upon the resources of his school district and ultimately upon the pocketbook of his parents. We find that such financing system as presently constituted is not necessary to the attainment of any compelling state interest. Since it does not withstand the requisite "strict scrutiny," it denies to the plaintiffs and others similarly situated the equal protection of the laws.

Four years after John Serrano's interview with the East Los Angeles principal, he had won his case.

### Reaction and Overreaction

Reaction in California to *Serrano* was quick and varied. Although no one defended the inequities of the existing finance system, schoolmen in the richest districts were plainly worried about the impact of the decision. Kenneth Peters, superintendent in Beverly Hills, feared that the legislature would halve his budget and hoped that the state would appeal the decision.* In San Mateo County, Tod Anton, superintendent of the wealthy Hillsborough elementary school district, expressed concern that "educational mediocrity would result" from the ruling. School officials in poor districts were jubilant. Glowed John Minor, superintendent of the largely black Ravenswood elementary school district in East Palo Alto, "we've been waiting for something like this for a long time."

At the state level, officials such as Wilson Riles, Superintendent of Public Instruction, and Houston Flournoy, the comptroller, both of whom had long advocated school finance reform, reacted favorably. "It's revolutionary," Riles

---

* Since, as noted above, the decision is technically not a final decision, no appeal is possible until the suit is heard again by the trial courts.

exclaimed. While Republican officials such as Governor Reagan withheld comment, Democratic politicians heaped praise on the court. "Why should parents of Beverly Hills school kids be entitled to gold-plated education when other districts can't paint their buildings?" asked former governor Pat Brown.

*Serrano* quickly attracted national attention. *Life,* the *New York Times,* the *Christian Science Monitor* and the *Wall Street Journal* re-echoed the court's view. Several states, including New York and Wisconsin, established special commissions to consider the educational finance question. While Philadelphia's school finance director "shuddered to think of the gyrations we'd have to go through to come up with a new system," Daniel Taylor, West Virginia's superintendent of schools, praised the result: "I don't think the accident of birth in terms of geography ought to be a significant factor in determining a child's educational opportunity."

*Serrano*'s implications for national politics were readily recognized. President Nixon, expressing "shock" over the inequities, proposed federal aid which would ease property tax burdens and reduce educational finance disparities. Sidney Marland, U.S. Commissioner of Education, called the ruling a "very fundamental breakthrough in the concept of state educational systems"; HEW Secretary Elliot Richardson praised *Serrano* as "the American ideal of labor rewarded." The President's Commission on School Finance concluded its efforts in March 1972 with a declaration that "the financial problems of education derive largely from the evolving inabilities of the States to create systems that provide equal educational opportunities . . . to all their children."

Within sixty days of the decision, lawyers in more than twenty states filed similar suits in state and federal courts throughout the country. These lawyers had earlier met in Washington, D.C., to discuss *Serrano*'s ramifications; the suits they filed borrowed heavily from the arguments initially advanced in that case.

The California court's opinion proved persuasive. It was often quoted with approval by judges in other states. The Wyoming Supreme Court was so impressed by it as to convert what had been a routine district consolidation dispute into a *Serrano* issue and to order statewide school finance equalization, a judicial action almost without precedent. Federal district courts in Minnesota and Texas and state courts in Arizona and New Jersey also struck down school finance statutes. Only one court, a trial in New York's wealthy Westchester County, dismissed such a complaint, concluding that *McInnis* foreclosed a favorable ruling.

Interest in the issue was not limited to politicians and judges. PTAs, taxpayers groups, teachers' unions, church organizations — seemingly everyone with a stake in education or tax policy wanted to know how *Serrano* might affect them. Those who praised the decision as a means of securing educational equity and those who damned it for imposing educational mediocrity shared Wilson Riles' view that, for better or worse, the educational revolution was at hand. In so doing, they failed to appreciate the limits of the modest fiscal neutrality standard which the California Supreme Court had adopted.

*David L. Kirp*

### Prohibited Inequity Is Not Compulsory Equality

Particularly with respect to controversial issues, people hear what they expect to hear. Often, their gloss on events assumes political significance equal to the event itself. The misunderstanding and confusion which *Serrano* occasioned proved no exception to this general proposition.

Those who sought state financing and control of schooling declared that the decision secured just that result. Writing in the *New Republic*, Jerome Zukosky, a onetime consultant to the New York education finance commission, asserted that school finance litigation

> is the equal of *Brown* — at least the equal because it provide[s] the lever of dismantling a system of shared power in all states . . . that undergirds the present school government structure . . . shifting to the state the power to make the major decisions in the political economy of public education.

Houston Flournoy, California's comptroller, concluded that the court decision "will force adoption of a uniform property tax." Those who opposed such a scheme were equally convinced that *Serrano* required its implementation. Thirty-eight of California's wealthiest school districts organized Schools for Sound Finance, a lobbying group dedicated to the defeat of the threatened statewide property tax.

Those who were concerned about equalizing educational resources for all children asserted that *Serrano* and its legal progeny required equalization. "School officials," *U.S. News and World Report* observed, "say the decision, if upheld, would require something like complete equalization of per-pupil spending on operations of public schools within each state." In poor districts, this was cause for joy; in rich districts, it evoked alarm. "Equal dollars does not mean equal education," warned the Beverly Hills school superintendent.

The "fiscal neutrality" principle of *Serrano* actually requires considerably less than the educators, politicians, and commentators hoped or dreaded. *Serrano* does not demand that the state distribute education dollars equally, securing the principle of "one dollar, one scholar." Nor does it require disequalization to favor the poor; none of the definitions of resource equality earlier described is constitutionally mandated. *Serrano* does not oblige the state to abandon local control of schooling, to provide funds sufficient to compensate for differences in cost of living in different areas, to spend more money, or to help (or hurt) big cities. In short, *Serrano* does not presage what commentators have called "the egalitarian revolution." The constitutional standard that "education may not be a function of wealth" requires *only* the adoption of a resource distribution formula which assures that poor districts are not shortchanged because of their limited taxable resources. Any formula which distributes education dollars on the basis of some rational criteria satisfies *Serrano*.

What school finance plans might a state adopt? It could choose either to raise all education money at the state level, or continue to rely on locally raised revenues to support schools. If it opted for state funding, a state might distribute education dollars on an equal per student basis. It could select a more refined formula which took into account cost of living differentials and transportation costs. The state might decide to fix dollar preferences for particular types of students, providing, for example, additional money for underachieving or physically handicapped students. It could give the school district discretion concerning educational expenditures or compel districts to spend fixed amounts for different kinds of students.

If the state decided instead to permit districts some choice in setting expenditure levels, it could allow districts to supplement the state's grant with locally raised funds. In order to satisfy *Serrano*, however, such a scheme would have to insure that a given tax effort produced the same revenue, regardless of the community's tax base; in other words, that equal tax effort yielded equal dollars. If, at a given tax rate, a poor district raised less than the guaranteed amount, the state would make up the difference; if a rich district, taxing itself at the same rate, raised more, the additional funds would be returned to the state.

## Will the States Comply?

If the U.S. Supreme Court affirms the "fiscal neutrality" principle, will state legislatures comply? While a decision of the Supreme Court in fact constitutes "the law of the land," the implementation of that law is not automatically secured, as earlier examples indicated. Noncompliance — or its kissing cousin, systematic evasion — is always a possibility which courts consider, unconsciously or self-consciously, in reaching decisions. The court's conclusion in *McInnis*, that the "needs" standard was nonjusticiable, might well be read as a declaration that the court lacked the wherewithal to define or enforce that standard. The Supreme Court's historic reluctance to venture into the "political thicket" of reapportionment, to attempt a definition of a "republican form of government," or more recently to pass on the legality of the Vietnam War, are each premised in part on a concern with enforceability. Courts do not have the power to rewrite legislation and, while they may stay the collection of revenues, courts cannot levy taxes. As Paul Carrington notes: "What is critically lacking to the judicial system is the power to raise a new tax. Federal and state constitutions are explicit about the process by which financial measures are to be enacted and the courts have no part to play."

Legislators confronted with an unpopular judicial decision have often threatened to defy it by continuing past practices, or to bypass it by amending the Constitution. Senator Everett Dirksen reacted to the "one man, one vote" decisions by pressing, with near-success, for an amendment to the Constitution which would have reversed them. The school prayer decisions were met with congressional truculence — as Congressman George Andrews of Alabama declared, "They put the Negroes in the schools and now they have driven God out of them" — and widespread popular defiance.

While noncompliance with a Supreme Court decision concerning school finance would be unfortunate and damaging to the Court's prestige, such a consequence is improbable. Unlike the school prayer and desegregation decisions, *Serrano* represents a widely acceptable resolution of the problem at issue. Even schoolmen and politicians in California's richest districts, while worried about the post-*Serrano* threat of "levelling" and "mediocrity," were unwilling to defend the pre-*Serrano* structure of fiscal inequity. Responsibility for complying with the decision rests ultimately with state legislators and governors, whose highly visible actions can readily be evaluated by the courts and the citizenry. The school prayer and desegregation decisions lacked a defined focus of responsibility for implementation; compliance could be secured only on a district-by-district or school-by-school basis. Despite the misunderstandings that *Serrano* produced, the "fiscal neutrality" standard establishes with clarity what may and may not be done by the state. In marked contrast, the first reapportionment decision merely announced that inequality in political representation could be considered by the courts and *Brown* v. *Board of Education* left school districts and federal courts with enormous flexibility in determining how to dismantle dual school systems. For those reasons — acceptability, political visibility, and clarity — compliance with the letter of the law can be anticipated.

## How Much Reform by the States Is Likely?

*The Inertia Factor.* What will become of the hope, voiced by the architects of *Serrano*, that the decision will "break the logjam of the status quo and thus free the state from a politically immovable system"? Will major structural changes in the financing and governance of education be adopted? Or will states do as little as they can to comply with the decision's limited requirements? What, in other words, is the likely extent of *Serrano*'s impact?

Those questions cannot be answered with confidence. While Minnesota and Iowa restructured their school finance systems in 1971–72, most other states will await the U.S. Supreme Court's decision before acting. The scope and substance of reform legislation will vary enormously from state to state, depending on such political factors as the size and diversity of the school population, the relative numbers of rich and poor districts, the costs of particular reforms, and the cogency of the arguments advanced for maintaining a structure which permits local control. It is nonetheless useful to speculate about what responses school finance cases may evoke, both in California and elsewhere.

*Serrano* is by no means the first occasion in which the inequity of educational financing systems has been pointed out. In many states, coalitions of teachers' organizations, parent groups, and poor and urban school systems have long lobbied for educational finance reforms. Their efforts have been resisted, for the most part successfully, by taxpayer groups and farmers' and industrial organizations concerned about the costs of those reforms. The Court's decision does not change these political configurations. As Arnold Meltsner notes, "while the [California Supreme] Court shifted the legislative agenda, it did not provide the political muscle to alter, in a significant way, the political forces behind the 'immovable' system." The very openness of the *Serrano* decree (in contrast with the "one man–one vote" standard, or the "educational needs" approach of *McInnis*) assures that no particular policy reform will be judicially favored. While legislatures may worry about what courts will settle for, legislative conclusions will hinge on political feasibility, not on anticipations of desirability or legal acceptability. For that reason, the states' fiscal difficulties — their unwillingness, or inability, to raise substantial new education dollars, or to demand that rich districts behave like Robin Hood, redistributing to poorer districts some of the money they raise locally — may overcome the arguments for significant change.

*Education Finance Reform: Whose Priority?* Increases in a state's education budget, made necessary in order to raise the expenditures of poor districts to those of rich districts, are unpopular in part because the assumption that more funds improve educational results is increasingly questioned. The widely known *Equal Educational Opportunity Survey* (1965), generally referred to as the Coleman report, concluded that the impact of school resources on student achievement was minimal. If education dollars do not matter, why should the state spend ever-more money on schooling? As one legislator asked, "Why should new money be poured down the same rat-holes?"

Attempts to equalize expenditures by centralizing funding, and bringing rich districts down to the level of their poorer neighbors, are resisted by the wealthy (who coincidentally exercise considerable power in the legislature) because they would, as one superintendent stated, "substitute mediocrity for excellence." Supporters of local autonomy also fear greater state involvement in education, predicting that an infusion of state dollars would carry with it strictures on how schools should be run.

Yet if the state adopts a decentralized plan, permitting local districts to raise some portion of their education costs through local taxes, the annual education bill will inevitably fluctuate. Since the state, in order to satisfy the fiscal neutrality principle, would have to guarantee that a given tax effort converted into a fixed number of dollars, the extent of the state's contribution would vary with the choices made by districts. If local tax

*David L. Kirp*

rates were high, a substantial state tax hike — political poison to legislators — might well be necessary. These are legitimate concerns. They also increase the difficulty of reaching agreement on any major change in the status quo.

That educational finance is at best a second priority for most of those directly involved in the decisions poses another roadblock to reform. Legislators worry about health and welfare reforms and tax relief — all of which compete with education for state money — and the always-impending election. Some school districts seek decentralization, while others regard consolidation with wealthier enclaves as a solution to their problems. Most state school officials view finance reform as but one priority among many others, including academic standard-setting, increased use of paraprofessionals in the schools, and desegregation. Teachers' organizations are concerned about the right to bargain, salary levels, and the protection of tenure.

That educational fiscal reform is the first priority of no one (except the cottage industry of school finance specialists) means that the constituency for major change is likely to be weak. While proposals to decentralize school governance or levy a statewide tax for schooling will be resisted by a host of groups, supporters are fragmented. The so-called school lobby is typically divided. State education codes effectively separate classroom teachers, counselors, and school administrators into different camps. Teachers and parents regularly find themselves battling with each other over issues of pedagogy and policy. To unite these groups poses a difficult but not impossible task.

*Complexity and Coalition-Building.*   Finance reform is a complicated business. Any legislative proposal must confront a range of issues. How much support will the state provide for public education? Will education resources be equalized, either through state-raised funds or redistribution of locally collected taxes? What changes will be made in the unpopular property tax structure? What choices — with respect both to substantive programs and to permissible variations in education spending — will be made by the state? Which will be made locally? In parceling out education dollars, will the state take account of the special needs of high-cost districts, or of the problems of particular groups of children?

The questions are inextricably linked. They are all treated by state education codes; more significantly, they are politically joined. Although property tax relief is not theoretically necessary in order to change resource allocation formulas, the fact that schools use fully half of all local property taxes weds the two issues. A decision to subsidize particular interests — of needy districts, needy children, or both — obliges the state to assume more control over educational decisions, and raise additional revenue. If districts are free to determine their own tax rates, funds to subsidize poor districts' choices will have to be provided — through redistribution, new state taxes, or district consolidation to reduce wealth disparities.

The political coalition that might be expected to endorse any one of these measures cannot realistically be expected to endorse all of them. Again, examples may prove helpful. A modest increase in state equalizing aid will probably generate consensus, particularly if the money can be raised with little political cost. Should that increase be coupled with a demand that rich districts share their wealth, or if all of the increase is to be spent on urban districts, the coalition is bound to splinter. Legislators concerned about wasted educational resources and spiraling teachers' salaries may insist that if new money is to be spent on schooling, teachers be held accountable for classroom success and a ceiling on ever-rising teacher salaries be established. Neither suggestion will sit well with school personnel, whose salaries constitute 85 percent of the typical district's education budget.

These several factors — concern that providing more educational resources is not worth the effort; the fact that educational finance is a second-priority issue for many; the unpredictable costs of any new decentralized scheme; the weakness of the education finance lobby (and the strength of the opposition); the complexity of the problem; the difficulty of maintaining broad coalitions for major educational change — indicate that, at least for the near future, state legislatures may not respond to the *Serrano* invitation by adopting major reforms.

*A Gloomy Prognosis?*   For these reasons, many states may make only modest adjustments in the existing school finance statutes. Some may comply with the letter of the fiscal neutrality obligation; others, including California, may hope to persuade the courts that "substantial compliance" — legislation which reduces interdistrict wealth disparities while not eliminating them — is sufficient. Yet any number of factors could alter this conclusion. One significant but often undiscussed incentive to major change is what Eugene Bardach terms "the opportunity to do something [a politician] believes is right . . . or in the public interest. All else equal, political men prefer to act in consonance with [these values] than contrariwise." If a state's economy grows or if the federal government increases its education budget, major new state taxes might not be needed to increase the state education budget. Yet whether those hypothetical new revenues would be spent on education, returned to the taxpayer, or used in other governmental programs depends in part on the capacity of the fragmented education lobby to pull itself together and regain credibility, rallying support for a common approach. The creation of an Education Conference of California, joining thirteen of the state's major educational associations, may represent the beginnings of this kind of unity. As Wilson Riles, the state superintendent who organized the group, said, "The time has come for all of us to join together to develop a single unified strategy to resolve the school finance crisis."

No one knows whether such a strategy will alter the gloomy political prognosis. But if *Serrano* proves merely a judicial invitation to tinker with the system, those who hope for more far-reaching reform may seek to persuade the courts to provide further relief.

*David L. Kirp*

# Will the Courts Push into the "Educational Thicket"?

*The Equal Protection Precedents.* Writing shortly before the *McInnis* decision, Phillip Kurland worried over what he called "the limits of constitutional jurisprudence undefined." In cases involving "fundamental interests," he noted, "what begins as a narrow decision supported by a broad principle is soon utilized by the court as authority for extending the rule's coverage to the limits of the principle."

Recent decisions concerning criminal process, segregation of public facilities and reapportionment illustrate this judicial penchant for expansion. The principle enunciated in *Brown* v. *Board of Education* (1954), that racially separate schools were inherently unequal, was rapidly applied, almost without judicial analysis, to other municipal services, such as swimming pools and golf courses. Fifteen years after the second *Brown* decision, which declared that schools should be desegregated "with all deliberate speed," the Supreme Court was insisting that racial quotas provided at least a reasonable starting point for judicial determination of compliance with the Court's mandate. The indigent's right to a free transcript in criminal appeals was broadened to apply to other matters thought necessary for effective defense against criminal charges. Five years after the Supreme Court declared, in *Baker* v. *Carr* (1962), that legislative malapportionment was subject to judicial review, the Court had adopted a rigid formula of "one person, one vote," and applied it to all levels of government.

Whether one views these decisions as embodying necessary elaborations of equitable doctrines or as unwarranted judicial adventurism, the dynamic of judicial intervention cannot be gainsaid. Are there principled explanations underlying this dynamic? Do they suggest what further judicial intervention, if any, can be anticipated in the school finance realm?

One explanation for what courts have done is that equality (or, more precisely, equal protection of the laws, a somewhat more bounded concept) cannot be defined in static terms. Its meaning changes with nebulous but nonetheless real shifts in a society's understanding of what constitutes fair treatment. The command to treat equally poses for a society, and for the courts which give substance to the command, a never-ending task. As Nathan Glazer has noted: "And just as there is no point at which the sea of misery is finally drained, so, too, is there no point at which the equality revolution can come to an end, if only because as it proceeds we become ever more sensitive to smaller and smaller degrees of inequality."

Open-endedness provides a second explanation. In the desegregation and reapportionment cases, the court's initial definitions of the equal protection requirement were loosely constructed. But the obligation to dismantle dual school systems did not convey a universally shared meaning. Similarly, the statement in *Baker* v. *Carr* that a "rational" reapportionment policy was readily understandable and constitutionally necessary (a statement likened by Alexander Bickel to "an arrow wafted skyward in the hope that some appropriate target might find it") served only to confuse legislatures and courts, and was abandoned by the Supreme Court within a year of its enunciation.

*Brown* and *Baker* did not constitute plausible judicial end-points. The end-points ultimately reached were not the only logically inevitable ones, but rather represented a conscious choice among policy alternatives. If state-imposed constraints on interracial association was the evil *Brown* sought to remedy, that wrong was eliminated once districts permitted black children to choose which school to attend. Ten years after the *Brown* decision, the Court rejected that approach, concluding that only measures "which promise realistically to convert to a system without a 'white' school and a 'Negro' school, but just schools" were constitutionally acceptable. Lower courts were thus instructed to consider not the choices made by white and black children, but the effects of those choices, the numbers of black and white children attending integrated schools.

"The achieving of fair and effective representation for all citizens is concedely the basic aim of legislative apportionment," Chief Justice Warren observed in *Reynolds* v. *Sims* (1964). Yet unnoticed by the Court, there lurked a tension between the values of fairness and effective representation. Apportionment schemes which concedely were not "fair" — that is, which considered such factors as existing political boundaries, shared economic and social interests, and geographic compactness, and which therefore produced districts of varying population — often might have secured the goal of effective political representation of minority groups better than strict numerical equality. Warren's conclusion in *Reynolds* — "Legislatures represent people, not trees. Citizens, not history or economic interests, cast votes" — missed the thrust of Justice Frankfurter's argument, voiced in *Baker* v. *Carr:*

> One cannot speak of "debasement" or "dilution" of the value of a vote unless there is first defined a standard of reference as to what a vote should be worth. What is actually asked of the Court in this case is to choose among competing bases of representation — ultimately, really, among competing theories of political philosophy — in order to establish an appropriate frame of government.

The tendency of courts to expand equal protection doctrine and to adopt increasingly rigid yardsticks with which to measure compliance can also be explained as a function of impatience with continuing noncompliance. Had southern school districts, in the years immediately following *Brown*, opened all schools to black and white students, freedom of choice plans might have proved constitutionally respectable. Instead, the South responded with outright defiance — as Dixie governors stood in schoolhouse doors to bar blacks from entering — and with subtler but equally effective foot-dragging devices. In that context, "freedom of choice" was rightly viewed, a decade after *Brown*, as another subterfuge, a euphemism disguising evasion of the Constitution. By 1968, the Fifth Circuit Court of Appeals, which has jurisdiction over much of the South, concluded that the flexibility which *Brown* had provided was in fact being utilized by obdurate school boards and recalcitrant lower-court judges to delay desegregation. For that reason, the Court of Appeals, in a decision subsequently affirmed by the Supreme Court, moved to establish uniform and rigid guidelines for all school districts in the circuit.

Is it likely that school finance litigation will follow a similar course, that a Supreme Court decision affirming the "no wealth" principle will be followed in short order by more explicit commands to the states? In approaching that question, several preliminary analytic distinctions are necessary.

*Proximate Means Versus Ultimate Ends.* The changes that a court can really secure often are but partial and gross approximations of what might be termed the ultimate goals of judicial intervention. While the "one man, one vote" principle has been almost universally implemented, the ability of judges to do more than that, to secure the effective participation of those who previously were unrepresented or underrepresented, is less certain. A decade after *Baker*, some interests continue to be influential well beyond their numbers; others remain disadvantaged in terms of their numbers. Nor has the pattern of state legislation (who gets what) changed a great deal. That fact is only a reminder of the obvious: political equality and influence are functions of more than a literal voting equality of citizens.

A similar distinction can be made with respect to the school desegregation cases. Almost two decades after *Brown*, most southern school systems are formally desegregated; there is greater segregation in the North than the South. Yet, if *Brown* sought ultimately to alter deeply engrained social and political beliefs, its hopes have not been realized. Whether blacks and whites eventually come together in this society or continue to function as "two nations — separate and unequal," is a matter which courts can influence but not determine.

By assuring that resources — educational inputs — are distributed equitably, *Serrano* satisfies the proximate goals of the school finance reformers. But the ultimate goals of some equalizers — raising the level of student performance, eradicating differences in educational achievement among race and class groups — are far harder to accomplish through judicial intervention.

The desire to improve educational outcomes, particularly those of poor and minority children, is laudable. It has its antecedents in President Eisenhower's hopeful but statistically improbable observation that all American children should be above average. Yet, as a hypothetical judicial decree, a standard framed in educational-outcomes language carries with it two unlikely assumptions: first, that schools can in fact teach with systematic differences in effectiveness to alter educational outcomes; and second, that it is appropriate to insist on their doing so as a matter of constitutional right.

Educators simply do not know how to equalize school success. Recent empirical studies such as the Coleman report suggest that manipulating educational inputs may not have much effect on school outcomes; the social class background of the child and his classmates has greater impact. And even if schoolmen knew how to equalize educational achievement, it is unclear whether the social costs, the inevitable coercion of children's behavior needed to accomplish the result, would outweigh the benefits. For those reasons, a demand that the courts move beyond proximate means to secure as a constitutional principle the ultimate end of racially and socially equal outcomes should be viewed, in Justice Holmes' words, as a "pedagogical requirement of the impracticable."

*The Educational Thicket.* To argue that the means of equalizing student success are unknown and hence cannot be mandated does not imply that courts will not attempt the task by applying a rigid formula akin to the "one person, one vote" standard. Two of the state court decisions on educational finance reform which followed *Serrano* have in fact adopted just such an approach.

In one, the Wyoming Supreme Court declared that uniform state financing of education is required. "We see no manner in which ad valorem taxes for school purposes can be made equal and uniform unless it is done on a state wide basis." While the Wyoming court indicated that dollar disparities, of 10 to 15 percent among districts, caused by additionally imposed local taxes, would be permissible, the benchmark of constitutionality was clearly dollar equality. In the other, a New Jersey trial judge also viewed state. financing as a constitutional necessity:

> Education serves too important a function to leave it also to the mood — in some cases the low aspirations — of taxpayers of a given district, even those whose children attend schools in the district. The uncertainty of raising sufficient local funds for school purposes is the very hazard that the uniform State tax was designed to meet.

Whether the New Jersey court would sustain any inequalities was left unclear. While both decisions were premised in part on state constitutional requirements, both cited equal protection cases to buttress their arguments.*

These two holdings demonstrate that an equalization-minded court, uncertain and even unaware of the consequences of its decision, can adopt its own definition of what equity commands. Yet such an approach seems unwise. It does not constitute a logical, much less inevitable, judicial extension of the *Serrano* principle, for unlike *Brown* and *Baker*, the "fiscal neutrality" standard does represent a plausible end-point for the courts. The command to equalize forces the legislature to undertake particular and significant budget-

---

* Most state constitutions contain both an equal protection clause and a provision requiring the maintenance of a "uniform, thorough, and efficient" public school system. Thus, however the Supreme Court decides the school finance issue, state courts could rely on the provisions of their state's constitution to compel either "fiscal neutrality" or funding equalization or even outcomes equalization.

*David L. Kirp*

ary reallocations undreamt of in the *Serrano* ruling and effectively precludes it from making its own judgments concerning the soundest means of distributing necessarily limited education resources. While equality represents an alluringly simple response to the problem, it does not consider the varying educational needs of children, the differences in the costs of providing education, and the importance of local choice-making. The "equal dollars" standard should satisfy only those with a penchant for mathematical exactitude.

*Proximate Means and Symbolic Consequences.* If there is little that courts can do — either by adopting a "no wealth" standard, a rigid dollar equality rule, or even commanding that students do better in school — to affect school outcomes, what justification exists for the limited judicial intervention of *Serrano?* Has the court embarked on a fruitless and quixotic journey, which can only raise false expectations? That question, pressed by several critics of this new judicial foray, implies that courts ought to act only when the result of their decision is measurable change. Even in those terms, *Serrano* is bound to have an impact for children in districts which suffer most for lack of school resources.

But the importance of *Serrano* cannot just, or even primarily, be defined in terms of educational outcomes. *Serrano* forcefully reminds us that government must behave fairly in allocating resources for the nation's most costly and most important good, that the poor as well as the rich have claim to even-handed treatment at the hands of the state. As John Coons has written, "if money is inadequate to improve education, the residents of poor districts should at least have an equal opportunity to be disappointed by its failure." Cast in terms of political principle and symbolic importance, *Serrano* is indeed a landmark decision, at once an initial and final intrusion by the courts into the arena of interdistrict school finance inequities.

### Intradistrict and Interstate Fiscal Inequities

*Serrano* speaks to inequities among school districts within a state. But what of inequities within districts, which result in more money being spent on white and wealthy children than on their poor and minority counterparts? And what of the education resource disparities that exist between states?

The problem of within-district inequality is not, as might be suspected, a trivial one.* In Washington, D.C., the per pupil expenditure in the wealthiest school was more than ten times that of the poorest, a gap as wide as that separating a typical state's richest and poorest school districts. In 1971, a child attending school in Rock Creek Park, Washington's only predominantly

---

* Editor's note: Murphy's study of Title I of ESEA touches on this same subject. See pp. 160–98, this volume.

white neighborhood, received 27 percent more teacher resources, measured in dollar terms, than did the average child attending school elsewhere in the city. Disparities of lesser magnitude exist in Boston, Chicago, Oakland, and other major cities.

While intradistrict and interdistrict inequalities are of similar dollar magnitude, the constitutional and political issues that they pose are quite different. In voting on school tax rates, parents in a given district lack even the illusion of choosing how much should be spent on their children relative to others living in the same district. The property tax rates are identical for all, and parents make the reasonable assumption that all children in a district will be treated equitably. The constitutional and political arguments justifying only limited judicial intervention into the interdistrict finance issue do not hold for judicial scrutiny of inequalities within a given school district. Unless the district can justify differences in allocation — either by identifying economies of scale (it costs more to operate a small school than a large one) or by adopting a formula that promises to confront the educational difficulties of particular groups of students — an "equal inputs" standard seems appropriate. Such was the approach taken in *Hobson* v. *Hansen,* a suit brought in Washington on behalf of children in poor and black neighborhoods. The court declared: "If whites and Negroes, or rich and poor, are to be consigned to separate schools, pursuant to whatever policy, the minimum the Constitution will require and guarantee is that for their objectively measurable aspects these schools be run on the basis of real equality, at least unless any inequalities are adequately justified." That standard embodies neither an extension of the *Serrano* principle nor a resurrection of *McInnis,* but borrows from the constitutional arguments advanced in *Serrano* to devise a remedy appropriate for a different, if related, educational finance issue.

Just as states contain rich and poor school districts, so too are there rich and poor states. The poorest state, Alabama, spends an average of $438 on each child's education, while the richest, New York, spends $1,237 — almost three times as much. This disparity may suggest the appropriateness of federal fiscal relief, but it does not clearly pose a constitutional problem. The equal protection clause of the Fourteenth Amendment, the constitutional basis of the school finance cases, speaks to the states (and their political subdivisions), not the nation. While the Fifth Amendment's guarantee of due process, which does constrain federal government action, might be read by the courts to incorporate the guarantee of equal protection, such a transposition is almost unprecedented and consequently unlikely.

### Will the "No Wealth" Standard Be Extended to Other Government Services?

*Serrano* and its successors focused on inequities in the provision of a particular public good, education, caused by reliance on local property

*David L. Kirp*

taxes to support schools. Other services provided in whole or in part by local governments — health, welfare, police and fire protection, streets and sanitation — are also financed from property tax revenues. Does the *Serrano* "fiscal neutrality" principle reach inequities in the provision of these other services also caused by differential property tax bases?

California's Supreme Court carefully avoided the question: "We intimate no views on other governmental services." Yet it was the "fundamentality" of education that allowed the court to reach its result. "[Its] uniqueness among public activities clearly demonstrates that education must respond to the command of the equal protection clause." For the poor person unable to obtain shelter, food, or medical assistance, however, education may well represent a luxury, not a necessity. If education is "fundamental," what of these basic human needs?

Confining the "no wealth" principle may prove no easy judicial task. As Kenneth Karst observes: "In *Serrano*, the court has made a crucial contribution to the progressive extension of equal protection doctrine to new subject areas, a contribution that seems certain to bear fruit when the winter that began in 1970 is over." Yet the general extension of that principle to other governmental services creates dilemmas both for the courts and for the structure of government. Which services should join education in the inner circle of fundamentality, and which should be left out? Does the claim that health and welfare are prerequisites for survival differentiate those services from police and fire protection? The lack of a satisfactory and inclusive judicial definition of fundamentality should make courts reluctant to travel down so uncharted a road. That education, but not other public services, can be directly and plausibly linked to the exercise of First Amendment rights also suggests the constitutional appropriateness of different judicial treatment.

Applying *Serrano* to all governmental services would have profound implications for the budgetary process and for the allocation of political power among local communities and the states. The revenue-raising or redistribution required would be of a magnitude dwarfing the demands made by a court order confined to education. The financing of public goods would, as a practical necessity, be centralized, thus limiting the capacity of cities to set their own fiscal priorities.

Yet the constitutional objections to the existing system do not lack force. The application of the "fundamental interest" argument to publicly provided services other than education has been noted above. An alternate legal approach extends the rationale of the reapportionment cases, asserting that the elector's power with respect to the same political issues — for example, how well equipped a fire department will a community have — should not vary according to the wealth of the municipality in which he happens to reside. Such an approach would require either substantial equalization of the tax base among all municipalities, or centralized funding of all public goods.

Will the courts eventually extend the *Serrano* principle to all municipal services? The practical difficulties that such an action would create argue against the wisdom, if not the eventuality, of such a broad-brush approach. Yet for certain services, such as health and welfare, which directly and profoundly influence individuals' lives, a limited extension of the "fiscal neutrality" principle may be forthcoming, as courts struggle to distinguish, on principled grounds, what is vital and what is constitutionally trivial. Whether or not that happens will depend on evolving and necessarily unpredictable understandings of the scope of society's obligation to assure that its members are treated equally.

### Concluding Observations

"The fascinating thing about the Supreme Court," Robert McCloskey has written, is "that it blends orthodox judicial functions with policy-making functions in a complex mixture. And the Court's power is accounted for by the fact that the mixture is maintained in nice balance; but the fact that it *must* be maintained in such a balance accounts for the limitations of that power." The impact of *Serrano* and related cases on school finance reform supports McCloskey's observation. Courts do not make policy in a vacuum; they are responsive to the articulated concerns of a variety of interests. Nor can courts implement policy decisions on their own; they necessarily depend on other political institutions to interpret and enforce their decrees. Yet courts do take part in shaping policy, and in so doing function as political institutions. They could not act otherwise and remain true to their constitutional obligations.

During the Warren Court era, many hoped that the Supreme Court would do more than participate in political decision-making. They urged the Court to address itself to the substance of fundamental and divisive issues, in the expectation that a favorable judicial response, affirming principles of social justice, would somehow revive the nation's spirit. But as an institution, courts often lack both the knowledge and the power intelligently to intervene. What would be the meaning of a judicial declaration that four presidents had exceeded their constitutional war-making powers in Vietnam? Should judges be dispatched to every schoolhouse to assure that teachers were ministering to the varied educational demands of children? These are dreams of a philosopher-king, not models for plausible judicial behavior.

"In the long run," Jack Peltason has observed, "a nation gets the kind of judicial decisions it deserves." In giving substance to a constitutional provision as unbounded as the equal protection clause, courts must ultimately look for guidance to the will of the society whose disputes it is adjudicating. Of course, judicial decisions need not (and ought not) faithfully reflect whatever national polls reveal that social will currently to be; what is needed is, as former Chief Justice Earl Warren has said, "a political conception of compassion." But if the actions of the judiciary are sufficiently out of step, they will be ignored or overturned. How does a court balance these factors?

*David L. Kirp*

The "fiscal neutrality" principle of *Serrano* embodies one such response. That principle imposes a limited check on state legislatures, constraining only decisions which preserve irrational inequities. It signals to the society that fairness in the allocation of as important a social good as education is constitutionally required. Most important, it does not insist upon a particular definition of equality, but rather serves as a catalyst, facilitating legislative reexamination of basic issues of taxation and school expenditure policy.

This quite limited approach is not without its detractors. Those who criticize *Serrano* as an exercise in judicial overreaching wonder whether the plight of poor districts merits the courts' attention, and whether poor children will in fact be any better off because of the decision. As the discussion of the likely legislative responses suggests, the prospect of limited benefit is real. Those who would have the courts act more venturesomely insist that it should be self-evident, even to courts, that America's schools fail millions of children each year, that poor and minority children suffer at the hands of an unresponsive school bureaucracy, and that the society would be better served if schooling did more than cement existing racial and social class differences. Sidney Wolinsky, who argued *Serrano*, asserts:

> [A]ll the commentators . . . focus on . . . what will happen if the courts get involved in one or another social policy question. I would throw the burden back on the system and ask what will happen if the courts do not respond. If on a matter of such gross inequities the United States Supreme Court will not respond, I see little hope . . . for the whole system. . . .

Yet, in examining these and similar issues in the context of proposed judicial intervention, the pertinent question remains, what can *courts* do about these problems? In reviewing education policy grievances, can courts render the public schools institutions of enlightenment, or make wise men of those who administer them? The claim that our society, through its school system, must rid itself of its ills will continue to be voiced, but it should be heard as a call for legislative and executive action, not as a plausible demand for further judicial intervention.

## SOURCES AND READINGS

This study rests on varied sources, including: judicial school finance decisions and briefs filed in those cases; interviews; drafts of legislation; and books and articles concerning the nature of the judicial role, the economics of school finance, the constitutionality of existing state school finance systems, and the politics of school finance reform.

The court decisions — notably, *McInnis* v. *Shapiro*, 293 F. Supp. 327 (N.D. Ill. 1968), *aff'd mem. sub. nom.*, *McInnis* v. *Ogilvie*, 394 U.S. 322 (1969); *Serrano* v. *Priest*, 5 Cal. 3d 584, 487 P.2d. 1241 (1971); and *Rodriguez* v. *San Antonio Ind. School Dist.*, 337 F. Supp. 280 (W.D. Tex., 1971) — suggest the evolution of the "fiscal neutrality" principle. The judicial reasoning in the post-*Serrano* school finance cases is not uniform, as a comparison of *Robinson* v. *Cahill*, 118 N.J. Super. 223, 284 A. 2d 187 (1972) and *Sweetwater County Planning Comm. for the Organization of School Districts* v. *Hinkle*, 491 P. 2d 1234 (1971) with *Serrano* and *Rodriguez* reveals.

The range of arguments presented to the California Supreme Court is reflected in the "friend of the court" briefs filed in *Serrano*, by organizations including the Urban Coalition, the San Francisco Youth Law Center, the National Association for the Advancement of Colored People, and the Center for Law and Education. The oral argument before that court, preserved on tape, suggests the nature of the judges' concerns and the responses of both sides. Interviews and correspondence with those intimately involved with the evolution of *Serrano* — John Coons, Harold Horowitz, and Sidney Wolinsky, who collectively prepared and argued the case, and Ellen Cummings, law clerk to Judge Raymond Sullivan, who wrote the *Serrano* opinion — broadened my understanding of the political and legal maneuvers in *Serrano*, and provided valuable assistance in final revisions of the manuscript. My own involvement in the school finance issue — as Director of the Center for Law and Education, and coauthor of the Center's brief in *Serrano* — necessarily helped shape my own views, and introduced me several years ago to the small world of school finance reformers. The Lawyers' Committee for Civil Rights Under Law, through staff attorney Steven Browning's never-ending efforts, kept me abreast of current cases and developments in the field.

The school finance cottage industry has produced a number of books and articles on the structure and constitutional implications of school finance plans. Charles Benson, *The Economics of Public School Education* (Boston: Houghton Mifflin, 1968), describes with clarity the operation of state finance systems. The Hearings of the Senate Select Committee on Equal Educational Opportunity (Part 16, 1971) and the reports of the University of Florida National Educational Finance Project (1971) provide additional empirical data. John Coons, William Clune, and Steven Sugarman, *Private Wealth and Public Education* (Cambridge, Mass.: Harvard University Press, 1970), sets forth the constitutional argument on which *Serrano* and its progeny rest. Two articles by Harold Horowitz — "Unseparate But Unequal — the Emerging Fourteenth Amendment Issue in Public

Education," 13 *U.C.L.A. Rev.* 1147 (1966), and "Equal Protection Aspects of Inequalities in Public Education and Public Assistance Programs from Place to Place Within a State" (with Diane Nietring), 15 *U.C.L.A. L. Rev.* 787 (1968)— and Charles Daly (ed.), *The Quality of Inequality* (Chicago: University of Chicago Press, 1968), debate the pros and cons of pre-*Serrano* legal approaches.

The politics of school finance reform is less well understood. Arnold Meltsner, Gregory Kast, John Kramer, and Robert Nakamura, *School Financing Reform — A Study of Political Feasibility: The Case of California* (New York: Praeger, 1973), is a noteworthy initial contribution.

On the general issue of judicial policy-making, Charles Black, *The People and the Court* (New York: Macmillan, 1961), and Alexander Bickel, *The Least Dangerous Branch* (Indianapolis: Bobbs-Merrill, 1962), develop contrasting views on the proper judicial role. The question continues to be argued, in law review articles by Archibald Cox, "The Supreme Court, 1965 Term. Forward: Constitutional Adjudication and the Promotion of Human Rights, the Supreme Court, 1964 Term," 80 *Harv. L. Rev.* 91 (1966), and Judge J. Skelly Wright, "Professor Bickel, the Scholarly Tradition, and the Supreme Court," 84 *Harv. L. Rev.* 769 (1971). David Kirp, "The Role of Courts in Education Policy," *Social Policy* (September/October, 1971), considers the problem in the context of school policy, while particular questions posed by the reapportionment cases are analyzed in Nelson Polsby (ed.), *Reapportionment in the 1970s* (Berkeley: University of California Press, 1971).

The classic statement concerning the scope of judicial review under the equal protection clause of the Fourteenth Amendment remains Joseph Tussman and Jacobus ten Broek, "The Equal Protection of the Laws," 37 *Calif. L. Rev.* 341 (1949). "Developments — Equal Protection," 82 *Harv. L. Rev.* 1065 (1969), analyzes the expansion of equal protection doctrine, while Frank Michelman, "Forward: On Protecting the Poor Through the Fourteenth Amendment, The Supreme Court, 1968 Term," 83 *Harv. L. Rev.* 7 (1969), reexamines recent equal protection decisions, and develops an alternative "minimum protection" rationale for the court's actions.

The "no wealth" principle has been subjected to extended legal scrutiny. See, for example, the reviews of *Private Wealth and Public Education* in 59 *Calif. L. Rev.* 302 (1971) (Steven Goldstein), 23 *Stanf. L. Rev.* 591 (1971) (Paul Brest), and 6 *Harv. Civ. Rights — Civ. Lib. L. Rev.* 619 (1971) (David Kirp and Mark Yudof). Steven Goldstein, "Interdistrict Inequalities in School Financing," 120 *U. Pa. L. Rev.* 504 (1972), Ferdinand Schoettle, "The Equal Protection Clause in Public Education," 71 *Colum. L. Rev.* 1355 (1971), and

Kenneth Karst, "*Serrano* v. *Priest:* A State Court's Responsibilities and Opportunities in the Development of Federal Constitutional Law," 60 *Calif. L. Rev.* 720 (1972), offer provocative and varied analyses of *Serrano*'s constitutional implications. The Winter 1971 issue of *The Yale Review of Law and Social Action* (Vol. 2, No. 2) is devoted to the subject of "Who Pays for Tomorrow's Schools: The Emerging Issue of School Finance." Gerald Lubenow, "The Action Lawyers," *Saturday Review of the Society* (August 26, 1972), provides a brief and competent review of the strategy on which *Serrano* was premised.

*David L. Kirp*

# STUDY FOUR

# THE BUREAUCRACY

Needed: the best thought. The two-page appendix.
Another task force. Picking up on the idea. Hurry to
the hopper. Hearings, and a forecast. The prophecy
proves self-defeating. By words we are governed. An
administrator's impress. Needed: new standards. The
case of Compton, California. Choosing the "winners."
More disappointments. Interagency relations. The pre–
Inauguration Day rush. Two voices of experience.
Concluding observations. Sources and readings.

Making a New Federal Program:
Model Cities, 1964–68

*Edward C. Banfield*

During the evening of the first full day of Lyndon B. Johnson's presidency — at 7:40 P.M. on November 23, 1963, to be precise — Walter Heller, chairman of the Council of Economic Advisers, came to tell him that three days before his assassination President Kennedy had approved a suggestion that the Council and the Bureau of the Budget develop a program to alleviate poverty. They were thinking, Heller said, in terms of pilot projects to be tried in a few cities. The president was enthusiastic, but he wanted something "big and bold." A program for just a few cities could never be propelled through Congress and, in any case, it would be regarded as another example of "tokenism" by black leaders whose growing anger was a matter of concern to him. A few weeks later, in his first State of the Union Address, he declared "unconditional war on poverty in America." The Office of Economic Opportunity (OEO) was created almost at once.

This initial attack was to be followed by offensives along a broad front. The Vietnam War was expected to fizzle out shortly and the federal treasury to overflow with a "peace dividend" as the economy expanded. No doubt, too, the president was confident that after the November election he would have comfortable majorities in both houses of Congress (as it turned out, he had the largest ones since 1937). Under these circumstances, he needed big ideas to put before the new Congress — a legislative program that would be distinctively his.

The following pages tell about one of the biggest and boldest of the programs that resulted — how the Model Cities effort was planned; how, through the intervention of the president himself it was pushed through a reluctant Congress; how its administrators grappled with dilemmas and constraints that were partly inherent in the conception of the program and partly in the harsh realities of the governmental system; and how, by the time the Johnson administration left office, the program had become very different from what its originators had intended it to be.

## Needed: The Best Thought

In May 1964, the president told a University of Michigan audience that it was in the cities, the countryside and the classrooms that the Great Society was to be built. While the government had many programs directed at these "central issues," he did not pretend to have the "full answers." To get them he would establish "working groups" to make studies and hold White House conferences. "We are going," he said, "to assemble the best thought and the broadest knowledge from all over the world to find those answers for America." That there *were* "answers" to large social problems and that thought and knowledge could "find" them he seemed to take for granted.

The president knew that John F. Kennedy had used task forces in his 1960 campaign. Because these groups had been too heavily weighted with scholars, the president thought, "very few suggestions emerged that were practical enough to exploit." He intended his to have a broad balance of "thinkers" and "doers." The presidential assistant who played the leading part in making up the Metropolitan and Urban Affairs Task Force was Richard N. Goodwin, a young lawyer who had been in the Kennedy entourage and was now a Johnson speechwriter. Although there were "doers" in the group that he assembled, its most active members turned out to be mostly "thinkers."

One of these was the chairman, Robert C. Wood, an amiable man just entering middle age who was a professor of political science at M.I.T. Before beginning his scholarly career he had served for three years in the Bureau of the Budget. His later work dealt with practical matters largely (his most recent book — *1400 Governments* — was an account of the intricacies of governmental organization in the New York region) and he had been active

*Edward C. Banfield*

in the Kennedy advisory group during the 1960 election campaign. He could, therefore, be considered both a "thinker" and a "doer." The other members of the task force were Paul Ylvisaker, director of the public affairs program of the Ford Foundation; Raymond Vernon, a Harvard economist who had directed the study of the New York metropolitan region; Jerome Cavanagh, mayor of Detroit; Saul B. Klaman, director of research for the National Association of Mutual Savings Banks; Ralph McGill, editor of the *Atlanta Constitution*; Dr. Karl A. Menninger, chief of staff of the Menninger Clinic; and four members of the faculty of the University of California at Berkeley: Nathan Glazer, a sociologist; Norman Kennedy, associate director of the Institute of Traffic and Transportation Engineering; Martin Meyerson, dean of the School of Environmental Design, and Catherine Bauer Wurster, professor of city planning. William B. Ross, a career civil servant from the Bureau of the Budget, was executive secretary. Goodwin was White House liaison.

The task force had less than three months in which to work. By the middle of November 1964, Goodwin, along with the assistants assigned to the other task forces, would have to begin "feeding" the president paragraphs for use in the various messages he would send to Congress in January 1965. Despite the lack of time, the group produced a report running to seventy double-spaced pages with an additional ten pages summarizing its recommendations. Often such reports consist largely of hot air; this one did not.

The report was politely but severely critical of the existing government programs for the cities. "Too frequently they operated within narrowly defined agency boundaries that fragment logically related services." This was true even of the newly created OEO ("admirable" but "designed to help primarily the temporarily disadvantaged"); the task of this and the juvenile delinquency programs "must be broadened to include health, education, recreation — the entire gamut of social development."

It went on to make many far-reaching proposals for change: the federal government should give block grants* to enable the cities to provide a wide range of services to all of their citizens as well as to care effectively for the poor; it should also make special grants for the support of community facilities (health stations, small parks, and so on); both the block and special grants should be contingent upon a *local* (this word was underlined) Social Renewal Plan (these words were capitalized); the government should also expand its technical assistance in many fields of public administration; and it should support planning by the cities, and endeavor in other ways as well to strengthen the office of mayor (or manager).

In polite — and therefore not very vigorous or vivid — language, the report said that most urban renewal projects had served the interests of down-

---

* A "block" grant is one that may be used for any purpose by the recipient or, at least, for a very wide range of purposes. By contrast, a "categorical" grant may be used only for a specified—often very narrowly specified—purpose.

town department stores and real estate operators and that public housing projects had not made a dent in the slums. If middle-income people were to be lured back into the deteriorating areas of the larger, older cities, a new strategy would have to be used. Timid efforts would be worse than none. "What is needed is an intervention so large and so profound as to alter the image of a neighborhood."

There were many other recommendations, including building large new cities from the ground up, reorganization of housing finance, aid to rail rapid transit, and creation of an Urban Affairs Council headed by the vice president. The emphasis, however, was on making federal efforts more comprehensive, improving their coordination, and giving local governments and the citizens most directly affected a greater share of control over the federal government's undertakings. The task force expected, it said (and these words were underlined),

> that the block service grants, the special local facility grants, the social renewal plan and the revised urban renewal plan would enable the mayor or other public bodies where appropriate, especially in larger cities, to bring together heretofore separate activities into a comprehensive strategy for local action.

Another report, this one prepared in the Bureau of the Budget and taking the form of a 100-page book, went to the president in May 1965. It reviewed various efforts to coordinate the many categorical programs through the voluntary efforts of the agencies themselves. (These included the Neighborhood Development Programs and One-Stop Welfare Centers.) These efforts had been almost fruitless and extremely time-consuming. The president, the Bureau of the Budget suggested, might deal with the coordination problem in one or the other of two ways: either by giving the cities block grants or by instituting a program under which they would be helped to make comprehensive plans that, when approved by the White House, would be implemented with federal funds.


The Two-Page Appendix

Whether because the president thought that they smacked more of "thinkers" than of "doers" or for other reasons, neither the task force nor the Bureau of the Budget report seems to have influenced his 1965 legislative program. Ironically, a proposal that was *not* among the task force's many recommendations turned out to have great importance. In the course of its discussions, at least three members of the task force (Wurster, Meyerson, and McGill) had more or less independently suggested that the federal government "adopt" two or three large cities and in addition build a brand-new one in order to show what could be accomplished by well-conceived, large-scale, concerted effort.

A concrete proposal along these lines had come to the task force in the form of a two-page memorandum titled "Demonstration Cities" written by Antonia Chayes, a former student of Wood's, in collaboration with her boss, Leonard Duhl, a psychiatrist who was head of the Office of Planning of the National Institute of Mental Health. Mrs. Chayes and Dr. Duhl proposed that all relevant federal agencies join in sending a team of experts to three large cities to make comprehensive plans for dealing with their particular problems in a fundamental way. When the plans had been made, agencies would concentrate their resources in a coordinated effort to carry them into effect. This might involve a good deal of slum clearance and rebuilding as well as the repair of much dilapidated and blighted housing. The emphasis, however, would be shifted from the "bricks and mortar" approach of the urban renewal program to a "social and psychological" one involving the improvement of school and health facilities, provision of neighborhood recreation centers, better police-community relations, participation by neighborhood residents in decisions affecting them, and whatever else offered some hope of raising morale and creating self-confidence among those who lived in the poorest districts.

This proposal may have been influenced by what was then happening in New Haven. Beginning in 1959, that city had sharply redirected its efforts from slum clearance to a wide range of efforts to improve the opportunities of the chronically poor, especially the young among them. What was happening in New Haven probably influenced the conception of "youth development projects" that were begun in New York City in 1961 with the encouragement and support of Robert Kennedy, then the attorney general. The central ideas behind these developments — the prevention (as opposed to the "cure") of poverty, especially among the young, through concentration of efforts by a wide range of public and private agencies in order to change the character of an entire district in accordance with a carefully made plan — were also the basic principles of the proposal that Heller carried to President Kennedy and then, a few days later, to President Johnson. (A Bureau of the Budget memorandum of November 21, 1963, had recommended "human investment expenditures through education, training and health" directed at "particular problem groups" or "where the yield will be high," with a focus on "human development" rather than physical facilities.)

The task force did not recommend the "adoption" of any cities; it attached the Chayes-Duhl memorandum to its report as an appendix, however. When Mayor Cavanagh showed the report to fellow Detroiter, Walter Reuther, the president of the United Automobile Workers, it was the appendix that caught Reuther's eye. He and the mayor arranged to have a brochure prepared — "Detroit, A Demonstration City" — which they put before Robert C. Weaver, the head of the Federal Housing and Home Finance Agency, and later before the president. Presumably this is what Mr. Johnson refers to in his memoirs, *The Vantage Point,* where he says that in May 1965, Reuther gave him a memorandum warning of the "erosion of life in urban centers."

Another Task Force

When Reuther's memorandum reached him, the president was beginning to think about his legislative program for 1966. He had directed his special assistant, Joseph A. Califano, a 33-year-old lawyer who had recently moved to the White House from the office of the secretary of defense, to "perform the spadework on a full-scale domestic program." "Rebuilding the slums," the president thought, represented "the first challenge." To help meet it, a new task force was created late in the summer. It was to work closely with Califano, and have its recommendations ready by the end of November 1965.

Wood was to be chairman of the new task force but "doers" were to dominate it. As the president wrote in his memoirs, "Business, labor, the construction industry, and the Congress were represented on that committee. The academic world was also represented. . . ." Reuther was the labor representative. Other members were Whitney Young, executive director of the National Urban League and a national Negro leader, Ben W. Heineman, president of the Chicago and Northwestern Railroad, Edgar Kaiser, president of Kaiser Industries, Senator Abraham Ribicoff (D., Conn.), Kermit Gordon, president of the Brookings Institution, William L. Rafsky, an economist who had served as program coordinator of the Philadelphia city government, and Charles M. Haar, a Harvard Law School professor who had written on city planning. Apart from the last three and Wood himself, none had any special knowledge of urban affairs.

This time there was to be no liaison with the Bureau of the Budget. The task force would get technical advice from its own professional staff, drawn from persons outside the government. Perhaps the differences between this task force and its predecessor reflected the president's belief that "big" and "fresh" ideas practical enough to be "exploited" would not come from scholars or career civil servants. As he explained later in *The Vantage Point,* he considered task forces better than the standard method of generating legislative proposals, which consisted of taking them from the departments and agencies and filtering them through the Bureau of the Budget and the White House staffs. He believed the bureaucracy was preoccupied with day-to-day operations, dedicated to the status quo, and not equipped to solve complex problems that cut across departmental jurisdictions. Scholars, in his view, had a different but equally serious limitation — that of impracticality.

In seeking to avoid these disadvantages, the president ran the risk of incurring others. For example, leaving agency interests out of account in the

*Edward C. Banfield*

design of a new program might mean that the program would be sabotaged by them later on. Apparently he was prepared to take such risks. From his standpoint, the crucial thing seems to have been to present Congress and the electorate with a program that they would regard as a bold and promising response to "the urban crisis." If this was the president's intention, it must have been enormously strengthened in August 1965, when — after the decision to set up another task force had been made — the black enclave of Watts in Los Angeles erupted in a long and destructive riot.

The terms of reference that the president gave the task force were very general. They did, however, include one particular: "Pick up on the demonstration idea."

### Picking up on the Idea

The task force was not fully constituted until early October 1965. Like its predecessor, it would have to do the best it could in weekend meetings over a period of about two months. Its proceedings (again like those of its predecessor) would have to be carefully hidden from the press. (The president's insistence that his advisers work without publicity resulted, his critics said, from his desire to monopolize the limelight. His own explanation, given later in his book, was at least as plausible: advisers tend to be more candid and critical as well as less cautious when they work on a confidential basis; moreover, when plans leak, opposition is given time to form.)

To preserve confidentiality and to avoid the bureaucratic interests which the president so much distrusted, the task force avoided contact with the agencies concerned. Even Robert D. Weaver, who seemed likely to head the soon-to-be-created Department of Housing and Urban Development (HUD), was not officially informed of what was going on. (As will appear, he managed nevertheless to find out.)

The professional staff of the task force wrote some two dozen background papers, all of high quality (they cost somewhat more than $70,000), but little or no use was made of them. The policy alternatives discussed in the papers were not considered sufficiently practical. It was all very well to document the need for metropolitan area governments, for example, but creating such governments was beyond the power of Congress and the president. Consolidating the 200 or more categorical grant-in-aid programs into a relatively few would doubtless (as the previous task force had stressed) improve coordination, but there was no point in studying this either, for Congress could not be persuaded to allow consolidations and, anyway, the press and public would not be much impressed by that sort of achievement. Califano stressed that the president wanted ideas that would yield spectacular results and yield them *while he was still in office.*

The members of the task force soon found out that they differed on important matters. Reuther wanted to bulldoze slum districts out of existence and replace them with "model communities." Young was opposed to this. Slum clearance, he pointed out, generally turned out to be Negro clearance; he favored tearing down or rebuilding housing where absolutely necessary, but he insisted that the emphasis go on measures like improvement of schools, provision of health services, job training, and protection of civil rights. Kaiser shared Young's preference for the "social and psychological" rather than the "bricks and mortar" approach.

Wood thought of the new program as having the purpose (among others) of coordinating existing programs; he saw it as a way of exerting leverage on the federal agencies that administered the categorical grants as well as on state and local agencies. In this way vastly more resources would be brought to bear on the causes of urban poverty and distress. (This, it will be recalled, had been the main thrust of the previous year's report.) Gordon, who recently had been director of the Bureau of the Budget and who had served with Wood on the other task force, was also much concerned with achieving co-ordination.

The differences were mostly of emphasis (no one envisioned a program *solely* to clear slums or *solely* to improve coordination), but they were important because they entailed further differences. For example, the "social and psychological" approach implied giving the residents of slum and blighted neighborhoods a large measure of control over programs, for only in this way, it was supposed, could the morale and self-confidence of the poor be improved. "Coordination," however, implied putting control firmly into the hands of elected officials. Wood was as irked as anyone by the arrogance urban renewal officials had often shown in their dealings with local people and he had no doubt that residents of affected neighborhoods should be consulted. But to give them *control* — that was out of the question.

The task force received a memorandum from the director of the Bureau of the Budget, Charles L. Schultze, which impressed it deeply. (As one of the president's staff, he was not subject to the ban against consultation with operating agencies.) He suggested that there might be a threshold below which public investment in poverty areas yielded little or no return. He had a hunch, he said, that by spending at a "saturation" level the net return might be increased by several orders of magnitude. But since this was only a hunch he favored trying "saturation" in no more than five or ten cities while making careful studies of the results. What he had in mind was an experiment, he told an interviewer later, not a national program, still less a national crusade.

Schultze's "hunch" was one that a first-rate economist might be expected to have. It is worth noting, however, that in 1963, as assistant director of the Bureau of the Budget, he had welcomed essentially the same ideas when he presided over the group which worked up the proposal for demonstration programs in several cities that Heller carried to President Johnson. He himself had then suggested appointing a "federal czar" in each area to open doors to Washington decision-makers and to "knock heads together when necessary to get cooperation" from local agencies. This idea also impressed the task force favorably.

The task force considered briefly giving one city "the complete treatment" but then decided not to, partly from fear that the administration would be charged with "tokenism" and partly because it would be impossible to choose between Detroit, Cavanagh's and Reuther's city, and Chicago, the city of the even more powerful Mayor Daley. Perhaps five cities should be chosen, someone said. Senator Ribicoff answered that five would not be nearly enough. Members of Congress would not vote large sums for a program which they knew in advance would not benefit their constituents. It was therefore a political necessity that enough cities be chosen to assure majorities in both Houses.

The task force began its report with a ringing declaration: 1966 could be the year of the urban turnabout in American history. For this to occur a dramatic new approach embodying three principles was required: *concentration* of available and special resources in sufficient magnitude to demonstrate swiftly what qualified urban communities could do and could become, *coordination* of all available talent and aid in a way impossible where assistance was provided across the board and men and money had to be spread thin, and *mobilization* of local leadership and initiative to assure that the key decisions were made by the citizens living in the cities affected. These principles were to be applied through a national program of city-building in which specially qualified communities executed plans of such size and scale as to transform existing urban complexes into new cities, by tying together physical and human resource programs, by developing and testing methods and programs, and by bringing to bear all the techniques of which technology was capable.

The task force proposed that all cities be invited to propose action programs designed to have a major impact on the living conditions of their citizens. After the most promising of these proposals were identified by a special presidential commission, the qualified communities were to prepare more detailed proposals. Each was to establish an appropriate administrative mechanism, not necessarily a formal unit of government, to assemble leadership and resources both public and private. A federal coordinator, the task force said, should be assigned to each city to bring all relevant federal aids together. Once selected as qualified, a city would receive two types of federal assistance: (1) the complete array of existing grants to the maximum extent authorized by law and on a priority basis, and (2) supplemental grants (at a ratio of 80 percent federal, 20 percent local) to make up any difference between what was available under existing programs and what the demonstration would cost.

The report recommended that there be sixty-six demonstration cities: six of over 500,000 population, ten of between 250,000 and 500,000, and fifty of less than 250,000. In the largest cities the typical program should build or rebuild about 24,000 units of housing, in the medium-sized ones about 7,500, and in the smaller ones about 3,000. In all cases the objective should be to eliminate blight completely in the designated area and to replace it with attractive, economic shelter in a neighborhood with amenities essential to a full life.

If there was anything new in these proposals it was the supplemental grants. Wood referred to these as "bait" and "glue" because they would attract federal grants to the cities and also bind them together in workable programs. (These images, incidentally, had been used in 1963 by the Bureau of the Budget officials who worked up the proposal that, much altered, became OEO.) In private, out of earshot of department and agency heads, the supplementals were also spoken of as "clubs," and this indeed was the principal function they were intended to serve and what made this proposal different from earlier ones. A demonstration city, knowing that it would get from HUD any funds that might be lacking to carry out its approved plan, would be in a position to bargain with the other federal agencies and to compel them to accept coordination on the basis of its locally made, HUD-approved plan on pain of being left out altogether from the biggest and most glamorous undertakings. Thus city governments, in partnership with HUD, would bring about the coordination that had so far proved unachievable. The result of all this, Wood hoped, would be to "suck the system together."

### Hurry to the Hopper

The task force's proposals did not get the close scrutiny from affected agencies, the Bureau of the Budget, and the White House staff that is usually given to policy proposals before they are publicly endorsed by the president. LBJ met with the task force once to say that they had his whole-hearted backing, but it was well understood that he did not want to be bothered with specifics. That was the job of Califano mainly, and he, of course, had countless other matters to attend to. Without much deliberation, then, the president committed himself in the State of the Union Address (January 26, 1966) to "a program to rebuild completely, on a scale never before attempted, entire central and slum areas of several of our cities. . . ." The next day he swore in Weaver and Wood as secretary and under-secretary of HUD, and a few days later he sent to Congress a special 4,000-word message on city development which began with words strikingly like those of the task force report: "Nineteen-sixty-six can be the year of rebirth for American cities." He went on to promise "an effort larger in scope, more comprehensive, and more concentrated than any before." The following day, the Cities Demonstration bill was introduced in both the House and the Senate.*

---

* A second bill, implementing other recommendations of the task force, was introduced at the same time; it provided "incentives for planned metropolitan development." Eventually the two bills were combined, becoming different titles of an omnibus bill. For present purposes this development, as well as the substance of the metropolitan planning measure, can be ignored.

*Edward C. Banfield*

The bill followed the task force report very closely. It declared improving the quality of urban life to be the nation's most critical domestic problem; its purposes were to enable cities "both large and small" to plan and carry out programs to rebuild or revitalize large slum and blighted areas and to improve public services in those areas, to assist cities' demonstration agencies to develop and carry out programs of sufficient magnitude "in both physical and social dimensions," "to remove or arrest blight and decay in entire sections or neighborhoods," substantially to increase the supply of low and moderate cost housing, "make marked progress" in "reducing educational disadvantages, disease and enforced idleness," and "make a substantial impact on the sound development of the entire city."

Demonstration programs were to be "locally prepared" and approved by the local governing body and by any local agencies whose cooperation was necessary to their success; they were to provide for "widespread citizen participation," "counteract the segregation of housing by race or income," and meet "such additional requirements as the Secretary may establish."

The secretary was authorized to make grants covering 90 percent of the cost of planning demonstration programs and 80 percent of that of administering them and, when a city's program was approved, to make grants ("supplementals"), amounting to 80 percent of the nonfederal contributions to the program, for the support of any or all of the projects in a city's program. In each demonstration city, an office of the federal coordinator was to be established with a director designated by the secretary. This gave HUD no authority over other departments, however, and the bill required it to consult each affected federal agency before making a demonstration grant. The bill did not say how many cities were to have demonstration programs, what the mix of city sizes was to be, or how funds were to be apportioned. Appropriations were to be authorized in "such sums as may be necessary" and the program was to terminate in six years.

Despite the speed with which the task force's recommendations moved into the legislative hoppers, they did not escape *all* high-level review. Weaver had arranged, doubtless with Wood's assistance, to have one of the task force's professional staff "leak" its doings to him, so that, when finally he was appointed secretary, he knew enough about the new program to be sure that (as he put it later) he "could live with it." HUD lawyers drafted the bill and this gave him a chance to go over it in detail and even to add a declaration that the new program would not supersede urban renewal. He was sure that without some such language, the bill would have no chance of passage.

Another cabinet member who was given an opportunity to express his views was Willard Wirtz, the secretary of labor. He told Califano that he did not think that the program would work. Concentrating federal spending in certain cities for purposes decided upon by the local officials might be desirable, but the hard fact was that practically all appropriations had to be allocated as Congress specified in statutes. Moreover, as a practical matter, department and agency heads had to exercise what little discretion the laws left them in ways acceptable to the congressmen and the interest groups upon whose goodwill they depended.


Hearings, and a Forecast

Hearings began at the end of February 1966 before the Subcommittee on Housing of the House Committee on Banking and Currency. Secretary Weaver was the first of some seventy-five witnesses whose testimony (not all of it concerning the bill) took four weeks and filled 1,100 pages.

When he entered the hearing room, Weaver believed that the president had in mind five to ten demonstration cities. (This, incidentally, was also the understanding of Schultze.) Before the session was called to order, however, it became apparent to him that congressmen expected there would be about seventy. After hasty consultation with Wood, he let that figure go unchallenged. He could see, he said later, that some of the congressmen would not discuss, let alone support, a program involving only five or ten cities.

After describing the provisions of the bill ("the most important proposal in the president's program for rebuilding America's cities"), Weaver responded to questions. He assured the chairman that many cities had indicated interest in the program, that its creation would not lead to any decrease of urban renewal funds for any city, that the federal coordinator's function was merely "to sort of lubricate the process" of reaching into the existing federal grant programs. When the ranking minority member expressed fear that the coordinator would leave local officials no discretion, Weaver explained that the demonstration program would be developed by the locality *before* the coordinator entered the picture. Spending decisions, he emphasized, would be made by the local government in accordance with a plan made by it.

A subcommittee member pointed out that a city's program had to meet "such additional requirements as the Secretary may establish . . ."

"Do we have to have that type of criteria?" he asked.

That provision, Weaver replied, would be used "very, very lightly" and "no major criteria will be added which is not in the substantive statute."

The witnesses who followed Weaver were mayors. Addonizio of Newark was first, then Cavanagh of Detroit, Lindsay of New York, Daley of Chicago and (eventually) a dozen others. The mayors, of course, were enthusiastic at the prospect of getting more federal money for their cities but they thought the sum proposed much too small. Lindsay said that as a rough guess the program to be "really meaningful" in New York would cost $1 billion for the "bare bones" on the physical side and another $1 billion on the human side. He proposed that the entire $2.3 billion for the six-year program be appropriated at once so that the cities could enter into long-term contracts right away. Chicago, Daley estimated, needed between $1.5 and $2 billion. Cavanagh's hopes ("dreams," he called them) were by far the most extravagant ("grand," he said). He envisioned building "a town within a town." "If we think," he told the subcommittee, "of a nation with a population of India by the end of the century and if we think of most of us living in cities, then we must not only dream grand dreams but we must also make them come true."

Opposition to the bill came chiefly from the National Association of Real Estate Boards, the U.S. Chamber of Commerce, the Mortgage Bankers Association of America and the National Association of Manufacturers. The chamber of commerce man remarked that with huge subsidies a few favored cities would show that they could get certain things done. What, he asked, would this demonstrate to cities in general? Other opponents doubted that the federal agencies could be induced to coordinate their programs, and one said that there were not enough skilled workers to rebuild the cities within a few years on the scale contemplated.

Although the bill seemed to be faring well in the hearings (in his opening remarks, the chairman termed the president's special message "inspiring" and declared that "our job is to give the Administration the legislative authority it needs to get the job done"), afterward the chairman and the ranking minority member agreed to report the bill out amended so as to authorize grants only for planning. Such a move would have amounted to killing the bill. Their decision cannot be accounted for by the weight of the testimony they had heard. Perhaps it reflected distress at the rising costs of the Vietnam War or a feeling that the administration should be satisfied with the many programs for the cities that had already been enacted. Wood, however, suspected a more particular cause: a committee staff man, miffed at not having been given a high post in HUD, had persuaded the chairman to scuttle the bill. Whatever the reasons, the outlook was now bleak. "All signs on Capitol Hill," the *New York Times* reported in mid-May 1966, "suggest that the program is dead."

### The Prophecy Proves Self-Defeating

When he read that in the *Times,* the president was furious. Calling in Vice President Hubert Humphrey and his assistant for congressional relations, Lawrence O'Brien, he told them to find a way to save the bill. If the most important item in his urban program could be dumped by a House subcommittee, his prestige would suffer and the rest of his legislative program would be in great danger.

O'Brien telephoned the chairman of the subcommittee and told him that the president's bill would have to be reported out intact — "or else." This was unusual language to use, but O'Brien considered it necessary and justified. In due course (on June 23, 1966), the bill was reported with only two amendments of importance. One, which Weaver had proposed, authorized an additional $600 million to be earmarked for urban renewal within demonstration city areas (the renewal "add-on," this was called); the other eliminated the office of federal coordinator.

Reproached in private by the ranking minority member of the subcommittee for having failed to abide by their agreement, the chairman replied as one politician to another. "There are times," he said, "when a man changes his mind and there are times when he has it changed for him. . . . I had mine changed for me."

Five days later, the full committee reported the bill favorably with other minor changes. "Metropolitan expediters" were provided in place of the coordinators. The committee report said that they were to have a "clearing-house" function and were not to pass upon applications. "This," it declared, "is to be a local program . . ." It also declared that the new program would not "in any way change the flow of funds, as among cities, under existing grant-in-aid programs." This could be taken as a mere statement of fact — the fact Wirtz had pointed out to Califano — or as a warning to federal administrators not to use what little discretion they had in such matters to bring about the concentration of effort that, in the opinion of some — Budget Director Schultze, for example — was the program's main justification.

Despite this progress, the bill was now stymied. It could not reach the floor of the House without clearance from the Rules Committee, seven members of which were strongly for it and seven strongly against. The swing vote was that of a southerner who objected to the provision requiring that demonstration programs promote racial integration.

Meanwhile, the vice president and O'Brien had been rounding up support for the bill. They got the AFL–CIO to lobby energetically for it. They organized a committee of twenty-two business leaders, including David Rockefeller and Henry Ford II, to issue a statement calling for its passage. With other high figures in the administration, they had scores of private meetings with members of Congress to make explanations, listen to objections, and, when absolutely necessary, offer assurances that a place would not be overlooked when the time came to select the "winning" cities. By the end of the summer, this promise had been made to more than 100 legislators, which was less than a third of those who asked for it.

By late summer, the Senate hearings had long since been completed (they began April 19 and lasted only a few days); the bill would by now have been brought to the Senate floor but for the fact that the senators who normally managed housing legislation were not willing to manage it.

Senator John Sparkman (D., Ala.), the chairman of the Subcommittee on Housing of the Banking and Currency Committee, although surprised that after passage in the previous session of (as he described it) "one of the most comprehensive housing bills of all times" the president was proposing important new legislation, had said when he opened the hearings that his first reaction to the bill was favorable. The objective — coordination of federal programs — was one he approved. He was up for reelection, however, and therefore too busy to lead the fight. Senator Paul Douglas (D., Ill.), who stood next to him in seniority, would not lead it either; he also was busy campaigning and, besides, his staff was critical of the bill.

138                                                              *Edward C. Banfield*

O'Brien then turned to Senator Edmund Muskie (D., Me.), who was much interested in intergovernmental relations, and found him reluctant. He, too, had received a critical report on the bill from his staff (among other things, it was badly drafted and did not provide adequately for "institutional change"). Moreover, Maine, having no large cities, could not expect much benefit from it. After an all-night session with Muskie's legislative assistant, in the course of which representatives of the White House, HUD, and the Bureau of the Budget accepted certain modifications in the bill, the senator agreed to be its floor manager. On August 9 the full committee reported the bill favorably.

Because of concessions that had been made to Muskie and others, the Senate bill differed considerably from the one bottled up in the House Rules Committee. The Senate bill reduced the term of the program from six years to three, authorized smaller amounts for supplemental grants and the renewal "add-on," did not require cities to plan for racial and economic integration, emphasized the importance of local initiative and instructed HUD to give "equal regard to the problems of small as well as large cities." During the all-night session in Muskie's office, it had been agreed that supplemental grants would be distributed according to a formula based on population, amount of substandard housing, percentage of families with income below $3,000 and percentage of adults with less than eight grades of schooling. This enabled three Maine cities — Bangor, Augusta, and Portland — to qualify. The formula was not written into the bill, however.

The committee bill reached the floor of the Senate on August 19. In the ensuing debate (which took parts of two days) it was made unmistakably clear that the small cities were to get their share of benefits.

> George McGovern (D., S.D.): Do I understand the Senator correctly that in his judgment some reasonable consideration will be given to the allocation of funds to our smaller cities, and that not all the funds will go to a few great metropolitan centers?
> Edmund Muskie (D., Me.): I would say to the Senator that I would expect that we would get demonstration city programs in these small areas, and I would be disappointed if we did not.

After the defeat of several threatening amendments, the Senate passed the bill by a roll-call vote, 53–22. Under the threat of a procedure (passage of a resolution for which twenty-one days' notice had been given) that would bypass it, the House Rules Committee finally (twenty-one days after the filing of such a resolution) granted a rule. After acrimonious debate in the course of which seventeen amendments were voted down and twenty others (all agreed to by the administration) were adopted, the bill was passed by a vote of 178–141 in a late-night session on October 14, 1966. (The lightness of the vote is accounted for by the fact that the 14th was a Friday not many days before an election; many members had left for their constituencies before the vote was called.) The conference committee report favored the Senate version, although conceding some details to the House. The Senate accepted it quickly on a voice vote. In the House, there were moments of uncertainty, but in the end it was approved by a margin of fourteen votes.

The president must have been well satisfied when on November 3, 1966, he called the chief actors to his office to witness the signing of the bill and to receive the souvenir pens that are distributed on such occasions. In all essentials and in most details, he had got what he had asked for. What was more, he had got it at the right time — election day was only a week away.

### By Words We Are Governed

If anyone had hoped that the hearings and debates would resolve, or even call attention to, the contradictions in the program proposed by the task force, he would have been disappointed. Some penetrating questions had been raised: Could the agencies administering the categorical programs concentrate on the demonstration cities? Would they if they could? Was it possible to have both "citizen participation" and control by elected officials? Could there be a "partnership" between HUD and local governments?

The matters that had been of most interest to the few congressmen who had familiarized themselves with the specifics of the bill were mainly of symbolic importance, however. What did it matter whether an official was called a "coordinator" or an "expediter"? (That provision had been put in the bill in the first place as a "loss leader" to attract support from the "good government" movement, Wood later told an interviewer.) Actually, the secretary needed no special authorization to employ assistants to try to bring about coordination. Dropping the requirement that city programs "counteract the segregation of housing by race or income" was also of purely symbolic significance. Cities were still free to counteract racial segregation if they wished and no one had ever supposed that a city making only a perfunctory gesture in this direction would be denied funds on that account.

In its final form the bill authorized only $900 million to be used over two years rather than $2.3 billion to be used over six years. This also made no practical difference; HUD had assured the subcommittees that it could not use more than that amount in the first two years anyway.

A few minutes before the president reached for the first of the pens with which he would sign the bill, Weaver told him of a congressman's objecting to the name Demonstration Cities on the grounds ". . . we got enough demonstrations already . . . we don't need any more" — a reference, of course, to the riots of the summer before. The president took the point seriously. As he signed the Demonstration Cities and Metropolitan Development Act of 1966 into Public Law 89–754, he referred to the new program as Model Cities. It would, he said, "spell the difference between despair and the good life."

*Edward C. Banfield*

## An Administrator's Impress

H. Ralph Taylor, the man chosen to administer the new program, had been the first executive director of the New Haven Redevelopment Agency (New Haven, it will be recalled, was widely regarded as having led the way in urban renewal) and had later worked for AID in Latin America. As assistant secretary of HUD for Demonstrations and Intergovernmental Relations, the Model Cities program would be his main but by no means his only responsibility. As his principal subordinate, he chose Walter Farr, a young lawyer who had also been with AID in Latin America. Farr was to be the operating head of the Model Cities Administration (MCA).

The staff was small by the standards of the government — about forty professionals in Washington and seventy in regional offices — but it had an unusually high proportion of its personnel in the upper salary ranges. Morale was high. Taylor and Farr got along well and conferred often, and relations between them and their subordinates were easy and cordial. As a new agency, MCA was regarded with apprehension by the long-established housing and renewal agencies of HUD. Farr and the young men around him were dubbed "Taylor's Green Berets" by the stand-patters in these agencies.

Although he had to spend most of his time in the first hectic months haggling with HUD administrative officers and the Civil Service Commission and meeting with mayors and others who were impatient for decisions, Taylor nevertheless managed to put the impress of his views on the program. The task force report could not, in his opinion, be taken seriously: its authors "did not understand housing." No one who *did* understand it would talk of rebuilding whole districts of the large cities: there were not enough carpenters, plumbers, and electricians to do the job and, anyway, it was obvious that Congress would not appropriate the scores of billions of dollars that would be required.

What Model Cities *could* do, Taylor thought, was, first, to document the vast extent of the cities' needs so that, when the Vietnam War ended, the nation might be persuaded to make a commitment on the scale required, and, second, to prepare local governments for effective action when the nation finally made that commitment.

His experience in New Haven had convinced him that excessive fragmentation of governmental structure was the major obstacle to getting things done. This was being made steadily worse by the almost daily increase in federal efforts — most conspicuously OEO's Community Action Program — which bypassed local governments. He was determined that Model Cities should not add to the governmental confusion. It would help the cities plan, but not impose plans on them. As one of his Green Berets wrote later,

> We had a great deal of faith at first in the latent power of the people "out there" in the cities, in their ability to come up with innovative solutions that could be replicated throughout the country if they were

left alone with a nice piece of federal change. We saw them as co-workers in an urban problems laboratory. Our job was to furnish equipment, assistance, support and occasionally a tube of catalyst. Theirs, was to innovate.

For Taylor, at least, "the people out there" were not primarily the residents of the slum and blighted neighborhoods. Model Cities, he told his staff, was to be "a mayors' and planners' program."

When the Model Cities bill was still before Congress HUD had set up a committee under the chairmanship of William Rafsky (a member, it will be recalled, of the task force) to advise on policies to be followed when it passed. In the committee's recommendations, Taylor found much to support his views. It urged HUD to insist upon high-quality programs. Before receiving a planning grant, a city should be required to describe and analyze the physical and social problems of its poor areas, lay out five-year goals for dealing with them and tell how it proposed to attain the goals. In addition, it should answer a long list of questions about its government and related matters. If its application did not meet HUD's stringent standards — if, for example, its projects were not innovative — HUD should demand something better. The cities making the best applications would receive grants for a year's further planning. An "action program" involving supplemental grants could begin only after satisfactory completion of "the planning phase."

The decision to require a one-year "plannng phase" had been made at a very early stage: Weaver had mentioned it in his testimony to the House subcommittee. (For that matter, the planners of the 1963 antipoverty proposals had intended to have the "pilot" cities spend a year planning and, as they put it, "tooling up.") Taylor, by following the recommendations of the Rafsky Committee and establishing an application process that might require several weeks or months, was in effect delaying the "action phase" still further. When the mayors realized how much delay there would be, they could be expected to protest vigorously. This would be awkward from a public relations standpoint, but Taylor was willing to pay the price in order to get information to document the extent of the cities' needs. With this in view, he established what he called a "high sights" policy: applications were to be made on the assumption that *all* of a city's problems were to be dealt with *within a few years.*

Fearful lest support for his agency in Congress melt away if more than a year passed without *any* "action," Taylor considered giving the cities small supplemental grants for "immediate impact projects," such as improved street cleaning, as soon as their applications were approved. Against the public relations advantages of this there were, however, two offsetting disadvantages: first, such "cosmetic" grants would do nothing to cure the cities' fundamental ills, and, second, they would distract the cities from the "in depth" planning that was crucial. Reluctantly, Taylor decided to withhold the supplementals until planning had been done properly. Somewhat to his sur-

*Edward C. Banfield*

prise, Weaver and Wood, who would have to bear the brunt of any criticism, agreed enthusiastically to these decisions.

In December 1966, MCA mailed out 3,000 copies of its program guide, a sixty-page brochure entitled "Improving the Quality of Urban Life." This explained that although Model Cities programs were to reflect local initiative, they had to conform to certain statutory requirements. The programs had to be of sufficient magnitude to (among other things) "make marked progress in serving the poor and disadvantaged people living in slum and blighted areas . . ." and "a substantial impact on the sound development of the entire city." Therefore the programs would have to deal with "all of the deep-rooted social and environmental problems of a neighborhood" and "make concentrated and coordinated use of all available federal aids . . ."

The guide emphasized another standard which, although not derived from the statute, was in Taylor's opinion fully consistent with it — namely, innovation. "Cities," it said, "should look upon this program as an opportunity to experiment, to become laboratories for testing and refining new and better methods for improving the quality of urban living."

The guide was soon followed by *CDA Letter No. 1*, "Model Cities Planning Requirements," which was the first of many formal instructions from MCA to city demonstration agencies. This letter made the "high sights" policy explicit.

> . . . cities must set their sights and their goals high. Model cities programs should aim at the solution of all critical neighborhood problems which it is within the power of the city to solve, and should be designed to make as much progress as possible toward solutions within five years. In most cases, it should be possible within five years to make all necessary institutional and legal changes at the state and local level and to initiate all necessary projects and activities which will, when carried to completion, achieve the long-range goals set by the city.

Applications, the instructions said, should describe and analyze each major problem, explain how and why each developed and give a preliminary judgment as to what should be done about them. Cities were to decide for themselves what to do, but they must show that they followed proper procedures in making their decisions. "Program analysis," MCA stated, "is the foundation on which the entire Model Cities undertaking rests."

"Program analysis" was fashionable in Washington at this time. In fact, the president had in 1965 instructed all agencies to institute PPBS —the Planning-Programming-Budgeting System — a procedure for analyzing and evaluating program alternatives that had been used in the Defense Department and much acclaimed by the press. The popularity of PPBS had little or nothing to do with MCA's enthusiasm for planning, however. Some of the principal Green Berets were graduates of city planning schools and, as such, products of a different planning tradition, one that derived from the city beautification movement rather than from economics. Taylor seems to have accepted on faith their claims to having skills that, if given scope, would cure the ills of the cities. Moreover, he saw in comprehensive planning a means of collecting information that would impress the country with the extent and seriousness of its ills.

Knowing that there would not be funds to support the full programs proposed by seventy-five cities (it had been decided to choose this number from a "first round" of applications; a "second round" would follow shortly), Taylor decided that the cities would have to concentrate their efforts on a single model neighborhood of not more than 15,000 persons or 10 percent of the city's population, whichever was larger; New York and a few other of the largest cities were to have more than one model neighborhood.

This decision left city officials wondering why they were required to describe and analyze the problems of *all* poor neighborhoods. It also raised the question why huge sums should be poured into one neighborhood while others nearby and equally poor got nothing. And it reduced whatever possibilities there were for collaboration between Model Cities and those federal and other agencies whose programs operated citywide. But Taylor really had no alternative. Given that there had to be seventy-five cities to begin with and more very soon, to make a "substantial impact" on a unit even as large as a neighborhood was hardly possible.

The essential decisions having been made, Taylor and some of his assistants set out in January 1967 as a "flying circus" to explain the program to local officials, answer their questions, offer help in filling out applications, and urge that applications be made early. "Analyze yourselves and your cities," Taylor told his audiences. "Walk the alleys and the streets and talk to people and get to the roots of the problem."


Needed: New Standards


Applications soon poured in, but Taylor and his assistants were disappointed when they read them. One Green Beret thought that less than a dozen showed any understanding of the experimental nature of the program. The projects proposed were not innovative, they did not constitute comprehensive or coordinated programs, and it was evident that they had been made with little or no consultation with the residents of the affected neighborhoods or even, in some instances, with the mayor and city council. "Our lab partners," he wrote, "didn't seem to get the hang of it."

With a view to improving the quality of future applications (the "second round" would begin within a few months) as well as of the first year's planning by the "winning cities," Farr brought his staff into a conference with consultant specialists. (Dr. Duhl, the psychiatrist who with Mrs. Chayes had written the 1964 memorandum proposing Demonstration Cities, was one.)

*Edward C. Banfield*

The result of these and other deliberations was revision of the instructions on planning and citizen participation.

The new planning instructions reflected the staff's conviction that most cities were incapable of "real" ("comprehensive") planning. Accordingly, the Five-Year Plan was deemphasized, becoming a "five-year forecast." City programs were henceforth to be based on analysis of *not quite* everything:

*CDA Letter #1 (the original version, October 1967)*

Each city's program should be based on a systematic analysis of all relevant social, economic, and physical problems which describes and measures the nature and extent of the problems, identifies their basic underlying causes, examines the inter-relationship between problems, and indicates the critical changes which must be made in order to overcome these problems.

*CDA Letter #4 (the revised version, July 1968)*

The problem analysis should cover all significant problems but the depth of the analysis can vary according to the significance of the problem and data available. High priority problems should receive the most attention the first year. Future planning should direct attention to these significant problems not adequately covered during the first year of planning. Although this section and its contents will vary according to local conditions and according to local understanding of problems, it should not avoid significant and historical causes of deprivation and inequality.

In a foreword by Taylor and in several footnotes, the new instruction described itself as "guidelines" which were to be interpreted "flexibly." The main purpose of the Letter ("40 pages of agonized noncommunication," one of its authors — the Green Beret already quoted — called it) was to *explain* the nature of planning, not to tell the cities what they must do.

A revised statement of policy on citizen participation was issued in order to keep peace within the staff. In the spring of 1967 Taylor had agreed to substitute "meaningful citizen participation" for "widespread" in a revision of the program guide. Later, when the first planning grant application began arriving it was evident that in most places citizens were not being consulted. The citizen participation specialists of MCA, OEO, and HEW then jointly wrote Taylor and Farr, the heads of MCA, proposing that the residents of model neighborhoods be given the right to choose their own representatives, have a "genuine" policy role, be provided a budget from which they could hire technical assistance of their own choice, and be compensated for their time and travel.

Farr knew that there would be trouble if these recommendations were not accepted. Citizen participation, however, was one of the few matters Weaver insisted on having brought to him for decision. Weaver believed that the recommended changes went far beyond what Congress had intended by the phrase "widespread citizen participation" but he recognized that concessions were necessary to mollify a part of the staff. Accordingly *CDA Letter No. 3* (it was dated November 30, 1967, but distributed to the cities about a month before) informed applicants that in order to build "self esteem, competence and a desire to participate effectively" on the part of neighborhood residents, there would have to be "some form of organizational structure . . . embodying" . . . the residents "in the process of policy and program planning and program implementation and operation." The leadership of such a structure "must consist of persons whom neighborhood residents accept as representing their interests" and these must have "clear and direct access" to the CDA's decision-making. Cities were to provide the residents' representatives with technical assistance "in some form" and were to compensate them when (but only when) doing so would remove barriers to their participation.

The compromise did not please the community participation specialist, who resigned before it was issued, but the rest of the staff was apparently satisfied.

## The Case of Compton, California

One of the cities to file an application was Compton (population 56,000), a predominantly Negro suburb of Los Angeles. Following the common practice of small cities, the city manager engaged a firm of planning consultants to prepare the application. This cost $5,000 and assured its failure. A city could not learn about its problems by employing outsiders, MCA wrote. The rejection came to a new manager, James Johnson, who put everything else aside in order to draw up a new application himself. The task took three weeks.

When he had accumulated 300 pages ("I put everything I could think of in it"), he sent the application to Washington. After several months' wait, he was surprised and elated to learn that Compton had been granted $110,000 for further planning. His elation faded somewhat, however, when he found that he might not use the money to work out the details of the projects that he had outlined in the application. His 300-page document, MCA told him, was not a plan, but a "plan to plan." He would now have to set in motion a planning process that would be carried on for a year by the City Demonstration Agency (CDA) and in which the residents of the model neighborhood would be "meaningfully" involved. Only when this was done and Compton's problems had been analyzed in depth, its goals defined, a five-year forecast made, and a first-year action program derived from it could he hope for an "action grant."

The action grant — assuming the city eventually qualified for one — would not necessarily be in an amount sufficient to support more than a fraction of the first-year action program. At best, Compton could get only its pro rata share of whatever supplemental grant funds Congress appropriated.

To Johnson it appeared that MCA was requiring that the planning grant be used to prepare a re-write of the 300 pages that he had already submitted: he doubted that the CDA and the citizens' advisory board could find much of anything to say about Compton's problems that he had not said in his application. It displeased him also that the further planning would have to be done by the CDA. This would tend to cut him, the city manager, off from a process which, if it were to lead to action, required his intimate participation. Perhaps in a large city such participation by a chief executive was impossible or undesirable, but why not let a city decide such matters for itself?

Johnson was also dubious about the citizen participation requirements. As in other black communities, politics in Compton was in a state of ferment; people who had had little or no experience in public affairs, many of them young and militant, were searching for leadership. In these circumstances, "citizen participation" was likely to mean endless talk at best. It was exasperating, too, Johnson thought, that the program could operate in only one neighborhood. Anyone could see that Compton's problems were citywide — indeed, *more* than citywide.

### Choosing the "Winners"

The "first round" applications were read by the MCA staff in Washington, which prepared brief appraisals of each. These included summary information about each city's political leadership, administrative capability, and understanding of its problems, along with a judgment as to the innovativeness of its proposals. These appraisals were read by an interagency committee of which Taylor was chairman. It found some applicants clearly unsuitable. The others were given an "advanced" review. After considering a proposal for assigning numerical weights to a long list of sharply defined criteria, the interagency committee fell back upon an unsystematic "common-sense" procedure.

A list of sixty-three cities recommended by the committee was forwarded to Weaver in June in the expectation that it would be quickly approved. It was not, however. A month or two before Weaver had spent a bad morning answering questions before an appropriations subcommittee which was considering MCA along with other HUD items. It was evident that the congressmen did not like the idea of appropriating $650 million without knowing where the money would be spent or (except in very general terms) for what purposes. When they were told that only eight cities had so far submitted completed applications, some of them were surprised and annoyed. Recalling their attitudes, Weaver decided not to announce the "winning" cities until the bill had been passed. This, he supposed, would be fairly soon: appropriations bills were normally passed before the start of a fiscal year, July 1. This time, however, there was disagreement over many items in the bill and, although passage seemed likely from week to week, it did not actually occur until November.

The delay in announcing the "winning" cities, the reasons for which could not be made public, caused the backers of some promising projects to lose interest in them. The MCA staff, however, thought that on the whole the effect of the delay was beneficial because most cities had not yet developed accounting procedures that met its standards.

All but nine of the sixty-three "winners" were in Democratic congressional districts. This was not surprising, since most sizable cities were Democratic. Asked by the press how much politics there had been in the selections, Weaver said, "As little as possible."

This was undoubtedly true. Taylor had resisted political interference because he knew both that his staff would lose respect for him if he "went too far" and that the prestige of the program — perhaps even its existence — would be threatened by including cities whose projects were ill-conceived or certain to fail for other reasons, such as administrative incapacity. In some instances, however, political influences could not be withstood. The White House was sure that Eagle Pass and Laredo, Texas, met all possible criteria. Smithfield, Tennessee, was the home town of the chairman of the House subcommittee that passed on HUD appropriations, and Pikesville, Kentucky, was the abode of another chairman. Montana, the Senate majority leader's state, had two especially deserving cities. Maine, Muskie's state, had three.

Some voices — Republican ones, of course — had been saying all along that Model Cities was just another Democratic pork barrel. To prove them wrong, at least one large city represented in Congress by a Republican had to be on the list. Happily, one — Columbus, Ohio — was found. A few cities that could not have qualified by nonpolitical standards were on the list (Laredo had not even submitted an application). In general, however, the "political musts" met MCA's standards as well or better than other applicants. Of the 150 cities eventually chosen, less than a dozen, Taylor said later, were accepted solely because of political pressure. If he had succumbed to it very often "the pressure would never have stopped . . . and the program would have been ruined from the start."

When he was asked how much politics there had been in the selections Weaver might have said as truthfully, "Less than necessary." For, despite his precautions, Congress in late 1967 gave Model Cities less than half what had been asked for — $200 million for supplemental grants and $100 million for the renewal add-on. The only item *not* cut was for additional planning grants — $12 million.

This meant that Congress was ready for a "second round" of applications, bringing the number of Model Cities to 150. By halving the appropriations and doubling the number of cities, it was making ridiculous Wood's continued declaration that the purpose of the program was "to determine the 'critical mass' for real change in the problems of human and physical deterioration in our cities."


More Disappointments

The first-year programs, which began to reach MCA in the fall of 1968, nearly two years after the passage of the act, were found to be even worse than the applications had been. This at least was the judgment of the Green Beret who had helped write the "40 pages of agonized noncommunication" that was *CDA Letter No. 4*. The cities, this man wrote later, were "willing to play our silly little game for money," but they did not understand that MCA was trying to get them to experiment and innovate; they found it easier to accept regulation than to make use of freedom.

Very likely he was right. The CDA planners, however, worked under certain constraints that should be noted. For one thing, the amount of the planning grant, ($150,000 for most cities) was not nearly enough for "in depth" fact-gathering and analysis of a great many problems. It was inevitable, too, that careful analysis would sometimes knock the props out from under proposals of the sort that the planners were expected to bring forward. In Binghamton, New York, for example, one survey of opinion in a model neighborhood revealed that more than 75 percent of blacks considered their housing either "good" or "excellent" and another survey showed that 78 percent of those polled (black and white) were satisfied with the public schools.

However hard they might have tried, the cities would have found it remarkably difficult to devise programs that were "innovative," "comprehensive" or "coordinative," and perhaps impossible to devise ones that were all three simultaneously. The words themselves were ambiguous in the extreme. (In Atlanta, researchers asked seventy local officials what they understood by "coordination" and got seven distinctly different replies.) Even if the objectives had been made perfectly clear, the cities might not have been able to devise programs to achieve them because of the inherent difficulty of the task. Innovation, for example — devising measures that are new, not unreasonably expensive, acceptable to the public, and that produce the effects intended — is not as easy as Washington seemed to think. (In Boston, where the Ford Foundation created a committee of "experts" to find "new ideas" for helping the poor, a long effort yielded next to nothing.)

It was probably impossible to achieve simultaneously and in a high degree all the standards MCA set because, however they might be interpreted, there were tensions if not incompatibilities among them. The more "comprehensive" a program, the less "innovative" it was likely to be; to the extent that it was "innovative" it would probably make "coordination" more difficult. (Taylor's determination not to worsen the fragmentation of local government led him to insist that projects be administered through *existing* agencies but innovation, sometimes if not generally, required creation of new ones.) And the more "innovative" a project the less its chance of making a "substantial impact," for new efforts usually have to start small. Similarly with citizen participation: the more seriously MCA took it, the more it had to sacrifice in terms of its other goals.

CDA directors seized different horns of these dilemmas. Some bore down hard on "comprehensiveness," appointing dozens, or even scores, of task forces that produced hundreds of projects which were offered as a "program," although they were really a sort of civic laundry list. Others emphasized "coordination" and drew up schemes for exchanging information among agencies by means of committees, conferences and the distribution of memoranda. Those who placed their bets on "innovation" usually hired consultants to think up ideas for them.

Whichever way they turned, the CDAs had to take account of something that *CDA Letter No. 4* overlooked: local politics. As perceived from Washington, a city government was an entity capable, if sufficiently prodded and when provided with a grant, of making decisions in a rational manner, i.e., of comprehensive planning. City officials, including of course CDA members, knew, however, that only in a rather limited sense did such a thing as a city government exist; for them the reality was bits and pieces of power and authority, the focuses of which were constantly changing. Bringing the bits and pieces together long enough to carry out an undertaking was a delicate and precarious operation requiring skills and statuses that few persons possessed. To those who saw governing from this perspective, MCA's rigamarole about program analysis, goals statement and strategy statement did indeed appear a silly game. "If the Feds tell us to jump through hoops for their money," a CDA director said, "we'll jump through hoops."

Interagency Relations

After two years of trying, MCA could not claim much success in "sucking the system together." When the act was passed, there had been in the larger cities a rush by local bodies to offer cooperation in the spending of the large sums that Model Cities was expected to control, but this enthusiasm faded fast. Some mayors (and city managers) used the CDA to strengthen their management. Others, however, more or less deliberately let their Model Cities program become the preserve, or playground, of persons who claimed to speak for the poor. The CDA letter strengthening citizen participation requirements, which appeared at the end of the second summer of urban riots (1966), made such mayors all the more inclined to (as an MCA official put it later) "turn the whole thing over to the noisiest citizens' group in order to keep them quiet." It is probably safe to say that where mayors *tried* to use the program to improve coordination they found it useful and where they did *not* try the result was confusion worse confounded.

*Edward C. Banfield*

Supplemental grants, it will be recalled, were intended by the task force to serve as both "bait" and "glue" — "bait" in that they would enable a city to attract categorical grants from federal agencies anxious to try things that they could not try elsewhere; "glue" in that they could be used to bring diverse projects (federal, state, and local) into internally consistent wholes. In this way, MCA and the city governments, working in partnership, were expected to bring about coordination.

To establish the relationships with federal agencies required for this, Taylor had sent them drafts of the program guide for review and comment. Except for OEO, which urged MCA to adopt its "confrontation" tactics in dealing with city agencies, their responses had been perfunctory. He had persisted, however. When the time came to select the first-round cities, he created regional interagency committees to make recommendations. These played little or no part in the selection process, probably for lack of time to give them training, but (as has been explained) a Washington interagency committee *did* pass upon the applications.

After the selections had been made, the interagency committees, both regional and Washington, were given the task of reviewing the cities' plans and giving them technical assistance. Since the funds for model cities' projects would presumably come mainly from departments and agencies other than HUD, it was necessary to bring these units into close contact with the CDAs, the local bodies making the plans.

That these arrangements sometimes did not work as they were supposed to is evident from the experience (perhaps not typical) of the Texarkana, Arkansas, CDA when it asked its regional interagency committee for advice. "We expected a dialogue on the purpose and potential impact of individual projects and groups of projects," a CDA official wrote. Instead, the federal agency representatives met first in a session from which the locals were excluded; later the locals found themselves answering questions about budgetary and other details of particular projects. It was apparent that most of the "Feds" had not read the city's five-year plan; they were interested only in its first-year action program and only in those parts of it that related to their agencies' programs. "Federal employees," the Texarkana official concluded, "are generally limited to specific project categories." This, of course, was one of the very conditions that the Model Cities program had been created to correct.

It is not surprising that the interagency committee members were not interested in Texarkana's five-year plan: each was there primarily to protect and promote the interest of *his* agency. It was all very well for MCA, which had cast itself in the role of coordinator, to preach the virtues of coordination. The other agencies did not have the same interest in the matter: on the contrary, they had reason to view coordination with some suspicion; its success would tend to subordinate them to MCA.

Relations between MCA and OEO were always difficult. In theory, CDAs did planning whereas CAAs (Community Action Agencies of OEO) operated programs. Naturally, CDAs contended that *all* programs in model neighborhoods should fit harmoniously into their plans; naturally, too, CAAs insisted that they had a right — indeed a responsibility — to extend any of their programs to the *whole* of any city.

What most concerned Weaver, Wood, and Taylor was the failure of supplemental grants to serve as "bait," "glue," or "clubs." "Supplemental" soon proved to be a misnomer. Most CDAs made little or no effort to get categorical grants; instead they asked for supplementals to finance projects that could have been financed with categoricals.

There were several reasons for this. CDAs found it less trouble to use supplementals because they did not have to find out about, and adapt to, the detailed restrictions with which Congress had loaded the categoricals and also because they were more used to dealing with MCA, their parent agency, than with others. The administrators of the categorical programs thought — or claimed to think — that model cities (the "winners" in the national competition) would be generously funded by MCA and that therefore their own grants should be given to less favored places. Thus when the Seattle CDA allocated $35,000 in supplemental funds to expand an OEO legal services program, OEO at once reduced its contribution to the project by that amount. From OEO's standpoint, this was the sensible thing to do: since the legal services program was now going to be supported at what it (OEO) deemed an adequate level, it could put its $35,000 into something else.

As Secretary of Labor Wirtz had pointed out to Califano (special assistant to LBJ), administrators of categorical grants had very little discretion in the allocation of them. For example, HEW, the department most disposed to cooperate with model cities, had appropriations of $6.4 billion in 1968 but only $181 million of this — roughly 3 percent — was not committed by statute or otherwise.

By the spring of 1968, it was evident that vigorous intervention from the White House would be required to establish MCA in a coordinating role. The president's prestige was now very low (he had announced that he would not be a candidate); even so, a few well-chosen words from him would greatly strengthen MCA's influence with the other agencies. Getting him to say the words was a problem, however. Only Weaver, the cabinet member, was in a position to approach him on the subject, and he sensed that to do so might irritate him and do MCA's cause more harm than good.

Accordingly, Weaver, with Wood, Taylor, and Farr in tow, went to see Califano and Schultze, the White House assistants most responsible for such matters. Both of them readily agreed to request in the president's name that the relevant departments and agencies earmark part of their discretionary funds for use in model cities neighborhoods.

Taylor meanwhile was doing what he could to get state governments to give the model cities neighborhoods more of what they got in federal grants as well as more from their other revenues. At his suggestion, Weaver invited nine states (later others as well) to participate in the review of "second round" applications. These efforts, however, yielded little. State agencies had not much more freedom of action than did federal ones and, besides, they too had their own axes to grind.

### The Pre–Inauguration Day Rush

Two years after the passage of the Model Cities Act, Richard Nixon was elected as president, and Weaver, Wood, and Farr made ready to leave the program to successors who, it seemed likely, would liquidate it. As matters stood on Election Day, this would have been easy. As yet only planning grants had been made, and not as many of these as intended. The "first round" cities were now approaching the end of their "planning year" but none had submitted its first-year program. Consequently, not a dollar of supplemental grants had been obligated.

To make liquidation of the program awkward for the new administration, MCA put the "first round" cities under pressure to make program submissions by December 1 so that funds could be committed to them before Inauguration Day. Sixteen cities met the deadline, and the programs of nine were approved. Selecting the remaining "second round" cities was easier and the quota was filled by the end of December.

The Nixon administration would be in office for six months before the beginning of the new fiscal year, but, unless great inconvenience and confusion were to ensue, the Johnson administration had to prepare a tentative budget proposal for fiscal 1970. In the previous two years, Congress had appropriated nearly $1 billion for Model Cities grants. Only a few million of this could be obligated, for lack of cities whose submissions were ready, or almost ready, to be approved. Nevertheless, the Johnson administration's 1970 budget proposed another $750 million for Model Cities. It was, of course, good politics to put the Nixon administration in the position of appearing unsympathetic to the poor and blacks by trimming from the Johnson budget funds that could not possibly be spent.

Weaver, Wood, Taylor, and Farr, although loyal members of the Johnson "team," were, it is safe to say, less interested than the White House in creating embarrassments for the next administration. They did, however, want to do what they could to assure the continuance, growth, and success of the Model Cities program. Taylor approved only nine of the sixteen program submissions because he depended upon a normal bureaucratic evaluation process, which took a certain amount of time and turned up only nine submissions that met the established standards. (One partial exception may be noted: Seattle's submission was taken out of turn because it was thought expedient to show West Coast Republicans that they had a stake in the continuance of the program.)

This was in fact a time when politics receded farther into the background than usual. "We were leaving office," one of those most concerned said later, "therefore we had nothing to lose by being *not* political."

Two Voices of Experience

Before they emptied their desks, Taylor and Farr wrote memoranda to be read by their successors.

Farr said that substantial progress had been made in strengthening local governments and in creating a federal organization that could respond quickly to the cities' needs. But so much time had been required to develop workable relations between city governments and neighborhood groups that little had been left for planning. Innovation had been hard to "pull off," both for lack of money and because of the commitment not to increase the fragmentation of local government. Coordination, when it occurred, had more often been information-sharing than program integration, and the federal agencies (except those in HUD itself) had made only nominal efforts to help the cities develop high-quality programs.

The promise of the program, Farr said, could not be realized unless there was a "quantum leap" in the amount of technical assistance given the cities and in the attention given to the evaluation of their results. The likelihood of MCAs ever having enough personnel to do these things adequately was, he judged, zero. But without vast expansion and improvement along these lines the Model Cities Program would amount to little more than block grants. This might be valid and appropriate, but it was not what Congress intended.

Taylor, in his memorandum, revealed that two years of trying had left him convinced that local governments could not be "tooled up" from Washington: the federal government simply did not have the capacity. The categorical programs, he said, were too many and too diverse to be managed, even by a "super-department" that some would like to see created. Moreover, the categorical system was an impediment to local planning: except as they had latitude to make choices, local governments were without incentives to plan. The number of categorical programs, he thought, should be reduced by at least one-half through consolidation; HUD should be made a "Department of Urban Affairs" with authority to coordinate federal efforts in urban areas, and revenue-sharing (an arrangement by which the federal government would regularly pass a fixed percentage of its revenue on to the states and cities to use as they saw fit) should be instituted.

The role Taylor envisioned for Model Cities was a limited one, and it was based upon assumptions that the rest of his memorandum seemed to contradict. MCA, he thought, should be the Department of Urban Affairs' instrument for developing and testing new techniques for improving local public services; in particular it should try to discover whether, by the use of block

*Edward C. Banfield*

grants and the concentration of resources, local officials could be induced to take responsibility for the solution of local problems.


Concluding Observations

There was not in 1965, when the second task force did its work, the slightest possibility of a federal program being brought into existence which could accomplish any of the various large purposes that Model Cities was supposed to serve. The president and his advisers, including the members of the task force, knew perfectly well that the boundaries of political possibility precluded measures that would change the situation fundamentally. Block grants, not to mention revenue sharing, were out of the question. (As Wood remarked later, "Congress was not about to collect taxes and then let the states and cities spend them with no strings attached.") Bringing the more than 200 categorical programs under central control was equally unfeasible.

It was also politically impossible to concentrate federal funds and efforts in a few large cities, let alone to "saturate" a few. Even if there had been no Vietnam War, the scores of billions that would have been required to make a "substantial impact" on the physical slum in the dozen or so largest cities would not have been appropriated and, even if it were, men could not have been found to do the work. Even to *stop* doing things that manifestly did not work — urban renewal, for example — was beyond the bounds of possibility; one had to expand what did not work as the price of trying something that *might*.

These constraints were all apparent to the designers of the Model Cities program. There were other constraints which a charitable reader may suppose were *not* apparent to them and are visible now only by the light of hindsight. That local political arrangements in the United States preclude anything remotely resembling "comprehensive" or "rational" planning is a fact familiar to all practical men and documented repeatedly by journalists and even by scholars. That inventing social reforms that are likely to work and that voters are willing to have tried is very difficult to do anywhere (and almost impossible to do in an American city where "veto groups" abound) is a fact hardly less obvious. As for citizen participation, very little judgment or experience was needed to see that this would be costly in terms of other goals — planning, coordination, and innovation.

Even if these constraints had not existed, the new program would have been the product of (at best) the "educated guesses" of persons with experience and judgment but without any sort of technical expertise on the basis of which they could answer the really important questions. That the "social and psychological" approach would achieve worthwhile results, for example, was mere conjecture. No "facts" or "tested theories" existed from which a remedy for any of the ailments of the cities could have been derived.

There *did* exist, however, a fairly good example of the very program that the designers of Model Cities were trying to create, one which, had they examined it closely (time did not permit) would have revealed the futility of what they were about to attempt. New Haven (as was remarked above) was a model city before Model Cities was invented. Its circumstances were peculiarly favorable: small (population 150,000) and without much poverty, it had (what was most unusual) a mayor who not only won elections but surrounded himself with able assistants, some of whom were unusually talented at devising innovative measures to improve the lot of those for whom poverty had become a way of life. While the Wood task force was at work, New Haven had more than twenty-five agencies, public and private, participating in about sixty programs that were coordinated by a special body. Federal and other spending there was close to a "saturation" level, amounting in 1965 to nearly $7,000 for each family with an income under $4,000.

If Wood and his associates had studied this ready-made "pilot program" they would not have found evidence that it was making a "substantial impact" on the "quality of life" in the city. But even if they *had* found convincing evidence of this, the significance of the finding for other cities would have been questionable. Weaver was optimistic, to say the least, when he told the House subcommittee that successful demonstrations in a few cities would be copied by thousands of others. This might happen if the demonstrations were of new methods that could be easily applied, although political or other circumstances might stand in the way even then. But if the nature of a demonstration were such as to preclude its general application — if, for example, it required extraordinary political or administrative skills — then Weaver's hope could not be realized. It was more than likely that any measures that could make a "substantial impact" would be so costly in money and other resources (e.g., political leadership) as to preclude their being generalized. To invest as much per capita in *all* cities as had been invested in New Haven was fiscally impossible.

Supposing, however, that from the example of New Haven or otherwise the task force had devised a simple and highly effective method for bringing about complete coordination of federal, state, and local efforts, public and private, while realizing simultaneously and to the full the ideals of comprehensive planning, citizen participation, and innovation. It is likely that this would have "solved," or much alleviated, the problems of the cities? There is very little reason to think so. Conceivably, the result might have been the more effective pursuit of courses of action that in the long run would have made matters worse. (Suppose, for example, that such successes had, by making life in the poorest parts of the city less dismal, reduced the pressure to move to the suburban areas where job opportunities would certainly be better in the long run.)

However this may be, President Johnson's prediction that the Model Cities Act would "spell the difference between despair and the good life" was far-fetched in the extreme. Possibly, however, his rhetoric and the act itself were

*Edward C. Banfield*

not intended to be taken at face value but rather were gestures intended to help create confidence in government and (what may have been the same in the president's eyes) in himself as a leader. If this is taken as the "real" purpose of the program, one may well wonder what was the nature and extent of the gains that accrued from holding out such promises and whether they were later offset — perhaps more than offset — by a loss of confidence when the promises proved unrealizable.

These questions will never be fully answerable and it is probably fruitless even to speculate about them now. The forces that converged in the making of the Model Cities program are still at work and what they will lead to eventually is anyone's guess.

### SOURCES AND READINGS

The reader is asked to bear in mind that this account does not carry the Model Cities program beyond January 1968. It should not be assumed that the program and the conditions affecting it have remained unchanged.

The following were kind enough to read an earlier version of the case in its entirety: Jay Janis, Marshall Kaplan, William L. Rafsky, H. Ralph Taylor, Robert C. Weaver, and Robert C. Wood. Others who were helpful on particular matters were: Antonia Chayes, William Cannon, James Johnson, Martin Meyerson, and Charles L. Schultze. It goes without saying that some of these may disagree with my interpretations.

The work is based largely upon interviews by the author with participants. He has also drawn upon interviews by Christopher DeMuth, for which privilege he is grateful. He is grateful also for much stimulating comment and criticism from Mr. DeMuth and from Lawrence D. Brown.

Only such source material is cited as is easily available in published form. This includes especially the hearings held in 1966 by the housing subcommittees of the Committees on Banking and Currency of both House and Senate. The House hearings are entitled *Hearings on Demonstration Cities, Housing and Urban Development and Urban Transit*. The Senate ones are entitled *Hearings, Housing Legislation of 1966*. President Johnson's special message on demonstration cities may be found in *Public Papers of the Presidents*, 1966, Vol. I. For the reaction of academic specialists to the president's message the student should read the symposium of comment in the November 1966 issue of *The Journal of the American Institute of Planners*. In the writer's judgment, Professor James Q. Wilson was particularly prescient in his contribution to that symposium.

The debates on the bill are to be found in the *Congressional Record*. The Senate debates were on August 18 and 19 (Vol. 112, Part 5) and the House debates on October 13 and 14 (Vol. 112, Part 20).

For the ideas and efforts that preceded and presumably influenced the planning of the Model Cities program the student is referred to Richard Blumenthal's chapter "The Bureaucracy: Antipoverty and the Community Action Program," in Allan P. Sindler (ed.), *American Political Institutions and Public Policy* (Boston: Little, Brown, 1969), Peter Marris and Martin Rein, *Dilemmas of Social Reform: Poverty and Community Action in the United States* (New York: Atherton Press, 1967), and D. P. Moynihan, *Maximum Feasible Misunderstanding* (New York: Free Press, 1966). For a full and careful account of what was done in New Haven, consult Russell D. Murphy, *Political Entrepreneurs and Urban Poverty* (Lexington, Mass.: Heath Lexington Books, 1971). Former President Johnson's (retrospective) account of his administration (which is quoted or paraphrased several times in the case study) is of course of unique interest and value; his book is *The Vantage Point* (New York: Holt, Rinehart and Winston, 1971).

Some who played active roles in the Model Cities program or who observed its beginnings at close range have written about it. One short but valuable article is by Fred Jordan (the "Green Beret" much quoted in the text above): "The Confessions of a Former Grantsman," in *City*, Summer 1971. Planning in three model cities is described at length by the members of a firm of consultants employed by MCA to evaluate its efforts; see Marshall Kaplan, Sheldon P. Gans, and Howard M. Kahn, *The Model Cities Program: The Planning Process in Atlanta, Seattle and Dayton* (New York: Praeger, 1970).

The Model Cities program has been described as a "coordinating structure" in one chapter of a study of coordination in the federal system by James L. Sundquist with the collaboration of David W. David; their book is *Making Federalism Work* (Washington, D.C.: The Brookings Institution, 1969).

# STUDY FIVE

# INTERGOVERNMENTAL POLITICS

The legacy of failure. Another stab at the "preposterous." Congressional passage of ESEA. Title I's origin and objectives. Title I's distribution of power. Federal administration of Title I: 1965–69. *USOE: a state-oriented agency. An avoidance of evaluation. Inaction on audits of abuses. USOE's timidity. Resisting USOE's initiative: concentrating the funds. Resisting USOE's initiative: local parent advisory councils.* State administration of Title I. *Management of Massachusetts' Title I. An explanation of the Massachusetts pattern.* A turning point in Washington? *Another try to establish parent councils. A new face for USOE.* Massachusetts revisited. New Title I enforcement: a post mortem? Concluding observations. Sources and readings.

# The Education Bureaucracies Implement Novel Policy: The Politics of Title I of ESEA, 1965–72

*Jerome T. Murphy*

On the floor of the House of Representatives, Wednesday, March 24, 1965, started off like many other days. There was a prayer, then an announcement; it was Bradford County Strawberry Day and each congressman was to be the lucky recipient of one pint of the "succulent berries." But March 24 was different in one significant respect. It was the first day of debate on the 1965 Elementary and Secondary Education Act (ESEA), a bill hailed by President Lyndon B. Johnson as "the greatest breakthrough in the advance of education since the Constitution was written."

Though many shared Johnson's view of the proposal, a vocal minority in the House raised objection after objection. Putting his finger on one problem bothering many congressmen, Judge Howard W. Smith (D., Va.), the venerable Chairman of the Rules Committee, commented, "Mr. Speaker, we apparently have come to the end of the road so far as local control over our education in public facilities is concerned. I abhor that." J. Arthur Younger (R., Cal.), a conservative ex-banker, embroidered that theme: "We are placing in the hands of the Commissioner of Education almost dictatorial powers. . . . He has the full power of a commissar, and I think that he ought to have the title that goes with his duties."

Such worried rumblings about federal control were hardly audible amid the clamor for reform from the executive branch. With President Johnson proposing and prodding, nearly three dozen major domestic laws were steered through the Congress between 1964 and 1966: civil rights guarantees, a war on poverty, aid to education, urban housing, Medicare, and other "landmark" legislation to help meet the needs of the poor. These accomplishments, together with the inflated rhetoric of the day, led to feelings of exuberance and optimism among government officials. Many of them, reformers at heart, had entered public service because of John Kennedy and had stayed on under Johnson. Believing that racial discrimination was being struck mortal blows, that poverty soon would be eliminated, and that Johnson's "Great Society" was on its way to realization, these reformers were cheered by Congress's endorsement of one after another of LBJ's programs.

Yet less than a decade later, most of these high hopes have been dashed. In their place there is a growing self-doubt, malaise, and skepticism about government's capacity to remedy pressing social problems. In the harsh light of 1972, the "era of good feeling" of the early and mid-60s seems marked by naïveté about the complexity of federal reform. This case study describes and probes that complexity by focusing on federal aid to education, an important part of the LBJ reforms.

The 1965 ESEA was a prime example of Great Society legislation. It was innovative and bold, calling for a redirection of local priorities. Its goal was to "buy reform," as one of its designers said, by providing the schools with more than $1 billion each year. The act had five parts or titles. Title I provided aid for the schooling of disadvantaged children in urban slums and poor rural areas. The second title provided funds for school library resources and textbooks. The focus of Title III was school innovation to enhance the learning of both children and adults, through the establishment of supplementary educational centers and services. Title IV called for a national network of regional educational laboratories to close the gap between research and educational practice. The strengthening of state departments of education, viewed as key agencies in the long-run improvement of education, was the goal of Title V. In a word, ESEA was a first step toward a new face for American education.

This study concentrates on Title I of ESEA, the largest program ever administered by the United States Office of Education (USOE). Its initial 1965–66 appropriation of $959 million almost tripled USOE's budget for elementary and secondary education. And by fiscal 1972–73 Title I's appropriation has increased to an estimated $1.6 billion, providing roughly 4 percent of the nation's school expenditures. Title I also called for the greatest change at the local level — a new focus on the needs of the educationally deprived, or so-called compensatory education. Moreover, Title I provided the federal government with substantial new authority to exert influence at the state and local levels.

No one policy area or problem can be a full surrogate for all others, but an account of the political and bureaucratic obstacles to federal educational reform suggests a general range of problems besetting federally initiated reform. Further, a better understanding of the problems of ESEA's implementation by USOE and by one state department of education (Massachusetts) should suggest remedies applicable to other agencies and policy areas as well. This study takes the approach that this understanding can best be achieved by viewing key educational administrators as primarily political figures — rather than as educators — subject to the demands of their constituencies and to the constraints of their bureaucracies.*

## The Legacy of Failure

Despite nearly 100 years of congressional effort to win extensive federal aid for the nation's public elementary and secondary schools, success was not achieved until 1965 because of four issues. First was the fear that federal money would lead to federal control of the schools, an anathema to those who treasured the nation's long tradition of local school autonomy. A second stumbling block was concern about the appropriateness of federal support of schools practicing blatant racial discrimination. Since the 1950s, whenever a school aid bill came up for a House vote, Adam Clayton Powell, a black Democrat from Harlem, routinely proposed an amendment prohibiting aid to segregated schools. Opponents of federal aid to education would join Powell and his liberal colleagues in voting for the amendment. Once the Powell amendment was adopted, southern congressmen would then join the bill's initial opponents to defeat the measure on the final vote.

A third barrier was the problem of reaching agreement on a "fair" formula for distributing federal aid. Great inequalities had long existed among the states in their level of support for education and in their need for assistance. National average expenditures for education in the 1963–64 school year, for instance, amounted to $455 per student, but state averages ranged from $241 to $700 per student. This inequality, and conflicting opinions about the proper federal role in alleviating it, stalled congressional action. The final, and perhaps most important, difficulty was the emotion-charged question of federal support for private education, particularly Catholic schools. Vehement op-

* Although Title I includes limited aid for handicapped, institutionalized, American Indian and migrant children, this study deals only with aid for educationally deprived children in the public schools. Its focus is not on how well compensatory education "works" or whether extra dollars result in higher school achievement, but on the capacity of the federal government to impose its priorities on localities.

position to private school aid was led by the National Education Association, a powerful Washington lobby representing public school teachers and administrators, which viewed such aid as a breach of the constitutional separation of church and state. Favoring aid to private schools was the National Catholic Welfare Conference (now the U.S. Catholic Conference), an influential organization speaking for the Catholic schoolmen of the nation.

Hopes were nonetheless high in 1960 that an education breakthrough was imminent. Just elected, President Kennedy pushed for general support of elementary and secondary education, calling his 1961 bill "probably the most important piece of domestic legislation of the year." Pigeonholed in the House Rules Committee by a vote of eight to seven, the bill's fate was the same as many of its forerunners; it was killed, mainly because of its failure to aid church-related schools. Theodore Sorensen, a top aide to President Kennedy, described the bind faced by his boss: "While it should not be impossible to find an equitable constitutional formula to settle the church-school aid problem, it is difficult for that formula to be suggested by the nation's first Catholic President."

The crushing defeat of the Kennedy bill in 1961, combined with the previous history of failure, led several political analysts to conclude in the early '60s that broad-scale federal aid to elementary and secondary education was not possible in the foreseeable future. One observer colorfully concluded:

> From all that has gone before, it can be said that the spontaneous arrangement of circumstances into the ideal pattern [necessary to pass federal aid] is possible — but only in the same way that it is possible for pigments thrown at a canvas to shape themselves into the "Last Supper." That is, it may happen, but it is not a good bet, and to have to count on it for the success of legislation approaches the preposterous.

## Another Stab at the "Preposterous"

In 1964, President Johnson asked U.S. Commissioner of Education Francis Keppel (the head of USOE, which is part of the Department of Health, Education and Welfare) to devise an education bill that would avoid another church-state controversy, and to build a "consensus" of support behind legislation that Congress would pass.

Keppel took to his new assignment enthusiastically. An ex-dean of the Harvard Graduate School of Education, he had been brought to Washington by President Kennedy in 1962 to break the school aid logjam, but had not yet accomplished his goal. Dapper, witty, and disarmingly deferential, Keppel had a knack for making even the least able congressman or lobbyist feel smart, important, and somehow above the political fray. Inspiring confidence, he put his talents to good use in hammering out compromises on ESEA.

In carrying out his task, Keppel had direct access to the White House, working closely with Douglass Cater, a special assistant to the president. In constant communication with Cater, Commissioner Keppel held a series of meetings with key education lobbyists, particularly those representing the long warring National Education Association and the National Catholic Welfare Conference. Keppel acted as a "broker" among the various interest groups, adroitly building a cohesive coalition for passage of the legislation. According to one USOE staffer, the task was approached as if ". . . the coalition was some sort of Chinese puzzle. With everyone in line we're all right. If one left the reservation we would lose the entire thing."

The negotiations were greatly helped by a fortuitous combination of circumstances in 1964. The Civil Rights Act passed that year, blunting debate over federal funds for racially segregated schools; such aid now was illegal and the Powell antisegregation amendment no longer was an issue. Also, there was a growing ecumenical mood in the nation, spurred by the reign of Pope John. This, combined with a Protestant president, greatly reduced opposition to aid to private school children.

The chances of passing a bill were also considerably enhanced by the overwhelming victory in 1964 of a president committed to federal school aid, and perhaps most important, by the election of sixty-nine freshman Democratic Representatives, thirty-eight of whom replaced Republicans in the House. The result was a huge Democratic majority (two out of three in the House), dominated by northern liberals. Southern Democrats and conservative Republicans could no longer join forces to form a working majority in the House. Finally, the continuing failure to obtain general aid made supporters of this time-worn approach more open to compromise.

What emerged from Keppel's labors was an "ingenious political contrivance" focusing on reform which had the support of all key interest groups. A church-state compromise was reached by channeling aid through public authorities which provided services for children, regardless of the schools they attended (public or private). Fears of federal control were reduced by complex arrangements placing substantial authority in the hands of state and local authorities. And a new formula for distributing funds to the states was devised which a broad coalition could support.

### Congressional Passage of ESEA

The administration sought to push ESEA through Congress as quickly as possible in early 1965, without major amendments, lest the fragile coalition fall apart. Flaws in the bill could always be "fixed" in subsequent years. President Johnson used the analogy of a Model-T Ford to describe the strategy to secure ESEA's enactment: just as the Model-T was improved over the years, so ESEA could be modified once off the drawing boards and in operation.

The bill raced through the hearing stage. In procedures unprecedented at the beginning of a legislative session, witnesses testified before the House Education Subcommittee eight to ten hours a day, including Saturdays. By February 5, less than a month after the bill was sent to Capitol Hill, it was ready for consideration by the full Committee on Education and Labor. Here the quick-passage strategy encountered its first major snag. Chairman Adam Clayton Powell was out of town and the committee could not meet without him. One furious Democratic committee member exclaimed:

> Why the son-of-a-bitch! The committee had nothing else on its schedule, the coalition was just barely sticking together . . . in danger of becoming unglued . . . we were all ready to go and he's down in Bimini [in the Bahamas]. If he doesn't make a contribution he shouldn't be chairman. There is no divine right of committee chairmen.

Rested and relaxed, Powell jetted back to Capitol Hill three weeks later. Quickly and effectively, he led the committee in reporting out a slightly modified ESEA by March 2, which received continued coalition backing.

Beginning on March 24, House debate went smoothly until the Republican opposition focused on the church-state compromise. Those defending the bill became confused under the rapierlike questions of Charles E. Goodell (R., N.Y.), the leader of the attack.* As the muddled debate got worse, the president's assistant, Douglass Cater, and Samuel Halperin, USOE's brilliant legislative tactician, sat huddled together in the gallery "scared to hell" that the bill was about to be lost, once more over the church-state controversy. But in the thick of the debate, John Brademas (D., Ind.), an urbane Rhodes scholar, managed to cut through the tension.† Standing before his embattled colleagues and the hushed galleries filled with lobbyists, he exclaimed:

> Mr. Speaker, I am the Methodist nephew of a hard-shell Baptist preacher. My mother belongs to the Disciples of Christ Church. My father is Greek Orthodox; and before coming to the Congress of the United States, I taught at a Roman Catholic college. If I could find myself a Jewish bride, I would represent the finest example of the ecumenical movement.

This lightened the debate and took the sting out of the opposition; Brademas and others clarified the meaning of the bill's imprecise language dealing with

---

* In 1965, Congressman Goodell, a six-year House veteran, represented a conservative rural district in western New York. In 1968, he was appointed to the Senate to fill the unexpired term of Robert Kennedy, and began to take more liberal stands, breaking with President Nixon over his handling of the Vietnam War. In 1970, Goodell lost his Senate seat to conservative James L. Buckley.

† Editor's note: The relation between Brademas and the education community is explored in Jack Schuster's case study in this volume.

the church-state compromise. Despite extended discussion of this issue, and some controversy over Title I, the bill quickly moved to passage by the House on March 26 by 263–153 vote. (Almost three-quarters of the Republicans and a majority of southern Democrats were on the losing side.)

Having the votes in the chamber as well as the strong support of Wayne Morse (D., Ore.), chairman of the Education Subcommittee, the administration adopted the strategy of "no amendments" and quick passage in the Senate. By avoiding a House-Senate conference to iron out differences, the Senate could prevent the House from having another chance to scuttle an education aid bill. After three days of floor debate, the Senate assented to the House-passed bill on April 9; the vote was 73–18, with nearly all Democrats in favor but 44 percent of the Republicans in opposition. The total elapsed time from introduction of the ESEA bill to LBJ's affixing his name to the law on April 11, 1965, was eighty-nine days. Since most bills average some two years from introduction to passage, it was little wonder that some critics of ESEA called it the "Railroad Act of 1965."

### Title I's Origin and Objectives

The reformist thrust of ESEA was to help eliminate poverty. Its underlying notion was familiar — poor children given the opportunity to do well in school will do well as adults — and it was embodied in the act's first and most important title. By allocating extra funds for educationally deprived children in poverty neighborhoods, federal reformers sought better education and improved opportunity.

In this, Title I was responsive to the "rediscovery of poverty" in mid-60s Washington. The 1964 Economic Opportunity Act had just passed and it was only natural that government officials would try to extend the president's "unconditional war" on poverty by providing quality education for poor children. This attitude also reflected the influence of what Daniel P. Moynihan calls the professionalization of reform:

> [President Kennedy's] election brought to Washington as officeholders, or consultants, or just friends, a striking echelon of persons whose profession might justifiably be described as knowing what ails societies and whose art is to get treatment underway before the patient is especially aware of anything noteworthy taking place. . . .

Moreover, federal school aid was viewed as desperately needed. In the nation's fifteen largest cities, 60 percent of tenth graders from poor neighborhoods dropped out before finishing high school. Conditions were no better in rural Appalachia and many areas in the South.

New school programs to aid the poor were promoted by Commissioner

Keppel, a strong advocate of concentrating resources on disadvantaged children. He was supported in his efforts by John W. Gardner (then President of the Carnegie Corporation, later HEW Secretary, and currently head of Common Cause), who had chaired a secret presidential task force on education in 1964. Keppel was also aided by a bill (S.2528) introduced by Senator Wayne Morse in 1964, which suggested a formula for concentrating funds on cities and rural areas at the same time, thus helping to assure a coalition of northern urban and southern rural congressmen. The administration's Title I formula, with its seeds in Morse's proposal, was attacked during House debate by Edith Green (D., Ore., who was supported mainly by Republicans) for discriminating against poorer states. Nevertheless, the formula did "solve" the historical problem of finding a method of distributing funds which would win congressional support. It did so by following the tested political strategy of distributing the benefits widely: the formula provided aid to school districts in 95 percent of the nation's counties.

These efforts of Keppel and others, in the context of LBJ's "war on poverty," explain Title I's intent to heighten local concern for the needs of the educationally deprived. But it is equally important to recognize those factors *not* playing a role in Title I's focus on reform. They demonstrate three things: the reform was based on few educational precedents; the reformers by and large stood alone in their special concern for the disadvantaged; and others viewed Title I as serving different purposes.

Title I was not a natural outgrowth of tried and tested programs at the local level. By 1965, only three states (California, Massachusetts, and New York) had passed legislation specifically geared to disadvantaged children, involving only small pilot projects. Other local efforts were new, few, and concentrated in a limited number of cities. Nor was Title I a response to public pressure. Unlike the great national programs enacted during the New Deal, the program did not result from public demand. The poor were unorganized and made virtually no demands for such legislation. Nor was Title I the creature of the established educational organizations or educational administrators. The "old guard" bureaucracy in USOE viewed its job more as a consulting firm offering technical assistance to the states and local schools than as providing a focal point for leadership or initiative. They had many reservations about Title I.

The reform likewise was not the product of the professionals who staffed the state and local school systems. In a national survey of school administrators in May 1966, approximately 70 percent stated that Title I funds should not be allocated on the basis of poverty. Moreover, schoolmen were confused and dismayed when they learned of the specific language of Title I showing that the program was not general aid to the schools. After all, congressional debate had *always* focused on general aid, and to those unfamiliar with the text of Title I, it appeared to be general aid because it provided substantial assistance to the great majority of school districts.

The educational associations in Washington were also primarily interested in general support for ongoing public school activities. They accepted ESEA's poverty focus as a compromise necessary to achieve passage of ESEA, but their emphasis was on breaking the federal aid logjam, on the ground that this would be a major step toward federal general support later. Andrew Biemiller, chief lobbyist for the AFL–CIO, expressed this theme:

> Let's get started . . . and get a bill through here, and begin to get some money into our school systems where we now know it is badly needed, and then we can take another good look and get closer to the goal that both you and I want; and we make no bones about it, that we want a general education bill.

Nor was the reformist intent of Title I the product of Congress. While legislators like Senator Morse influenced the ideas behind the formula for distributing aid, the guts of ESEA was developed "downtown" by the executive branch. Moreover, congressmen also differed on whether Title I was an antipoverty measure or a thinly disguised general-aid-to-education bill. That divergence in outlook stemmed in part from the House Committee Report on ESEA which contained a "laundry list" of forty-nine possible Title I expenditures ranging from reading programs to health services to class size reduction to school equipment. Without ever saying that Title I was general aid, the report provided a basis for making that inference.

Title I's focus on the disadvantaged, then, reflected neither pressure from the poor nor from professional educators. The former were quiescent and the latter supported Title I as providing the general aid they had long sought or as the major initial step in that direction. Their objective clearly was the provision of new federal assistance funds, not reform, a viewpoint shared by many congressmen. It was the executive branch which pushed for a new focus on the special needs of the disadvantaged. That concern included, to be sure, establishing the principle of federal aid to the schools, but it went beyond that to press for a redirection of local priorities to remedy educational deficiencies for the poor. As a result of these two quite different conceptions of Title I, confusion and ambiguity about its "real" intent bedeviled and weakened the administration of the law — even though Title I's language clearly targeted aid for the educationally deprived in poverty neighborhoods.

Title I's Distribution of Power

The successful implementation of federal reform depends heavily on the distribution of governmental power. But prior to the '60s, the federal government had played an inconsequential role in elementary and secondary education. The chief administrative unit, USOE, was a small nondescript agency buried in the Department of Health, Education, and Welfare. Stephen K. Bailey and Edith K. Mosher described its impotence:

> Aside from grants-in-aid for vocational education and to Land Grant Colleges under automatic, nondiscretionary formulas, USOE managed next to nothing. It had few friends apart from the National Education Association, the American Association of School Administrators and the Council of Chief State School Officers. . . . There was at least some validity to the widely-held assumption [in 1965] that USOE was, in fact, the "kept" Federal agent of these major private educational associations.

Given USOE's weak position in American education, the reformers recognized that federal leverage required new legal authority. The legislative record, however, was mixed on this point. While the reformers were anxious to use federal power to improve schooling for the poor, they were acutely aware that the old bugaboo of "federal control of the schools" was still a major concern at the time the bill was being drafted. Political reality required caution; every increment in federal power could be perceived as a corresponding decrease in local authority. Besides, Commissioner Keppel strongly believed that successful reform in the long run could not be accomplished by going around the states and dealing directly with the schools; state departments of education had to be strengthened.

These contradictory pressures were resolved by providing in the ESEA legislation a complicated set of arrangements which distributed power among the three levels of government. The formula grant mechanism was used to bypass the states and localities in determining roughly for whom the money should be spent. Funds were to be distributed down to the county level based on 1960 census data on the number of children, aged five through seventeen, from families with an annual income of less than $2,000. (During congressional debate a second poverty indicator was added: the number of children, aged five through seventeen, from families with incomes exceeding $2,000 in the form of aid to families with dependent children (AFDC), under Title IV of the Social Security Act. This amendment guaranteed large cities with high welfare payments their share of Title I.) Each county's allotment was equal to the product of its total number of poor children multiplied by one-half the state's average school expenditure per child.

Beyond the county allocations, the formula was even more complicated in determining eligible children. Funds were to be distributed to school districts within counties based on the latest available indicators of relative poverty, and within each school district Title I would be spent for supplementary programs to meet the "special educational needs of educationally deprived children" in areas of "high concentration" of poverty. New York City, for example, would be required to expend its Title I money in the poorer neighborhoods of Harlem, rather than in the richer suburbs of Queens. And once

*Jerome T. Murphy*

the money reached the target schools in Harlem, educationally deprived (not necessarily poor) children would be helped. In short, the poverty formula was a device to get compensatory funds to those geographic areas of greatest need within most of the nation's school districts for their expenditure, based on the premise that a high correlation existed between poverty and educational deprivation.

The formula grant system cut both ways, however. While it bypassed state and local governments, it established a virtual entitlement, once the total appropriation was known. Each state and locality "knew" how much it would receive. The absence of local competition for federal funds reinforced local views that the federal money was rightfully theirs, immensely weakening the ability of federal officials to bargain with states and localities over improvements in administration.

The determination of eligible children and program design was left with the states and localities. The local school district was to identify target schools and the eligible educationally deprived children within them, determine the children's needs, design programs to meet them, and apply to its state department of education for approval. State departments of education were to approve projects of sufficient "size, scope, and quality," monitor them, insure the participation of nonpublic school children, and submit fiscal reports and evaluations of the effectiveness of the local projects to USOE.

As a counterweight to this almost complete delegation of responsibility, USOE was authorized to accept or reject "assurances" submitted by each state "in such detail as the Commissioner [of Education] deems necessary" that the law would be followed. If the assurances were not met, USOE could withhold state funds. (In practice, USOE accepted a pro forma two-page letter of assurance from each state and virtually never attempted to exercise its unwieldy withholding authority.) Also, USOE was authorized to provide federal guidance of state and local administration of Title I through "such basic criteria as the Commissioner [of Education] may establish." Failure to meet these basic criteria, which were to be developed after the law's passage, also could lead to USOE withholding state funds.

The "basic criteria" provision of Title I was a source of contention in Congress's consideration of ESEA. For example, at the hearings before the House Subcommittee on Education, HEW Secretary Anthony J. Celebrezze argued that the LBJ administration strongly supported localism and had no intention of instituting federal control of education. Nevertheless, he and Commissioner Keppel were bombarded with questions about the meaning of the basic criteria provision. Congressman Charles E. Goodell, single-handedly mounting the attack, asked the secretary: "Tell me about 'basic criteria.' . . . Can you tell me what 'basic criteria' — not 'control' but 'criteria' — you are going to impose on the States?" After a long day on the witness stand, Celebrezze, a politically seasoned former mayor of Cleveland, finally exclaimed in exasperation, "We have been arguing all morning and afternoon about Federal control. . . . We don't impose anything on the states." Although the language on "basic criteria" emerged from the House and Senate unchanged, the Senate report on ESEA stated:

> The minority pointed out that the language of the bill was ambiguous with respect to the authority of the Commissioner of Education under Title I to establish 'basic criteria.' . . . *The Senate Report now acts to restrain the Commissioner from adding criteria beyond those written in the law.* [Emphasis added.]

The controversiality of the basic criteria provision and the congressional wariness of it suggested the difficulties to come in USOE's attempts to use this authority to control Title I expenditures.

In sum, Title I contained a complicated set of provisions, providing some influence for each level of government, but at the same time setting limits which favored the influence of local school districts. The USOE bypassed the state departments of education in determining the allocation of grants and established basic criteria to be met by local districts, but it had no operating control over the projects. The states had the responsibility for approving projects, but they had to apply federal criteria in carrying out this responsibility. Local districts had access to earmarked funds and latitude in designing projects, circumscribed only by the effectiveness of state supervision and federal criteria. Thus, even on paper, the local school districts had the greatest say in how Title I funds were to be spent.

### Federal Administration of Title I: 1965–69

*USOE: A State-Oriented Agency.* As we have seen, reformers read Title I's intent as assigning resources for the educationally deprived, particularly the poor, while others understood it as providing general aid to education. This disagreement, of course, would have to be "resolved" during the program's administration, and primarily by personnel who had not pushed for Title I in the first place. The executive-branch reformers who promoted the passage of ESEA were largely uninvolved in its implementation; they continued to develop and propose new policies in other areas. It fell to USOE officials to administer the program, so that Title I's effectiveness would depend heavily on USOE's inclination to act aggressively on the managerial and political dimensions of its task.

Federal administration of ESEA was turned over to lower levels in the 98-year-old USOE. This staff had not influenced the development of Title I, and would have preferred general aid. Lacking experience with grants-in-aid of the size and scope of Title I, the agency had never been called on to write "basic criteria" governing the approval of projects. Herculean efforts to bring in new blood and to be responsive to its ESEA responsibilities produced some changes within USOE. But the "old guard," if not always controlling policy, continued to staff the program and to make the day-to-day decisions setting the tone and much of the substance of the federal operations.

Even if USOE had been less rigid in its attitudes, it did not have enough people to monitor the program effectively. Title I was administered by the Division of Compensatory Education in the Bureau of Elementary and Secondary Education of USOE. Monitoring was carried out by area desk officers, generally professional educators, in the Operations Branch. Although Title I policy was usually set at higher levels, the area desk officers were the links with the states and had day-to-day responsibility to assure that the states were following the law, regulations, guidelines, and basic criteria. In the early days of the program, the division approached its authorized personnel strength of eighty-two (including professional and clerical staff), but the staff size subsequently dwindled. By the end of 1969, there were some thirty professionals working on all facets of Title I — technical assistance, accounting, program support — but only three area desk officers for the entire nation. The one dealing with Massachusetts, for example, also had sole responsibility for twenty-three other states. He felt overworked and believed that he could use at least four assistants to provide adequate technical assistance to the states.

In addition, the USOE staff had traditionally taken a passive role with respect to the states. USOE's job was to write checks, not to meddle in state and local affairs. "Everything in the Bureau was assistance and state-oriented," commented a Title I staffer. "Anytime you mentioned compliance in [Bureau Chief] Lessinger's presence, he would have a fit." This deferential attitude toward the states was adopted by the Massachusetts desk officer at USOE who described his relationship with the Massachusetts Title I director as "very nice." In the six months preceding a 1969 interview, they had met together once and talked occasionally on the telephone. The area desk officer viewed his job as one of trouble-shooting, answering complaints, and providing service. He did not want to provide leadership, nor did he view himself as a program "monitor" in the sense of being an enforcement officer. He readily admitted that he did not have the time to know what was going on in his states, and thus was dependent on information supplied by state officials as to whether they were enforcing the law. He found the limited staff situation frustrating, not because he was unable to monitor the states, but because he could not give them assistance.

The prevailing modus operandi was succinctly described in 1969 by an official in the Division of Compensatory Education who had been with the program since its start:

> Title I is a service-oriented program with predetermined amounts for the states. This sets the framework where the states are entitled to the money. Other than making sure states got their money and making sure it was spent, there was no role for the Office of Education. I don't know anyone around here who wants to monitor. The Office of Education is not investigation-oriented, never has been, and never will be.

*An Avoidance of Evaluation.* Since the program's beginning, evaluation of its impact has been high on the list of federal rhetorical priorities but low on the list of actual USOE priorities for a variety of reasons. One was the desire not to upset the federal-state balance. Another was recognition that little expertise existed at the state and local levels to evaluate a broad-scale reform program. A third was fear of disclosing failure; no administrator is anxious to show that his program is not working well. Aside from these impediments to effective evaluation, the diverse purposes of Title I left unclear just how one would determine whether Title I was "working." Title I could be seen as serving quite different purposes: to break the federal aid barrier; to raise school children's achievement; to help pacify the ghettos; to assist private school children; or to provide fiscal relief to school districts. By the latter standard, for example, if fiscal collapse had been avoided, Title I was successful regardless of its effects on children. Yet the ESEA legislation, at the insistence of Senator Robert F. Kennedy (D., N.Y.), called for objective measurements of educational achievement. This created a bind for many congressmen. While viewing achievement data as irrelevant, it was difficult for them to oppose efforts to measure enhanced learning of children. The result was public statements of congressional concern about inadequate evaluations of achievement, but only limited genuine support for improvement. Inconclusive findings were politically acceptable.

*Inaction on Audits of Abuses.* Federal audit reviews, conducted by the HEW Audit Agency, constituted another important area of federal responsibility. Their purpose was to determine whether funds were being spent in accordance with the legislation, regulations, and guidelines. These reviews were fairly comprehensive, and comprised the only full-scale investigations of Title I operations at the state and local level undertaken by HEW between 1965 and 1969. The results were always referred to the Division of Compensatory Education for action.

These audits disclosed numerous violations of the law across the country. Title I supplied general aid for *all* children in some school districts, rather than focusing on the special needs of the disadvantaged. Title I was used *in place of* state and local funds, rather than adding *supplementary* services in others. In addition, a variety of questionable, if not illegal, purchases were made: classroom carpeting, bedroom sets, football jerseys, air conditioners, and even swimming pools. In the judgment of HEW auditors, the misuse of funds was "severe"; they estimated that it was "substantially greater" than 15 percent of Title I's total allocation. (In fiscal 1968, for example, the auditors' estimate meant that more than $150 million was being expended in violation of the law.) Despite these documented abuses, USOE virtually ignored the audit findings. In the winter of 1969, a backlog of more than thirty audits existed, some of them more than three years old, with no action yet taken and little prospect of reduction.

*USOE's Timidity.* Why was USOE so hesitant to administer Title I aggressively and to follow up on the audits? Its limited staff and its overall service orientation are important parts of the answer, but other complicating factors also came into play. First, the pressure was on in the early days of Title I for the program to move quickly, to get federal-state relations off on the right foot. Hence there was little disposition to inject conflict by striking at alleged misuses. Second, the administration's need to demonstrate the program's success to the public and the Congress meant that program administrators were obliged to generate favorable statistics on the number of schools involved, the number of children affected, and so forth. Third, there was confusion among Title I staffers as to what stance they should take with the states. Those who wanted to enforce Title I usually received little support from their bureau-level bosses, many of whom believed that Congress "really" meant Title I as general aid. Not coincidentally, many of these officials were philosophically committed to that same goal and viewpoint. Finally, other Title I staffers feared that if USOE pushed too hard, Congress would indeed replace Title I with general aid, in which case USOE would have even less influence over the schooling of the poor.

That fear was not simply a cover for timidity. It is one thing, after all, to try to persuade a state to follow certain criteria, but an altogether different thing to accuse it of misusing funds which it views as its money. While politicians never tire of abusing bureaucrats who countenance waste, exceptions are made for individual cases, particularly when they occur in their own backyards. USOE staffers knew all too well of Commissioner Keppel's attempt, in October 1965, to cut off funds from Chicago for civil rights violations. When Mayor Richard J. Daley found out, he was "sputtering mad," according to Keppel. The fiery mayor hopped a plane to New York to confront President Johnson, who was meeting there with Pope Paul VI. Daley accused federal bureaucrats of trying to undermine him politically, and the president sent Wilbur J. Cohen, a trusted HEW lieutenant and later Secretary of HEW, to "straighten out the mess." The money was released; it may not be a coincidence that shortly thereafter Keppel left his job.

With this precedent etched in their minds, it is not surprising that top federal education officials were reluctant to arouse political wrath, especially when it was not likely that states would honor their "instructions" to return funds improperly spent. Moreover, they recognized the political nature of their jobs and of their agency's power, and knew they needed congressional and interest group support to survive. Hence top officials were willing to "bury" embarrassing audit reports that could threaten their position of influence and undercut their ability to persuade Congress and interest groups to support USOE's activities.

The states recognized these constraints on USOE's exercise of its authority and realized that orders or threats from USOE were not likely to be backed up with penalties. With USOE's limited influence based on its capacity to persuade and with its small staff almost totally reliant on the states for information about local programs, the states knew it was essential for USOE to maintain cordial relations with them. Exploiting these bargaining conditions, the states could exact a price for their good will. Consequently, USOE was willing to overlook and therefore sanction state/local deviations from the statute in exchange for retention of open communications. Given its dependency position, USOE's service orientation and its deference to local officials can be understood as strategic behavior designed to achieve the greatest possible influence in an environment unsupportive of a more aggressive stance on its part. USOE's problem, then, was not only lack of staff, but primarily the reinforcing weaknesses of lack of will and of political muscle. Like other politicians in similar circumstances, many key federal education administrators were unwilling to take risky actions unless pressure persuaded them that their failure to do so might be no less risky.

*Resisting USOE's Initiative: Concentrating the Funds.* USOE's role was not entirely passive. Occasional attempts to assert initiative and leadership also dot its record. More often than not, however, its more aggressive efforts met with less than crashing success. Two examples of USOE's unsuccessful initiatives merit discussion. Both involve the agency's authority and obligation, under Title I of ESEA, to establish "basic criteria" governing the program's administration at the state and local levels. The first example, discussed in this section, involves setting standards to control the concentration of funds. The second illustration, discussed in the next section, deals with local parent advisory councils.

One of the critical issues addressed in the original draft guidelines was the concentration of limited resources for a limited number of students. Title I officials believed that if the program was to have significant impact, the money could not be spread thin. The original provision in the draft guidelines (fall 1965) stated that the number of children served had to be approximately the same as the number of children counted under the formula for allocating funds. This meant that each of about 5.4 million students would receive about $200 extra for the cost of their education.

This standard came under fire from congressmen and professional interest groups opposed to this effort to concentrate funds. They argued that the standard was inconsistent with congressional intent; the number of children counted for purposes of distributing money had nothing to do with the number of children to be served. They also reminded Commissioner Keppel of the language in the 1965 Senate report which directed USOE not to go beyond the criteria written in the law. In November 1965, the word came down from Commissioner Keppel to "slenderize" the guidelines, and the concentration provision subsequently was removed. More than 8 million children participated the first year with an average expenditure of just under $120. This early defeat of the Division of Compensatory Education's attempt to exert leverage

*Jerome T. Murphy*

made it clear that federal guidelines and criteria were "fair game" for political intervention in the future.

More than two years after the law was passed, USOE issued the first set of "basic criteria" on April 14, 1967, responding to what the memorandum described as a "definite need" for states to apply specific criteria in approving local projects. Twelve criteria were proposed, backed up by a "supporting statement of the types of evidence or indications that the applicant's proposal should contain . . ." The criteria regarding concentration simply stated: "Title I services will be programmed so that the services provided will be concentrated on a limited number of children." The supporting discussion, however, established a new standard:

> The investment per child on an annual basis for a program of compensatory educational services which supplement the child's regular school activities should be expected to equal about one-half the expenditure per child from State and local funds for the applicant's regular school program.

Suppose, for example, that Bayside School District spent $600 each year per pupil. Under the standard, each Title I student would receive an extra $300 in services, making a total of $900 per participating disadvantaged child.

Exactly ten days later, under congressional pressure, the USOE issued a "clarifying" memorandum, which read in part:

> The criteria statements are the requirements to be met, whereas the discussion matter *provides guidance* in meeting the criteria. It should be expected, of course, that the discussion guides *may not be fully applicable to every project application.* [Emphasis added.]

Translated, then, the "clarifying" memorandum meant simply that the new standard had been rendered impotent.

Some nineteen months later, not satisfied that funds were being adequately concentrated and disturbed by several evaluations showing Title I's failure to raise achievement test scores, USOE issued another memorandum (November 20, 1968) focused on improving the quality of Title I programs. The draft memorandum that went to Commissioner Harold Howe's desk for signature specifically called for the implementation by 1970 of the initial concentration standard of 1967. At the last minute, the draft was pulled back by the USOE Bureau of Elementary and Secondary Education and revised. Bureau officials, sympathetic to their public school lobbyist friends, were reluctant to impose precise standards on the states. Instead, a hastily drawn statement was inserted: "Plan the program so that by 1970 the average Title I expenditure per child . . . *is raised to a significant level*" (emphasis added). Nowhere in the memorandum was "significant level" discussed or the previous standard mentioned. Thus, a memorandum which had begun in the Division of Compensatory Education as an attempt to accomplish greater concentration of resources emerged from the USOE bureaucracy with no standard even as "guidance." In the meantime, dollar expenditures per Title I child were decreasing each year, and 30 percent of the students participating in 1968 were neither educationally nor economically disadvantaged while several million eligible students went unaided.

*Resisting USOE's Initiative: Local Parent Advisory Councils.* Since the beginning of the program USOE has sought to involve parents in the local Title I programs on the theory that the more parents were involved, the better their children would do in school. The first set of basic criteria, issued by USOE on April 14, 1967, called for parent participation in Title I programs, but was not specific on its form beyond saying it should be "appropriate." The second set of basic criteria (issued on March 18, 1968) went a step further. It called "essential" the requirement that parents be involved "in the early stages of program planning and in discussions concerning the needs of children in the various eligible attendance areas." Four months later (July 2, 1968), USOE took a much bolder step. In response to the Poor People's March on Washington, the USOE directed the establishment of a formal mechanism for community and parent involvement. Its memorandum stated that:

> each Title I applicant *must* have an appropriate organizational arrangement. This means, in effect, that *local advisory committees will need to be established* for the planning, operation, and appraisal of a comprehensive compensatory educational program. [Emphasis added.]

This directive aroused considerable concern. It was one thing to suggest parent involvement in vague terms, but quite another to call for formal committees which could be identified, counted, and perhaps exert some influence over the program's direction. Many educators viewed these committees as a threat to professional control. Less than three weeks later, under pressure from interest groups, local educators, and the Congress, a clarifying memorandum was sent to the states retreating from the previous position:

> In most instances it will be advantageous for a local educational agency to establish a local advisory committee. . . . In some instances, however, local conditions may favor other arrangements. . . . Whatever arrangement is decided upon, it should be one which your office, in the light of its understanding of the local situation, finds likely to be effective. . . .

In effect, USOE told the states to do as they pleased.

Four months later (November 1968), the Title I regulations were amended to require "maximum practical involvement" of parents in Title I programs. Although this reaffirmed the need for parent involvement, total discretion and flexibility was left to the states and local schools to decide what constituted "practical" participation. When asked in 1969 about the status of local advisory committees in Massachusetts, the USOE area desk officer for Massachusetts stated: "Frankly, I've heard nothing about them. Haven't heard any complaints." Nationwide, an average of three out of five school districts in 1969 did not have Title I parent councils. Hence, another attempt by USOE to work out specific guidelines to influence Title I's implementation was thwarted through political intervention in the administrative process.

This account of guideline changes and program management illustrates the context in which USOE officials operated through 1969. They were indisposed to compliance activities to begin with, but even if that were not the case, the staff to operate an effective compliance program did not exist. Furthermore, even if both the staff and the will had been present, USOE lacked the political support to assert leadership. Given the nation's strong commitment to local autonomy, most legislators were sure to be more responsive to the wishes of state and local schoolmen than to the desires of federal bureaucrats. This was particularly true because there were no counterpressures from a constituency with differing values from public schoolmen, for example, from the program's clients (the poor). The result was that USOE officials acted as though their main constituencies were the Congress and state and local administrators, to the exclusion of the poor people whose children Title I was designed to assist. In those few instances when USOE tried to exert leverage, its efforts were challenged and frustrated. State and local interests, speaking through the Congress and their Washington-based lobby groups, by and large kept the lid on USOE's efforts to influence local priorities.


State Administration of Title I

Despite USOE's failure to gain control over Title I, federal priorities theoretically could be met by state departments of education, which had major responsibility for administering the law and guaranteeing that educationally deprived children benefited from Title I. As noted earlier, the states were authorized to review and approve local projects, monitor and audit ongoing activities, evaluate results and provide leadership in the development of program improvements. Title I's effectiveness, then, depended in large measure on the strength of these state agencies and on their relationships with both federal and local governmental units.

But in 1965 state education agencies varied widely in their capacity to carry out their Title I tasks. A few states had the administrative structure and staff capable of establishing state education priorities and, occasionally, the political support and the will to go beyond federal priorities in implementing Title I vigorously. For most states, however, the administrative apparatus was weak and unable to exercise significant leverage over local school policies. Inadequate staff capability and a strong tradition of localism promoted a general pattern of limited state educational leadership.

The Massachusetts Department of Education certainly was no exception to this pattern of weakness. A 1970 study found:

> The Department of Education, for many reasons, continues to carry out a wide variety of mandated functions, most of which have little to do with educational leadership or which have any visible impact on improving quality of education for students in our schools.

While Massachusetts' handling of Title I may not necessarily be typical, an examination of its problems highlights important political, bureaucratic, and intergovernmental barriers to Title I's implementation that are found in many states.

*Management of Massachusetts' Title I.* Each year from 1966 to 1969 Massachusetts school districts received approximately $16 million to support about 420 Title I projects in some 325 school districts. An average of about 100,000 children participated annually in these locally determined projects. The overall program was administered by a Title I unit in the Bureau of Elementary and Secondary Education in the Massachusetts Department of Education.

Although the state had major responsibility for administering the law, the Title I unit adopted an essentially passive attitude, leaving almost total program discretion to local school districts. Robert L. Jeffery, Massachusetts' Title I director, saw his job mainly as that of a consultant providing technical assistance and service to local schoolmen. This entailed regional meetings, workshops, and "helpful" visits to local Title I projects. But it did not entail an insistence on strict adherence to the law. In effect, Jeffery was as reluctant to interfere with local prerogatives as federal officials were to interfere with state prerogatives; he saw his role vis-à-vis local districts — a service role — the same way that his federal counterparts perceived their role toward Massachusetts.

Jeffery's negative attitude toward strong state action was reflected in Title I's management, as indicated by the department's project approval process, program monitoring, local audits, and program evaluation. For many school districts, the approval process was handled informally through telephone conversations and visits to the state office prior to the submission of the formal application. If local schoolmen planned to employ questionable Title I practices, the state Title I unit tried to discourage them through "friendly persuasion." Only a few projects were ever turned down and no money was ever withheld. And for many schoolmen the assistance available through informal discussions was not tapped; they simply submitted their applications to the state for approval without prior consultations. A 1969 HEW audit of Massachusetts pointed out one consequence of this substandard procedure:

> We found that applications submitted to the SEA [state education agency] for approval did not contain complete criteria as . . . required by the U.S. Commissioner of Education. . . . The SEA officials did not have pertinent information to effectively discharge its responsibilities in determining the adequacy of LEA [local education agency] proposed projects for meeting the special needs of educationally deprived children.

Visiting four Massachusetts cities, the auditors found inadequate or no documentation of the procedures used for choosing eligible Title I schools. Since the state would never discover that defect through its application procedure, localities could be spending Title I funds in the wrong schools for the wrong children.

Such laxity at the local level sometimes came to light through state visits to schools. State officials selectively monitored projects, especially those receiving more than $100,000 a year under Title I. But state officials often were reluctant to take strong action, even when they knew that the law and regulations were being loosely "interpreted." For example, Boston was permitted to spend Title I on *all* children in some target schools, despite a regulation that the money must be expended for supplementary services for those children identified as most in need. This was "blatant general aid," noted one unusually outspoken state official. Subtler violations of law were either ignored or never uncovered by the state. Some Boston schools, for instance, did go through the ritual of identifying the neediest educationally deprived children. According to the Boston criteria, a child had to perform below the so-called sixth stanine to be eligible for Title I assistance. This sounded objective, official, and educationally sound. But, in fact, this criterion opened the program to students performing *above* average for the nation, hardly those most in need. In short, the state's project approval procedures and subsequent monitoring were not effective in preventing local misuse of funds. Localities could pursue their own priorities, even if the law was stretched in the process, without fear of being called to account by the state.

The department's financial management procedures were equally weak. A 1969 HEW audit report on Massachusetts found that for the fiscal years 1966, 1967, and 1968 the department allowed Title I allotments of more than $1 million to lapse each year because of ineffective management. The audit concluded that "significant improvements in procedures and practices are needed at both the State and local levels. . . ."

The absence of adequate state audit procedures also precluded close scrutiny of the program. Although three auditors were paid with Title I funds, only one actually audited local projects. Working slowly without written procedures, he was unable to cope with the backlog of unaudited projects. As of November of 1968, less than one-third of the 1967 projects and none of the 1968 projects had ever been audited. Moreover, the only audit report local districts were required to submit to the state was a one-page sheet which broke down Title I expenditures by such categories as instruction, food, and administration, and divided the expenditure into salaries, contracted services, and other expenses. Data supplied in that form could not be reviewed to determine whether funds were spent in accordance with the law.

A similar pattern existed in the state's execution of its responsibilities for program evaluation. Title I required local districts to make annual evaluation reports to the states, including "appropriate objective measurements of educational achievement." Unlike previous federal programs, this provision called for the public disclosure of information which schoolmen knew might be used against them in the enforcement of new priorities. It also strained many local and state education units which had little evaluation experience or capability. Not surprisingly, persistent resistance to providing full and objective evaluation was evident. After all, in the absence of evaluation, local districts could meet their own priorities without being subject to challenge based on evidence of failure.

A 1970 study found that less than half of the local projects sampled had an evaluation design at all and that two of every three made little effort to analyze their evaluation data. In keeping with that pattern, the Title I director did not turn down projects because of failure to show success. On evaluation standards as with enforcement, then, the Massachusetts department related to local districts as the federal level related to the states: little direction.

*An Explanation of the Massachusetts Pattern.* The weakness in Massachusetts' management of Title I implementation by local school districts — in project approvals, monitoring, auditing, and program evaluation — can be traced to several factors. Title I was a new and complicated program thrust on a weak department, unfamiliar with managing large-scale programs. On top of that, the Title I office was chronically understaffed: prior to the 1968–69 school year, the unit had only two full-time professionals and only three more by 1970. Managing seven other programs related to the disadvantaged, the Title I unit's work load made it impossible even to visit each Title I project once a year, let alone to understand what each was doing with the money.

The root causes of Massachusetts' limited attempt to impose federal priorities go deeper than even these severe management problems. In America's federal system, states are independent entities with their own sources of political support. They have no incentive to enforce federal directives conflicting with state priorities unless they are suitably penalized or rewarded for such action. But, such penalties and rewards were not part of the Title I program.

*Jerome T. Murphy*

The states received their full entitlement of funds by simply "assuring" USOE that the law would be followed, as opposed to having to submit an approvable plan, produce some specified result, or do a good job by some agreed-on measures. Although *legally* USOE could cut off funds for violations of the law, state officials knew that USOE *politically* was reluctant to do so.

Not only were compliance incentives missing, but the states received mixed signals from Washington on what they were expected to comply with. Whether USOE saw Title I as a program providing supplementary services for the disadvantaged or really as general aid to education remained unclear. Federal efforts to persuade the states to follow the law rigorously were virtually non-existent. The Massachusetts department practically never heard from USOE except for occasional memoranda, and USOE was looked on mainly as a consultant. Remarked Title I Director Jeffery:

> USOE provides technical and administrative assistance. They are helpful. They won't come out and say what you can't do. I don't feel any kind of control. It just isn't there.

Knowing that USOE directives would not likely be enforced stringently, Jeffery and other Massachusetts education administrators felt free, in turn, to follow those policies helpful to the state department and to slight the others.

The Massachusetts department was no more able or willing to impose its priorities on local districts than USOE was to dictate to Massachusetts. The formula grant system, by eliminating competition for Title I funds, weakened the state's bargaining position as it did USOE's. And the kind of individuals administering the state program were like USOE's veteran staffers. They viewed themselves as professional educators assisting their professional colleagues on the local firing line. The role of an enforcer or a regulator, of monitoring and reviewing the judgment of their local peers, was repugnant to them.

The historical dedication in Massachusetts to local school autonomy also constricted state action, whether in the form of implementing federal priorities or their own. Local school control is " 'The Battle Hymn of the Republic' of New England educators," noted Jeffery. In the absence of strong pressure from USOE, the Massachusetts department could not buck local autonomy even if it wanted to. Consequently, the department was virtually deprived of leverage to control local Title I expenditures. Implementation depended on local priorities which often differed from those of the federal and state governments. A 1970 study of Title I evaluation in Boston underscored the typical problem of intergovernmental action:

> Looking back over this period of five years since Title I evaluation was brought to Boston, we can see there has been a clear absorption of all federal and state attempts (especially state attempts) to improve the

quality of the evaluation. . . . [N]ot only has the federal thrust toward reform been absorbed by the school system, it has been turned to the advantage of Boston to serve Boston's own needs.

### A Turning Point in Washington?

In the spring of 1969, a small group of civil rights organizations met to discuss the growing evidence that Title I funds were not being used to help educationally deprived children. In their view, the "accepted experts" in USOE had "failed to inform the public honestly about the faulty, and sometimes fraudulent" use of Title I. And they had little faith that timid federal bureaucrats would ever face up to the problem. Believing that poor children ultimately would be blamed if Title I failed, the group agreed to pool its resources to undertake a full-scale investigation of Title I's operation.

Their final report, *Title I of ESEA: Is It Helping Poor Children?*, was released in the fall of 1969. The so-called Martin-McClure report (named after its principal authors Ruby Martin of the Washington Research Project and Phyllis McClure of the NAACP Legal Defense and Educational Fund, Inc.) scathingly attacked Title I's administration. Relying heavily on the secret HEW audits discussed earlier, the report listed multiple abuses identified by the auditors and known to USOE officials, concluding:

> The audit reports have brought to light numerous violations of the law and have recommended that millions of dollars be recovered by the Federal government. Yet in only three cases has the Office of Education sought and received restitution of funds illegally spent. . . . Even in the most flagrant cases of unlawful use of the money — the two swimming pools in Louisiana for example — the Office of Education has failed to act.

The report also scored state departments of education for having not "lived up to their legal responsibility to administer the program" and charged that poor people were "excluded" from the planning of Title I programs. Indeed, in some communities "school officials refuse to provide information about Title I programs to local residents."

The report shifted the Title I debate from behind the closed doors of federal offices to the front pages of newspapers across the country. Public officials at all levels of government were shaken by the embarrassing publicity. The immediate effect was twofold. First, the report helped to coalesce a new Title I constituency, representing the interests of the poor, which set out to challenge the total control of Title I by the established powers in education. Strong parent council regulations were viewed as a crucial first step. The report's second effect was seemingly to alter the balance of power between the national and local levels of government. The public attention focused on local

Title I violations virtually compelled the central government to enforce the law better. These developments are discussed in the next two sections.

*Another Try to Establish Parent Councils.*   In 1968, as discussed earlier, USOE Title I staffers had failed in their attempt to require mandatory Title I parent and community councils. Trying a new tack in 1969, the Division of Compensatory Education (not without opposition within USOE) convinced the Nixon administration to recommend that the law specifically require Title I councils.

The administration's recommendation received short shrift in the House. Although a provision calling for Title I parent and community councils was adopted by the House Committee on Education and Labor, it was defeated during floor debate on the 1969 amendments of ESEA. An influential guardian of local school autonomy, Congresswoman Edith Green (D., Ore.), led the fight to have the "extremely obnoxious" provision deleted. Her amendment, she argued, eliminated the "unnecessary and pernicious requirement that the Commissioner of Education from Washington force every school board in the country to set up local advisory councils to superintend the work school boards themselves are elected or chosen to do." The Green amendment, attracting Republicans opposed to federal control and southerners fearful of community participation, carried.

The Senate also rejected the administration's recommendation that the law specifically require councils, preferring to keep the law "flexible." But its bill did authorize the Commissioner to promulgate regulations for parent and community involvement in any program if he thought such regulations "would increase the effectiveness of the program. . . ." In effect, the Senate's bill passed the buck back to USOE to fight the battles over requiring parent councils. This time, though, USOE would at least have specific legislative authority authorizing some type of parent involvement, instead of simply the "basic criteria" authority.

The House-Senate conference committee accepted the Senate language on parent participation but deleted any reference to community involvement. Both houses accepted this limited provision, despite Congressman Roman Pucinski's (D., Ill.) objections that it could result in "all sorts of people breathing down the neck of the school principal." The law was signed by the president on April 13, 1970.

During the following six months draft guidelines were circulated among interested groups for comment. At one end of the spectrum stood the "Big Six": the National Education Association, the American Association of School Administrators, the Council of Chief State School Officers, the National School Boards Association, the National Association of State Boards of Education, and the National Congress of Parents and Teachers. Spokesmen from these establishment groups fought against strong guidelines, meeting with USOE officials and flatly asserting that mandatory councils were unacceptable.

But unlike the past, the public school lobbies were not without opposition.

Following the publication of the Martin-McClure report, tough, single-minded, and articulate Phyllis McClure put together a broad coalition ranging from establishment groups (League of Women Voters, National Committee for Support of the Public Schools) to "radical" groups (like the National Welfare Rights Organization). Meeting regularly to plot its strategy, this "Title I Coalition" exerted constant pressure on USOE to issue strong guidelines. At the same time, local pressure for Title I change was mounting. Working with parents and poverty groups, the OEO-funded Harvard Center for Law and Education was pressing for reform through Title I law suits and threats of legal action. A scrappy young attorney from the Harvard Center, Mark G. Yudof, was also pushing hard for Title I councils, viewing them as potential avenues to greater community control. The Center acted as counsel for the Title I Coalition.

Against this backdrop of growing parent concern, the Title I Coalition met in September and October of 1970 with Acting Commissioner T. H. Bell and with new Acting Title I Director Richard Fairley. The Coalition demanded an elected council, with veto power over Title I projects, for every Title I school. Trying to find the course of least resistance, Fairley shuttled back and forth in negotiations between the "Big Six" and the Title I Coalition. A compromise emerged from USOE on October 30, 1970, requiring "systemwide" parent councils, and "encouraging" councils for each Title I school. But the battle was not over yet. Poverty spokesmen raised the possibility that the councils could be "stacked" with parents employed by Title I schools. After further negotiations USOE agreed that parents of eligible Title I children, not working for the school district, had to "constitute more than a simple majority" of a council's membership. Finally, eighteen months after the 1970 amendments, an estimated thirty drafts of guidelines and regulations later, and more than four years after USOE's first try to encourage parental participation, regulations were accepted on October 14, 1971. "Systemwide" parent advisory councils were made mandatory, with broad rights of access by their members to information about Title I projects spelled out in the regulations.

Looking back on this tortuous sequence of events, it seems clear that without the Martin-McClure report and the effective pressure of the Title I Coalition, USOE would not have come out with a reasonably strong regulation. As a somewhat bewildered National Education Association spokesman commented, "USOE has been getting pressure from some groups I've never heard of. I don't know whether they represent a constituency or not." Yet if the strength of the regulation demonstrated that groups representing the poor could influence federal action, its weakness also suggested the limits of that influence. "It was a win," says Phyllis McClure, "but it was a win that was easiest for the schoolmen to take. Those regs [regulations] confer no power on the local people."

*A New Face for USOE.* The Nixon administration responded to the Martin-McClure report by establishing a task force made up of middle-management HEW bureaucrats. Their charge from HEW Secretary Robert Finch included making immediate changes in the program as well as working toward a final report. Indeed, some HEW reformers saw the bad publicity on Title I's enforcement as a good "excuse to clean up a program which was an abysmal failure." According to their still-secret report, the task force found "considerable evidence" that USOE was not "meeting its management responsibilities," and continuing confusion about "what Title I really is." They "strongly" recommended "actions to clarify the intent that Title I be a compensatory education program."

At the urging of the task force and with the support of upper echelons in HEW, the Division of Compensatory Education was reorganized and its authorized staffing level significantly increased. While three area desk officers had covered all the states at the end of 1969, there were twenty-five to do so by late summer of 1970. In all, thirty new positions were authorized for the division. This jump in job slots, plus vacancies in already authorized positions, provided a unique opportunity for Acting Director Fairley to build the kind of staff he wanted. A tough and shrewd bureaucratic politician, he recruited about forty individuals from in and out of the agency, many of whom were oriented toward strict Title I compliance. "There was sort of a crusade atmosphere going on at the time," commented one of Fairley's new deputies. "A lot of poverty worker atmosphere."

With the support of his bosses, Fairley sent his new staff out to every state between July of 1970 and July of 1971, an unprecedented undertaking for Title I. Many of his troops carried a new USOE determination to enforce the law. "While we were giving the states technical assistance, we were monitoring the hell out of them," noted a new-breed area desk officer. These trips were followed by another Title I first: letters to the states not filled with ambiguous recommendations, but calling for specific "corrective actions." Moreover, USOE developed handbooks and other materials spelling out the procedures states and localities should follow to meet the law's requirements. In short, USOE shifted discernibly from a passive service-oriented agency providing limited direction to a somewhat aggressive unit stressing expanded technical assistance but also a reasonably strong effort at compliance.

Beginning in September 1971, USOE took a first step toward settling the outstanding audits publicized in the Martin-McClure report. Letters were sent to eleven states requesting the return of almost $10 million in misspent Title I funds. Also, with the backing of the task force, USOE pushed for strong, explicit guidelines to eliminate discriminatory expenditure patterns found in many school districts, and documented in the Martin-McClure report. For example, in Washington, D.C., the per pupil expenditures in five *poor* school districts ranged from $394 to $432 and in five *nonpoor* schools from $511 to $601. As long as such discrepancies continued, the addition of Title I to the budget of poor schools could hardly be considered a source of *supplementary* services.

In February 1970, USOE revived and strengthened a long-ignored regulation requiring state and local expenditures to be generally equal among all schools within a district before the addition of Title I funds. Simply put, this "comparability" requirement meant that Title I would provide something extra for disadvantaged children. Interest group opposition immediately developed. The new requirements were held to be confusing and unworkable, and to encourage federal interference in school policy. Meeting on the 1969–70 ESEA amendments, the House-Senate conference committee killed the guideline and wrote its own provision. Implementation of comparability was postponed from 1970 to 1972, and a gaping loophole was added. Longevity pay, or that part of a teacher's salary resulting from length of service, was excluded from the determination of comparability. This meant that more experienced (and hence higher paid) teachers, often concentrated in "better" schools, would not be affected by the new provision. Since teacher salaries account for about 70 percent of instructional outlays, this loophole also meant that the Congress sanctioned potentially sizable disparities in expenditures between poor and rich schools within the same school district.* The Congress's action provided yet another illustration of the difficulty of overcoming local dominance in American education.

In sum, important changes in Title I's federal implementation took place in 1970 and 1971. For the first time since ESEA's passage in 1965, USOE seemed serious about Title I's enforcement. Action was taken in eleven states to recover money for Title I violations and, even if the money were not returned or action not taken in other states, HEW audits would be highly publicized and not buried in bureaucratic channels. New guidelines, watered down but nevertheless specific, were promulgated. It would be harder in the future for local schoolmen to fudge parent involvement or to avoid providing *supplementary* services for the disadvantaged — parent councils could be counted and objective comparability data could be examined. Title I's bad publicity combined with new counterpressure from the poor seemed to have shifted the balance of power in the federal system. What impact, if any, these changes had on the states and localities and on the children Title I was designed to serve can be suggested by another look at the Massachusetts experience.


Massachusetts Revisited

Five months after the official release of the Martin-McClure report in late 1969, Massachusetts' Title I unit was visited by a four-man team of USOE officials who found serious deficiencies in monitoring, evaluation, fiscal control, and application review procedures. Specific remedial action was

* Editor's note: The study by David Kirp treats this issue briefly; see pp. 82–122.

*Jerome T. Murphy*

recommended by USOE, which then kept reasonably close tabs on Massachusetts' Title I operation. This, together with tougher directives from Washington, presented a new federal image to the state: USOE seemed to expect state accountability for Title I's implementation.

Although withholding Title I funds was not threatened by USOE, Massachusetts was anxious to avoid an embarrassing public report and thus responded to the altered federal role; Massachusetts' Title I unit has changed slowly but surely since 1970. Its professional staff doubled and the state's project approval procedures have been made more rigorous, with multiple reviews within the department and more information and documentation required to justify local expenditures. School district audits were regularly conducted, and for the first time the department in 1972 started an audit of Boston's Title I program. Evaluation, although still weak, has improved somewhat with the use of performance objectives and of more detailed evaluation procedures.

The attitude of the state Title I staff toward compliance changed a bit. While state officials in 1972 remained reluctant to "act as policemen," the regulations were followed more closely. For example, the department refused to approve fiscal 1973 Title I applications until school districts demonstrated compliance with the new comparability requirements. Also, the department initiated management reviews similar to those used by USOE with the states. The report on Springfield publicly disclosed Title I violations and in strong language called for remedial action.

USOE's tougher stance has in turn provided Massachusetts with new political muscle in its dealings with local school districts. By pointing to demands from Washington, state officials could mask their greater activity and thus avoid a state challenge to the tradition of localism. "[Local school administrators] are very conscious that HEW is requiring more of us in accountability and in turn we are requiring more of them," remarked Claire Walsh, a long-time state Title I coordinator. "There is certainly much more demanded of us."

Although implementing federal priorities somewhat more aggressively, the department has done little to exercise its own authority to upgrade local projects. A state-suggested focus on early childhood education was accompanied by the assurance to schoolmen that this was simply a recommendation, not a mandate. The department generally has avoided taking any strong stands on Title I matters that might challenge local prerogatives; the tradition of localism still limited state action.

There is one notable exception, however, which merits brief discussion. The department has gone beyond the federal guidelines and has mandated *elected* Title I parent advisory councils. This development reflected the pressure of a coalition of poverty organizations in combination with a state commissioner of education sympathetic to the idea. It was resisted vigorously by local schoolmen, who salvaged victory from defeat when the initial guidelines of late 1970 requiring elected parent councils were neutralized by their noncooperation. As the Massachusetts League of Women Voters characterized the subversion of the guidelines in an untypically harsh report in mid-1971:

> Most school officials begin with a negative attitude toward parent participation. They responded to the new state guidelines by unenthusiastically contacting parents by grossly inadequate means. Having excluded all community organizations, having explained nothing to the parents, and having done little to engender parental enthusiasm, school officials are then confronted by what they describe in self-fulfilling prophecy terms, as parent "apathy." Administrators then take control and appoint or elect their own choices to the PAC [parent advisory council] — thereby guaranteeing the continuation of parent "apathy."

The Massachusetts Board of Education adopted even stronger parent council guidelines in early 1972. Each school district's Title I application must now include compliance reports signed by the chairman of the parent council. Further, a 1970 provision allowing a local parent council to appeal to state administrators if it objects to the local Title I project was strengthened. The Springfield parent advisory council was scheduled in late 1972 to have a public hearing, represented by counsel, before the Massachusetts Commissioner of Education to discuss its objection to Springfield's Title I project. This would be the first such hearing in the nation.

The Massachusetts Department of Education became accountable to two new constituencies — the federal government and local poverty groups. No longer totally beholden to local schoolmen, it was more willing and more able to take a somewhat stronger stance in the administration of Title I.

The impact of these expanded state efforts is not yet clear. On the one hand, Jeffrey pointed to several signs of change. More money was reportedly concentrated on fewer children than was true in the program's early years. Also, attendance had increased recently at state meetings to discuss Title I regulations. Jeffrey stated:

> People who are responsible for developing local projects are much more open and willing to consult with the state. . . . The locals sense the increasing accountability and are conscious too of the states and localities that have been asked to refund money. They don't want to be caught in the bag.

On the other hand, it is worth noting key USOE recommendations made after a team of seven officials spent a week in Massachusetts in 1971:

> Re-emphasize to local agencies the requirement that projects must be designed to meet the special educational needs of educationally de-

prived children. . . . Approve only those applications that meet that criteria.

If it was necessary in 1971, six years after ESEA's passage, to reemphasize the basic requirements about eligible children, then one could not say with any certainty that Massachusetts schoolmen had gotten the message by 1972.

### New Title I Enforcement: A Post Mortem?

In late 1972, almost three years after the release of the Martin-McClure report, it is worth examining how things have really changed. Have USOE and the Title I Coalition sustained their 1970 and 1971 efforts to implement the law? What progress has been made nationwide at the local level? To what extent was the report a turning point in the administration of Title I?

At the federal level, the Title I Coalition which joined forces for different reasons to fight for parent councils no longer functions. After the final version of the new USOE regulations were agreed on about January 1971, this diverse group disbanded and moved on to other issues. "Title I was only in the sun for a little while," observed a disappointed USOE supporter. "They all let down." Currently two individuals carry on the battle at a national level: Phyllis McClure of the NAACP Legal Defense and Educational Fund, and, on a part-time basis, R. Stephen Browning of the Lawyers' Committee for Civil Rights Under Law. Indeed, Browning commented, "The Title I Coalition *is* Phyllis McClure." While energetic and able to make sentries appear like an army, McClure and Browning can accomplish only so much.

Things have also changed in USOE's Title I office. The initial excitement of enforcing the law in 1970 and 1971 has been replaced by growing frustration and fatigue. For one thing, USOE has failed so far in its attempt to recover the $10 million in audit exceptions from the eleven states sent letters; less than 1 percent has been returned, with most states ignoring USOE's demands. The outlook for future success is at best uncertain. As one area desk officer stated:

> It's a big political game. I don't believe that any money will be recovered over and above a little amount that won't hurt anybody. . . . I just don't think a Congressman or a Senator is going to stand to have his state pay money back when others are getting away with things just as bad.

For another, USOE desk officers are tired from constantly being on the road, and frustrated by the unwillingness of some states to follow the regulations. "For a lot of us everything was in the act of becoming," remarked one of Fairley's aides. "The fun was in getting things started." He and others, who joined the office in 1970, are thinking about new jobs. Not only are the area desk officers tired, but so too are their higher-level bosses who have to deal with congressional and interest group complaints about USOE pushing "too hard." "This is about the only program in the Bureau which is compliance oriented," commented another Title I official. "This program is the only one causing problems with the chief state school officers."

Title I staffers are also frustrated by growing signs of weakening commitment to the program in the executive branch. Education revenue sharing with the states is being pushed by the administration; this would mean less federal influence as power and resources are turned over to the states. Also, Title I staffers have been circulating with dismay a May 1972 letter from HEW Secretary Elliot L. Richardson to Senator Jacob K. Javits (R., N.Y.). Discussing the general lack of effectiveness of Title I, Richardson notes, "It [Title I] has been used as a means of increasing teachers' salaries and other forms of general assistance; it has not succeeded in the aggregate in improving poor children's educational performance." Title I officials wonder about the program's future.

In the wake of this uncertainty, Title I Director Fairley seems less concerned in 1972 than in 1970 with disclosing violations. Preoccupied with showing his bosses that the program, now *his* program, is working, Fairley's command to his troops has changed from "charge" to "protect your flanks." One slightly disillusioned Title I staffer captured the mood in the summer of 1972:

> If I thought this program was a priority then I could be excited. There are big question marks about how far up the line there is support for what we're doing. This is a Lyndon Johnson program with lots of problems and people are getting tired of them.

These signs of a return to USOE's pre-1969 posture are further evidenced in the agency's efforts to monitor the comparability regulations which require that Title I funds provide something extra for educationally deprived children. Rather than developing a staff to work closely with states and localities, USOE assigned one full-time employee to oversee compliance in some 16,000 districts. This was sufficient since "the word filtered down not to press the states on comparability data until July 1, 1972." Consequently, it is not surprising that USOE has only the sketchiest notion of how well comparability is being implemented.

In fact, Steve Browning at the Lawyers' Committee for Civil Rights Under Law, rather than USOE, heads the major compliance effort. In the summer of 1972, he hired several students to analyze comparability data from eighty large cities. The study was designed to serve two purposes: to provide the basis for possible litigation, and also to make it clear to the state and localities that someone was monitoring their enforcement procedures. Believing that

*Jerome T. Murphy*

some USOE officials want the comparability requirement implemented, Browning thinks that they are "afraid" to confront the Establishment. "I think they like the idea that we are trying to enforce it." But Browning's problem is the same as Phyllis McClure's: limited resources to monitor a complicated program requiring constant attention.

At the local level, the nationwide impact of the federal efforts since 1969 seems mixed at best. First, most school districts apparently have set up parent councils. The battle has now shifted to making them work; there are signs in some communities that poor parents are gaining more control over Title I expenditures and school policies. Second, all school districts were required to be in compliance with comparability by July 1972. Although no one in USOE has monitored implementation, the *Washington Post* revealed that an HEW audit (marked "not to be made available, even upon request, to members of the press and the general public") found that comparability data are based on "unreliable estimates and inaccurate figures." And the Lawyers' Committee study, released in September 1972, concluded that seventy-nine of the eighty school districts studied had one or more noncomparable schools.

Finally, there are conflicting opinions and data about the success of USOE's attempts at greater local compliance. On the one hand, a 1972 study commissioned by USOE concluded:

> Clearly, violations of Title I regulations and criteria have continued since 1969 in at least 37 states and this situation cannot be explained away either in terms of the newness of the Title I programs or the short time available to adapt management systems to its requirements. After six fiscal years of Title I funding, the program has not yet been implemented nationally as intended by Congress.

On the other hand, USOE officials argue that violations in some states have been reduced, and many states are working harder to enforce the law. Also, they say that more money is being concentrated on fewer children. Finally, USOE officials claim that, if nothing else, all the states have learned what is in the guidelines and now understand that USOE views Title I as a compensatory education program, not general aid. One wonders whether the new uncertainty in the Title I office might soon change this perception by the states.

In sum, the initial burst of energy accompanying the Martin-McClure report has subsided. The Title I Coalition and USOE have both let down. The momentum of change and the crusading atmosphere at the federal level have all but disappeared. The current mood is one of uncertainty about Title I's future. Hence, if the Martin-McClure report was a turning point in the implementation of Title I, the turn has been less than enduring. And even with the improvements that have been made, the question is whether they can be sustained. As one new-breed area desk officer noted somewhat sadly, "That's the question we all talk about at lunch."

## Concluding Observations

More than seven years have passed since President Johnson pointed to ESEA as education's greatest breakthrough, and Congressman J. Arthur Younger suggested that Francis Keppel be designated a commissar because of his new dictatorial power under ESEA. Seven years later, the program is beset with problems. Currently it is not even clear to what extent Title I is expended on eligible disadvantaged children in poverty neighborhoods. Even when it reaches them, it is uncertain that the money buys services in addition to the level provided other school children in each district. USOE and the Massachusetts Department of Education have made some attempts since 1970 to correct this situation, but these efforts may be waning. Prior to that time, enforcement problems were hardly debated, much less acted on; USOE and Massachusetts exercised little effective direction and had only superficial knowledge of how Title I funds were being spent. To say the least, neither the hopes nor the fears of ESEA's legislative framers have been realized in Title I's implementation.

Why has Title I been administered in this way?

Many reasons help to explain USOE's and Massachusetts' lack of leadership — inadequate staff, absence of managerial know-how, a complicated law, and a service orientation. But three more fundamental factors explain the specific difficulties with Title I and may also suggest general impediments to the implementation of innovative federal policy in the American political system.

First, the politics of passing legislation frequently requires that a bill's intent be unclear. This allows diverse interests to join forces behind a particular proposal; each group hopes that its objectives will be met during implementation. But while the absence of clarity may facilitate congressional approval, it subsequently impedes effective implementation. Former Commissioner of Education Harold Howe describes the basic conflict:

> ESEA was the only type of Federal activity in education which was likely to be politically viable in 1965. . . . I doubt that anyone could have dreamed up a series of education programs more difficult to administer . . . but ESEA was not designed with that in mind.

Although the language of Title I was clear as to eligible children, the bill's legislative history provided the semblance if not the reality of general aid. This confusion, and the fact that those reformers who had pushed for passage left implementation to lower-level officials, meant that USOE administrators could see in Title I what they wanted to see. Where there was vague language in the law, it also created later problems. For example, if a concentration standard had been spelled out, then its implementation might have been somewhat smoothed. This would have made sense administratively, but would have been a mistake politically. The vague phrase "basic criteria" postponed controversy over specific issues which might have threatened passage of the legislation.

The price of winning federal reform, then, may well be the appearance of ambiguity. That this was true in 1965 with the overwhelming Democratic majority in the Congress underscores the point. This also suggests that typically the implementation phase will be marked not only by standard managerial problems, but also by the more difficult political problems of continually defining a bill's "real" objectives. Hence, passing a law is only a small step toward the achievement of reform. Indeed, if reformers want *their* goals to be met, then they must somehow be significantly involved in the day-in and day-out battles of implementation.

A second major obstacle to Title I's implementation stems from the sharing of values and function by schoolmen at the national, state and local levels of government. Viewing themselves and each other as professional educators, they are inclined neither to act as policemen nor to embarrass their colleagues. Problems are solved by "working things out" quietly through bureaucratic channels, not through controversy in the public media and certainly not by confrontation. The emphasis is on maintaining "good working relationships" and on providing friendly assistance.

Moreover, state and federal schoolmen know the problems faced by school administrators — anxious parents, problem children, striking teachers, empty coffers, and demands from all sides for more services, particularly if federal money is available. Sympathetic to the plight of their local peers and respectful of their professional judgment about the needs of children, federal and state officials are inclined to give local schoolmen freedom in developing their programs. As a result of the shared professional mentality of educators and the intergovernmental empathy among colleagues, their unity of action is promoted despite the formal barriers of governmental levels and of legal technicalities. Unless constantly pressured by other interests, state and federal schoolmen will tend to defer to local professional priorities.

A third major obstacle to Title I's implementation, and perhaps the most important, results from the decentralization of power in the American political system; authority and influence are dispersed among national, state, and local constituencies. In part, this derives from the American federal system with its sharing of power among different governmental units; from a history and tradition favoring state and local initiatives; and from the fact that decentralization continues to benefit important interests in society. Perhaps most important, this dispersion of power results from (as well as reflects) the decentralized nature of the American political party system.

The lack of party solidarity and of party commitment to a range of policies has important decentralizing effects in the administration of federal programs by freeing legislators to pressure federal program administrators on behalf of their local constituents. The result is persistent political intervention by legislators acting as watch dogs for local interests. The administrator typically must respond to this pressure. After all, if the president cannot consistently control fellow party members, such as a congressional subcommittee chairman who sets a program's funding level, then the federal administrator must develop his own source of political support in order to survive. This requirement, of course, makes it difficult for a program administrator to impose federal directives conflicting with local priorities, since the affected local interests can speak through the Congress and their Washington-based lobby groups. Morton Grodzins describes how a successful federal administrator must behave:

> [The absence of party solidarity] compels political activities on the part of the administrator. Without this activity he will have no program to administer. And the political activity of the administrator, like the administrative activity of the legislator, is often turned to representing in national programs the concern of state and local interests, as well as of other interest-group constituencies. . . . [A]lways [the administrator] must find support from legislators tied closely to state and local governments. The administrator at the center cannot succeed in his fundamental political role unless he shares power with these peripheral groups.

The pattern noted is accentuated for educational administrators, of course, because of the pronounced tradition of local control of the public schools.

As we have seen, Title I administrators have shared power with those interest groups able to pressure USOE. Prior to 1969, these groups consisted entirely of state and local schoolmen who were opposed to strong enforcement of ESEA and to specific basic criteria for Title I expenditures. When USOE officials occasionally tried to assert leadership they were forced, by and large, to retreat. Furthermore, this absence of federal leadership had direct consequences for the states, particularly those like Massachusetts with especially strong traditions of localism. It was the limited accountability of Massachusetts to the federal level which, in turn, promoted the neglect of local district accountability to the state. The localistic bias in the politics of federal educational reform provided a major barrier to Title I's implementation.

Since 1969, Title I has developed a new constituency, speaking for the interests of the poor, which has been able to influence USOE behavior mainly through adverse publicity and, in some cases, lawsuits or threat of legal action. This countervailing power has provided the political pressure, and sometimes support, for USOE to act more affirmatively with the states in Title I's administration. In turn, these greater federal demands have increased somewhat Massachusetts' efforts to see that the law is properly implemented. The impact of these efforts to date, as discussed earlier, seems mixed.

Reviewing the 1965–72 record, the problems of effective implementation of Title I were administrative-managerial in part, but at bottom they were political. A necessary though not sufficient condition of Title I's vigorous administration on behalf of compensatory education would appear to be the

*Jerome T. Murphy*

maintenance of political pressure by poverty groups and their allies, and meaningful participation by such interests in local school district councils or other comparable devices. Ironically, success in such efforts might unintentionally hasten Title I's demise. If no large-scale federal general aid to education develops and Title I monies were expended entirely for supplementary compensatory education for the disadvantaged, 1965's broad coalition of support for ESEA could well dwindle. Were the powerful public school lobby to shift to the opposition on Title I, it is far from certain that sufficient countervailing power could be developed to retain the present program.

Quite apart from the tug and haul of contending school interest groups, Title I could become a general aid program anyway as a result of other forces. Among other straws in the wind are the rising interest in revenue sharing and the growing feeling that compensatory education has not justified its costs by its results. Viewed in this light, perhaps there should be no great optimism about the future of Title I. Still, given the unpredictability of the future, a strategy of increasing the countervailing power of the poor probably makes the most sense. As one USOE official, sympathetic to the needs of the poor, commented about Title I: "You use it for what it's worth while it's there."

## SOURCES AND READINGS

A variety of means were used to gather the information for this study. Interviews were conducted between 1969 and 1972 in the United States Office of Education, in the Massachusetts Department of Education, and to a limited degree at the local level. Other information was gathered through congressional documents, government reports and memoranda, newspaper articles, correspondence, articles in professional journals, and a number of books. In addition, some of the material reflects my experience with the program, gained while working for the Department of Health, Education and Welfare between 1964 and 1969. An earlier product of some of these efforts was a substantially different version of this case study which appeared in the *Harvard Educational Review*, Vol. 41, No. 1, February 1971.

The story of the long fight to pass a major aid to education bill, of ESEA's passage, and of its earlier implementation has been told in several books. In this study, I have drawn heavily on three. Robert Bendiner, *Obstacle Course on Capitol Hill* (New York: McGraw-Hill, 1964), is a lively account of the failure to pass education legislation prior to ESEA. The details of congressional passage are well told in a volume by Eugene Eidenberg and Roy D. Morey, *An Act of Congress* (New York: W. W. Norton, 1969). And a volume by Stephen

K. Bailey and Edith K. Mosher, *ESEA: The Office of Education Administers a Law* (Syracuse: Syracuse University Press, 1968), is particularly valuable in describing the executive branch initiatives in developing ESEA, and in delineating the complicated process in USOE of gearing up to administer a major new program. One final source is particularly worthwhile in describing the mood of reform in 1965, the hopes for ESEA, and the bill's many objectives: a short account by Samuel Halperin, "ESEA: Five Years Later" (*Congressional Record*, p. H8492, September 9, 1970).

Some highly selective further reading on the problems of implementing governmental programs may be suggested. Morton Grodzins, *The American System: A New View of Government in the United States* (Chicago: Rand-McNally, 1966), effectively treats American federalism, including problems of political intervention in the administrative process. Martha Derthick, *The Influence of Federal Grants* (Cambridge, Mass.: Harvard University Press, 1970), explores federal efforts to influence local and state welfare policies. It provides interesting parallels and contrasts with my study of Title I. Finally, Graham T. Allison, *Essence of Decision* (Boston: Little, Brown, 1971), applies organizational and political theory to a crucial international event — the Cuban missile crisis. It is extremely useful in understanding how any governmental bureaucracy operates, not just those concerned with international affairs.

Those interested in the countervailing strategy adopted by poverty groups working on Title I are referred to two volumes. First, of course, is the Martin-McClure report, *Title I of ESEA. Is It Helping Poor Children?* (A report of the Washington Research Project of the Southern Center for Studies in Public Policy and the NAACP Legal Defense and Educational Fund, Inc., 1969). This study lists by state a variety of abuses of the Title I program. Also, the Harvard Center for Law and Education has gathered into a single volume a variety of materials ranging from copies of the Title I regulations to sample complaints for bringing Title I lawsuits to case studies and brochures on Title I community action: *Title I Litigation Materials* (Cambridge, Mass.: Harvard Center for Law and Education, 1972).

*Jerome T. Murphy*

# STUDY SIX

# ELECTIONS AND INTEREST GROUPS

Brademas: the man, the politician. 1968: a foreboding year for Democrats. Brademas' difficulties in 1968. *Indiana congressional redistricting. The new Third District. Intraparty dissension. Nixon's coattails. The Wallace problem. The Republicans' choice.* Campaign strategies: images and resources. *The incumbent's edge. Mobilizing allies. Image and party. An exhausting pace.* Mobilizing the education community. *The Washington "education lobby." The "education congressman." Education as a campaign issue. Cultivating the education interest groups. The federal educators — legislative-executive coordination. Rallying the local educators. Seeking an "education community-at-large." A well-timed education conference. Recruiting student support in the year of disaffection. National mass media endorsements.* The election outcome. Concluding observations. *Postscript. Some larger questions.* Sources and readings.

# An "Education Congressman" Fights for Survival: Congressman John Brademas' Bid for Reelection, 1968

*Jack H. Schuster*

Article I, Section 1, of the United States Constitution [decrees] that once every twenty-four months Congressmen sweat blood on Election Day. To be sure, Congressmen ought to be free, and are free, to do their work, without excessive public interference, but when they have done their work, they go back to the people and stand trial for their political lives.

This observation of a noted political scientist, the late E. E. Schattschneider, was amply confirmed in 1968 in Indiana's Third Congressional District election. Commenting on John Brademas' quest for a sixth consecutive term, the *South Bend Tribune* reported:

U.S. Rep. John Brademas, trying to cope with a Nixon tide, a Wallace splinter, a GOP-flavored redistricting and an industrious Will Erwin, will be struggling for his political life Tuesday.

For Brademas and many of his colleagues in the House, the 1968 campaign had begun very soon after the previous election in November 1966. To be sure, many of the nation's 435 congressmen — well over half and probably closer to three-quarters, depending on the criteria employed — occupied safe seats; for them, general elections were little more than legitimating rituals. But for marginal congressmen everywhere, the House of Representatives was a jealous mistress; the condition for continued House membership was incessant political campaigning.

Deeply concerned about his prospects for reelection, but no less concerned to maintain his reputation for integrity, Brademas attempted to make full and legitimate use of whatever political opportunities he had and whatever special resources he might be able to tap. As a congressman, he had made his mark primarily in shaping education policy. Could he, then, he speculated, find some way to capitalize on his special relationships with educators? Could an education-oriented constituency — at national, state, and local levels — be mobilized to support him? And, if so, was this potential support, in terms of volunteer help and financial contributions, significant enough to justify a sizable commitment of his own time and that of his staff? Or was the "education community" too amorphous to be reached, too impotent politically to recognize and act on its stake in the election, in all, merely an illusory asset?

In concentrating generally on Brademas' reelection efforts and particularly on his relationships with varied education groups, this study raises a more general question: how a congressman seeks to collect political debts, in the form of campaign support, from his special interest constituencies. Examination of an "education congressman's" attempt to draw upon the education community for campaign support, informative in itself, should also provide insights into comparable techniques used by, say, an "agricultural congressman," a "labor congressman," or a business-oriented congressman to mobilize his particular policy-related constituencies. At the same time, a review of the response of the education community to Brademas' appeals for assistance tells us something about how educators seek to fashion national education policy and, more generally, about the dynamics of education politics.

Brademas: The Man, the Politician

Addicted to "combat politics" (to borrow the term of his political hero, Adlai E. Stevenson), John Brademas is perhaps as much at ease among scholars, artists, and theologians as among tough-thinking politicians and sophisticated diplomats. As much as anyone in Congress, Brademas could be regarded as "an intellectual"; indeed, the juxtaposition of the worlds of politics and scholarship is a topic on which Brademas has reflected at length.

Intense and exacting, John Brademas nonetheless possesses a warm and engaging personality. He tackles his work with inexhaustible energy, operating from behind an unbelievably cluttered desk. ("Order," he explains with a smile, quoting Spinoza, "is in the mind.") Perennially identified by Washington social columnists as one of the town's most eligible bachelors, he is a frequent escort of chic women at embassy parties and smart Washington soirees. Always the teacher, he is ever ready to discuss, especially with students, the realities of political life.

He was born in 1927 in Mishawaka, Indiana, the eldest of Stephen and Beatrice Goble Brademas' four children. His father emigrated to this country from Kalamata, Greece, as a young man, and, before his retirement, managed a restaurant in South Bend. His mother taught in the public elementary schools and kindergartens of Indiana and Michigan for over forty years. His father is Greek Orthodox; his mother, Disciples of Christ Church, but son John was raised a Methodist. (Brademas maintained sufficient involvement in the affairs of the United Methodist Church to be designated in 1968 a delegate to the Fourth Assembly of the World Council of Churches and to be elected to its 120-member Central Committee.) He has always spoken proudly of his Greek heritage — "it was the Greeks, after all," he points out, "who were the first genuine educators of the Western world" — and until 1967 enjoyed the distinction of being the sole American of Greek ancestry then serving in Congress.

Brademas graduated from Central High School in South Bend in 1945, an outstanding student and less spectacular quarterback on the football team. Then it was on to Harvard College on a scholarship. Earning a Phi Beta Kappa key and graduating *magna cum laude* in 1949, Brademas remained at Harvard for a year of graduate study in political science. During that year, he was designated a Rhodes scholar. He enrolled in Brasenose College, Oxford University, and chose to stay beyond the customary two-year stint for Rhodes scholars to complete a doctorate in social studies. His dissertation treated the anarchist movement in Spain in the 1930s, a topic that enabled him to make use of his fluency in Spanish.

After his sojourn at Oxford, John Brademas, A.B., D.Phil. (Oxon.), returned to South Bend. In college he had developed a keen interest in politics, and in 1954, at age twenty-seven, he boldly sought the Democratic nomination for Indiana's Third Congressional District. Brademas won the nomination in a sharply contested seven-way primary, but was narrowly defeated in the general election by the two-term Republican incumbent. (His 49.4 percent of the vote left him short of an upset victory by just over 2,000 votes.)

Moving to acquire more practical experience, he served in 1955 as an aide to U.S. Senator Pat McNamara (D., Mich.) and then as administrative assistant to U.S. Congressman Thomas "Lud" Ashley (D., Ohio). In 1956 he was an aide to Adlai E. Stevenson during the first months of the Governor's second bid for the presidency; his major responsibility was preparing material on campaign issues. Later that year he again received the Third District congressional nomination, this time, on the strength of his near-victory two years earlier, without serious primary opposition. But his second bid for Congress failed; Brademas' share of the vote slipped to 46.9 percent, some 12,000 votes short. Deciding to remain close to home, Brademas became Assistant Professor of Political Science at Saint Mary's College, Notre Dame, Indiana, teaching courses in American government.

For Democrats across the nation, 1958 proved to be a bonanza year. (Though a very popular president, Dwight D. Eisenhower had limited "coat-tail" power in his own reelection in 1956 and markedly less influence in the 1958 off-year election.) With a net gain of thirteen Senate and forty-seven House seats, Democrats won greater margins in both houses of Congress than they had enjoyed for many years. Indiana Democrats fared especially well, defeating six incumbent Republican congressmen, picking up one Senate seat, and retaining two other House seats. (Having held just two of Indiana's eleven House seats in the previous Congress, the Democrats' new total of eight House seats represented their best postwar margin.) Brademas was one of the victors. Taking advantage of the Democratic tide, the 31-year-old bachelor handily unseated the Republican who had beaten him in 1956. Capturing 57 percent of the vote, Brademas won by almost 24,000 votes.

The South Bend Democrat won reelection the next four times. But aside from 1964, the year of a national Democratic landslide (when he garnered 60.8 percent of the vote), he never achieved a comfortable margin: 52.5 percent in 1960; 52.2 percent in 1962; 55.8 percent in 1966.

### 1968: A Foreboding Year for Democrats

The Third District of Indiana, like the Hoosier State itself, was politically volatile. Neither Democrats nor Republicans were dominant; the party outcomes shifted uncertainly from one election to the next.

In statewide balloting, Indiana had voted Republican in presidential elections since 1940, excepting only the Lyndon Johnson runaway of 1964. On the other hand, both U.S. Senators from Indiana — Vance Hartke and Birch Bayh — were Democrats, though their respective holds on high office were precarious. Bayh, former Speaker of the Indiana General Assembly, had won in 1962, defeating conservative Republican Homer Capehart, a Senate stalwart since 1945, by an 11,000 vote margin of 1,800,000 ballots cast. Bayh now faced a stiff reelection challenge from William Ruckelshaus. Hartke, the state's senior senator, had been elected in 1958, succeeding another conservative Republican of long Senate service — William E. Jenner — and was reelected in 1964, both vintage Democratic years. But 1970, when Hartke would have to face the voters again, might not be nearly so promising.

The Statehouse in Indianapolis had alternated between the parties in the postwar years: Democratic candidates for governor won in 1948, 1960, and 1964; Republicans in 1952 and 1956. Now a Democratic governor, Roger D. Branigin, was stepping down. At that time in Indiana a governor was ineligible to succeed himself, and both parties were intent upon capturing the vacated Statehouse. The governorship was always a particularly rich prize — liter-

*Jack H. Schuster*

ally — for a full-scale patronage system still flourished in Indiana. Political appointees by the thousands contributed 2 percent of their salaries to party coffers, providing a substantial sum for the war chest of the party in power. (Indiana historian Donald F. Carmony has commented wryly that "Indiana politicians have fought for and then distributed governmental positions as if such a right were as inviolate and deeply imbedded in the Bill of Rights as freedom of religion!")

The Third Congressional District, prior to Brademas' first win in 1958, had been represented in Congress by Republicans for eighteen of the previous twenty years. In all, five of Indiana's eleven congressional seats were occupied by Democrats. Of the five, only one was considered completely safe in 1968, another was regarded as relatively safe, but three of the five, including Brademas', were thought to be very vulnerable.

In sum, from the Democratic party's viewpoint, the political stakes in Indiana were unusually high that year: Indiana's thirteen electoral votes for president, a Senate seat that had been won with barely 50 percent of the vote six years earlier, at least three of the House seats, and the Statehouse all were in jeopardy. Moreover, control of the Indiana General Assembly (the Senate was Democratic; the House, Republican), as well as innumerable city and county positions, were on the line.

### Brademas' Difficulties in 1968

Given the advantages of incumbency, five-term incumbents do not ordinarily have to "sweat blood" in their campaigns for reelection. But late in the campaign, the banner headline of an article in *Look* aptly described Brademas' situation: "Congressman John Brademas — A Liberal Fights for Survival."

*Indiana Congressional Redistricting.* The first blow fell in February 1968. A three-judge federal court handed down a decision which redrew Indiana's congressional district boundaries to bring about compliance with the "one man, one vote" standard for the House of Representatives first enunciated four years earlier in the U.S. Supreme Court's momentous decision, *Wesberry* v. *Sanders.* Speaking for a majority of six in *Wesberry*, Justice Hugo Black declared that

> . . . construed in its historical context, the command of Article I, Section 2, that Representatives be chosen "by the People of the several States" means that as nearly as practicable one man's vote in a Congressional election is to be worth as much as another's.

The *Wesberry* case itself involved only the state of Georgia, whose ten congressional districts (created by state statute in 1931) ranged in population (in 1960) from over 800,000 in the urban Fifth District to fewer than 300,000 in the rural Ninth. The Fifth District congressman, Black argued, had to represent "two to three times as many people" as did the congressman from the Ninth and from other sparsely populated Georgia districts; a voter in any of the thinly inhabited districts, Black reasoned, had a greater voice in Washington than a voter in the more populous districts. The Court's opinion concluded:

> While it may not be possible to draw congressional districts with mathematical precision, that is no excuse for ignoring our Constitution's plain objective of making equal representation for equal numbers of people the fundamental goal for the House of Representatives.

*Wesberry* was a historic — and controversial — decision. Three Justices dissented, John Marshall Harlan most vigorously. Harlan argued that Article I, Section 2, had been intended to deal only with the apportionment of representatives *among* states, rather than to impose a rule of equality *within* each state. Speaking from the bench, Harlan lamented that "one would have to search the pages of history to find a case whose importance equals what we have decided today." On that point, at least, all could agree, for in the wake of *Wesberry*, almost all states, including Indiana, set about to redraw their congressional district boundaries more equitably.

The Indiana General Assembly, though, had failed to find an acceptable solution in its 1967 biennial session; the Republican-controlled House and Democratic-controlled Senate had reached an impasse. (In 1965, the Democrats, then dominant in both legislature and Statehouse, had enacted a reapportionment plan that favored Democrats.) Moving into the vacuum created by the 1967 legislative stalemate, the federal court, in *Grills* v. *Branigin*, imposed its own redistricting solution. The plan, however, damaged Democratic interests more than Republican, and hence triggered partisan attack and defense. With respect to the Third District, *Look* observed: ". . . a three-judge Federal court (two were party-loyal Republicans) this year gerrymandered the Third District." (The third judge, a Democrat at the time of his appointment, had written an emphatic dissenting opinion.) Brademas and two other Democratic congressmen were badly hurt by the redistricting decree, and Democrats were quick to denounce the court's action. Ray J. Madden, a twelve-term Democrat from Gary (whose district was not adversely affected by the decree), launched the attack in the House:

> Mr. Speaker, I rise to voice my protest against what can only be described as a "St. Valentine Day Massacre" which took place in my State of Indiana yesterday, February 14, 1968.
> The massacre to which I refer is no less than the massacre of the legislative process by two judges of the U.S. court, and their decision yesterday poses a problem so grave in terms of the fair and equitable

process of our system of government that I call on the House Committee on the Judiciary to conduct an investigation of their action.

*The New Third District.* The court had performed major surgery on Brademas' Third District. The district, since the election of 1942, had consisted of the same four north-central counties; the redrawn district retained two of them and replaced two others with new counties. Thus, St. Joseph and Marshall counties remained in the Third District; Laporte and Starke counties, both of which Brademas had narrowly carried in 1966, were severed from the district. The new Third District, with approximately 446,000 inhabitants, was demographically diverse; urban, suburban, and rural, a rich mosaic of nationality, racial, and religious backgrounds, a veritable microcosm of the American polity. The 2,000-square-mile district was viewed by a visiting British political editor as:

> . . . fairly typical of the semi-industrial middle of America: a hotch-potch of drab township, pleasant suburban housing, sprawling shopping centre and uncompromising factory set down in the flat, wooded, watery country at the foot of the Great Lakes . . . [The Third District] constituents . . . are predominantly middle and lower-middle income but they are drawn from every imaginable race and creed — Poles and Hungarians, Belgians and Greeks, Irish and WASP, white and coloured, Catholic, Methodist, Lutheran, Baptist.

A quarter-million of the new district's population was clustered in St. Joseph County, which included industrialized South Bend (a city of 130,000), adjacent Mishawaka (35,000) — Brademas' birthplace — and the University of Notre Dame. "St. Joe" was the home of several large industries, two of the first locals of the United Automobile Workers, and a number of strongly ethnic neighborhoods. Brademas' political strength was centered in his home county. He had carried the county easily since 1958, though his margin had dipped below 15,000 in 1966. Since that size margin might not be sufficient to offset a strong Republican showing in the other three counties, Brademas was understandably apprehensive.

Flat and fertile Marshall County — over 90 percent of the land is farmed — numbered 35,000 citizens. Brademas had carried the county only once in seven tries. However, he had been steadily building up his support, losing in 1966 by only 600 votes. One of the two newly added counties, Elkhart (120,-000), previously had been part of the Third District. (The 1965 redistricting by the Indiana General Assembly had shifted the county to the Fourth Congressional District.) The county's largest city was Elkhart (40,000), a relatively wealthy community noted for its mobile home and band instrument industries. Brademas had carried Elkhart County only once — during the Johnson landslide of 1964 — out of six attempts. In the 1966 election, the Republican incumbent congressman, E. Ross Adair, swept the county with over 62 percent of the vote; indeed, prior to 1964, Elkhart County had not voted Democratic in a congressional contest since 1936.

The addition to the Third District of predominantly rural Kosciusko County, which Brademas had never represented, was even more disquieting to him. The county (population about 42,000) had regularly gone Republican within the memory of living man, including 54.5 percent support for Senator Barry Goldwater — his third highest percentage among Indiana's ninety-two counties — in his disastrous 1964 presidential race. As a part of the Second Congressional District, the county had always supported the veteran Republican congressman, Charles A. Halleck (first elected in 1935); in fact, Halleck's margin had dipped below 60 percent only once (1958) in the previous eighteen years.

The redistricting raised for Brademas one overriding question: could he build up a sufficient margin in his home county, St. Joseph, to offset anticipated losses in the two new counties? On that question hung his political fate.

*Intraparty Dissension.* In Indiana, as across the nation, Democrats were growing restive. The party was polarizing over the continuance of the Vietnam War, an issue further stirred by Senator Eugene J. McCarthy's (D., Minn.) candidacy for the presidency, announced in late 1967. Initially assumed to have no chance of dislodging the incumbent president, McCarthy's surprising capture on March 12, 1968, of 42 percent of the New Hampshire primary vote greatly encouraged dissenters within the party. In Indiana, antagonisms erupted between insurgents and the "old guard" as anti-LBJ partisans began to prepare for the Indiana presidential preferential primary of May 7. Then, in rapid succession, Senator Robert F. Kennedy (D., N.Y.) on March 16 announced his presidential bid and two weeks later President Johnson told an astonished national television audience that he would not seek reelection. The Democratic presidential primary in Indiana quickly became a three-way contest, and of national significance because it featured the first electoral confrontation between McCarthy and Kennedy. A third contestant, Indiana Governor Roger Branigin, presumably was trying to hold the line for Vice President Hubert H. Humphrey, who had declared his candidacy on April 27, too late to be listed on the Indiana ballot. With tensions proportionate to the high stakes, hostility flared between the McCarthy and Kennedy camps throughout the Indiana campaign.

Kennedy won the Indiana primary with 42.3 percent of the vote; he led the Third District with 46.6 percent. The comparable figures for McCarthy were 27.0 and 31.7 percent and for Branigin, 30.7 and 21.8 percent. Together, Kennedy and McCarthy, the two "anti-administration" challengers, had won 69.3 percent of the statewide primary vote and 78.3 percent of the Third District vote.

The presidential primary provoked deep cleavages within the Democratic party in Indiana, and relations were further strained when Senator Kennedy's assassination released Indiana delegates to the national convention from their obligation to support his candidacy. At the Chicago convention in August, Humphrey captured forty-nine of Indiana's sixty-three votes (78 percent). (McCarthy received eleven votes, Senator George S. McGovern (D., S.D.), two, and Rev. Channing E. Phillips of Washington, D.C., one.) Many Indiana dissidents contended that the primary vote had clearly demonstrated repudiation of administration policies; the people, they argued, had insisted upon a change. The wounds of May, exacerbated by Kennedy's death in June, the vote at the national convention, and the violent Chicago street scenes near the convention site, were far from healed by November; Democratic unity had suffered grievous damage.

Caught in the withering crossfire between party regulars and dissidents, Brademas declined to endorse publicly any of the presidential primary candidates. Why alienate supporters of two of the candidates in exchange for the goodwill of a third faction? Had Brademas not been a delegate to the national convention, he could have left ambiguous his preference until the party had nominated its candidate; his status as a delegate forced his hand. At the national convention, Brademas cast his vote for McCarthy, but as reported in *Look* magazine, "with no great passion or joy . . . to indicate my desire for change and, secondly, because of so many young people in my campaign. I did not want to disappoint them." His vote for McCarthy incurred the wrath of a number of party leaders in the Third District; one angry county chairman fumed that in his county it would cost the congressman 3,000 votes in November.

*Nixon's Coattails.* The candidacy of Richard M. Nixon constituted yet another ominous sign for Indiana Democrats. Indiana had voted heavily Republican both times Nixon had run for Vice President with Eisenhower in 1952 and 1956, and in 1960, Nixon, then at the head of the ticket, led John F. Kennedy by 223,000 votes. In the 1968 Indiana Republican primary, Nixon attracted a large vote despite being unopposed and having to compete for the electorate's attention with a Democratic donnybrook that was page-one news across the nation. In the Third District Nixon ran ahead of the combined Democratic primary vote in three counties, but considerably behind in St. Joseph, the most Democratic county, and emerged with 41.2 percent of the 105,000 total votes cast in both primaries. Following the debacle at the Democratic National Convention in Chicago, Nixon was expected to run even better in Indiana than he had in 1960. Several nonprofessional polls conducted after the August convention showed that Humphrey was favored by fewer than 20 percent of the Third District voters.

Political scientist Milton C. Cummings, Jr., points out that "Congressmen whose prospects for re-election are uncertain are well aware of the stake they have in the success of their party's national ticket." In presidential election years, the district-by-district strength of presidential candidates affects the outcome of House races, though generally less so in districts with long-term incumbents running for reelection than in those with less senior incumbents or no incumbents in the race. If an incumbent congressman's presidential affiliate carries his congressional district and wins the White House, his prospects for victory are very high: Cummings found that for the eleven presidential elections from 1924 through 1964, only eighteen incumbent congressmen from the party that won the presidency were defeated in districts carried by their presidential standard-bearer while 1,675 were returned to office. However, when an incumbent congressman is paired with a presidential candidate who loses both his district and the White House, the odds on his reelection drop substantially: for the eleven elections just cited, one-third of such congressmen were defeated.

Assuming a strong Nixon showing in the Third District in November, what were the possible consequences for Brademas? Voter turnout is highest in presidential elections. As a corollary, in congressional races a substantially higher percentage of the electorate votes during presidential election years (something over 55 percent since 1948) than in the off-year (roughly 45 percent since 1950). The literature suggests that these voters tend to be different from the more regular voters. According to Professor Lewis A. Froman, Jr., they are for the most part "unstable" voters, people "who do not have strong party identification, who have no lasting interest in politics, who are not terribly knowledgeable about politics, and who have little concern with the outcome of the election." In presidential elections most of these unstable voters are likely to vote for the presidential candidate they regard as most exciting or as promoting the most significant issue position. Moreover, and this is the crucial point for a congressional race, many of these once-in-four-years voters will cast a straight party ballot for others of the same party as their choice for president, especially candidates for House and Senate. As Froman observes: "Being neither very knowledgeable about the other candidates nor motivated to vote for political offices other than for President, they have little reason to split their tickets."

Accordingly, differential turnout rates always influence and sometimes determine the results of particular House contests. And in Indiana's Third District the differential was higher than in most of the other districts: an average of 165,000 votes were cast for congressional candidates in off-years since Brademas' first race in 1954, as compared to 210,000 in presidential election years. Thus, the presidential-year increment of voters — 45,000 on the average — constituted a sizable and volatile chunk of the Third District electorate. Just as Brademas had benefited handsomely by Lyndon Johnson's popularity in 1964, he could expect Richard Nixon's popularity to be damaging in 1968. How damaging was not clear, for Brademas could not estimate how many of the voters who were attracted to Nixon would split their ballots to vote for him in the congressional contest.

*The Wallace Problem.* An additional problem was posed by the presidential candidacy of Governor George C. Wallace of Alabama. It was difficult to gauge the extent of Wallace's popularity in the Third District. In the 1964 Indiana presidential primary, Wallace won 30 percent of the state-wide Democratic vote and carried nearby Lake County, which includes the industrial complex of Gary, Hammond, and East Chicago. Hence, it was assumed that in 1968 Wallace would draw more votes away from Humphrey than from Nixon in the industrial portions of northern Indiana. Local labor leaders, fearful of numerous rank-and-file defections to Wallace among blue-collar workers in South Bend, mounted a vigorous campaign to dissuade their members from bolting. Two troublesome questions remained for Brademas: how many Democrats would cross over to Wallace and, of those that did, how many would return to the Democratic column — and to Brademas — for the rest of the ballot?

*The Republicans' Choice.* Brademas was opposed by William W. Erwin, a 42-year-old farm manager and state senator from the hamlet of Etna Green in Kosciusko County. Described by the *New York Times* as an "old-line" conservative, he formerly served as state chairman of the Indiana Young Republicans and as chairman of the Indiana Advisory Commission to the U.S. Civil Rights Commission. He was an experienced and industrious campaigner, a calm, steady man. Regarded as heir apparent to the Second District seat which Charlie Halleck had occupied since 1935 and was now vacating, Erwin had unexpectedly become a casualty of the judicial redistricting decree. Erwin's home county, Kosciusko, was annexed to the Third District. In the Republican primary in May, by readily outdistancing a 31-year-old South Bend attorney, Erwin had earned his chance to unseat Brademas.

### Campaign Strategies: Images and Resources

No two elections are alike and neither are any two campaign strategies. All campaign strategies, though, are shaped by certain salient factors: the particular characteristics of the constituency, the personality, style, and issue orientation of the candidate and his opponent, the availability of funds, the role that party plays, and so forth. Given those determinants, some candidates approach campaigns without highly developed strategies. In practicing their political art, they avoid tightly structured campaign formats and tend to rely on their time-tested general sense of the electorate's mood.

Increasingly, though, the age of science is penetrating electoral politics: sophisticated polling (in-depth probes on candidates and issues, "quickie" telephone and shopping center surveys to detect shifts in voter attitudes and intentions); the wonders of electronic data processing (computer-generated "walking lists" for canvassing, computer-printed "personalized" letters, computer-assisted election return analyses); thoroughly professional media campaigns — especially centered on television — utilizing every selling technique known to Madison Avenue to project a buyable image. Some observers refer to these sophisticated techniques as "the new politics"; others fail to discern in them anything fundamentally "new."

Whether novel methods or not, these technologies are invariably expensive. Hence, their principal users to date have been candidates in statewide and, of course, national campaigns — would-be governors, senators, and presidents who have multimillion dollar campaign budgets. But the resources available to most candidates for the House, unless they have access to unusual wealth, are usually insufficient to underwrite a generous use of campaign technology.

John Brademas' 1968 campaign occupied something of a middle ground between the new and the not-so-new. His campaign budget imposed very real constraints on what political goods and services he could buy. He did employ more polling than he had in the past, but it was a modest effort. He did attempt to identify key "swing" precincts through a statistical analysis of voting data and demographic characteristics, but that, too, was a relatively primitive effort. His greatest indulgence was hiring one of the nation's most renowned political filmmakers, Charles Guggenheim, to prepare most of his TV spots — and they were highly artistic creations. But on the whole, the Brademas campaign featured familiar techniques.

Serious planning for Brademas' sixth-term quest began in December of 1967. Over the next several months, dozens of campaign topics were discussed at a series of meetings with staff and advisers. Detailed planning began on such matters as fund-raising, organizing notebooks on issues, monitoring the speeches of the Republican nominee, organizing "Citizens for Brademas" committees in each of the counties, locating a suitable campaign headquarters, formulating a detailed budget for the campaign, projecting the use of media, newsletters and other mailings to constituents, coordinating plans with other Democratic candidates (including access to polling information that might be available from Democratic candidates running statewide), and planning the frequency of Brademas' visits to the district.

Four aspects of Brademas' campaign strategy, all of which apply generally to a congressman's relationship to his constituency at election time, merit attention: exploiting the advantages of incumbency, mobilizing favorably disposed groups, projecting (in this particular election) a less partisan image, and maintaining an intensive pace.

*The Incumbent's Edge.* The advantages of incumbency for a congressman are numerous, formidable and, judging from the very high proportion of incumbents returned to office, readily exploitable. From 1954 to 1968, House incumbents won no less than 92 percent of the primary and general election contests in which they sought renomination and/or reelection; the comparable figure for Senators was 85 percent. Most congressmen believe, according to Charles Clapp, that aside from unusual circumstances where an overriding issue is present, an incumbent has little excuse for defeat.

The stature of the office tends to confer on its occupant an aura of valuable experience and expertise, assets which would be wasted (so the incumbent argues) if he were replaced. Moreover, the visibility of a congressman's activities provides a built-in advantage in gaining the attention, hopefully favorable, of his constituents. The advantage of exposure, like the supposition of expertise, is cumulative; the longer a congressman holds office, the more valuable these assets become. True, the names of most congressmen may not be known to almost half of the voters in their districts, but the names of their challengers, in most instances, are even less well known. Further, there are tangible resources which congressmen have generously allocated to themselves, and which are fully exploited by incumbents seeking reelection.

One major element of Brademas' campaign strategy was to emphasize his ten years as congressman. When he formally announced his candidacy for reelection, on March 25, his message was clear: "With five terms in Congress, I believe my experience and seniority will enable me to be even more effective in representing the interests of all the people of our district — Democrats, Republicans and independents — and in serving the entire nation. . . ." His campaign buttons and billboards proclaimed, simply, "Congressman Brademas for Congress." His campaign literature displayed such themes as "the right man in the right place" and "we have a good man in Congress — it makes sense to keep him there!" And, of course, in virtually every campaign speech, Brademas emphasized his "decade of service" to the district. In sum, he lost little opportunity to remind voters of his lengthy service as their congressman.

Also available to any member of Congress were the concrete advantages of incumbency: the use of staff for campaigning, of the House Recording Studio, and of special allowances for travel, office equipment, postage, stationery, and telephone and telegraph services. All of these perquisites of office could be used for campaigning purposes. For example, at levels in effect in 1968, congressmen were entitled to an allotment of more than $100,000 a year, known as a "clerk-hire allowance," which ordinarily supported an office staff of about twelve. (Challengers find it difficult — and expensive — to compete with incumbents in this respect.)

Another advantage of incumbency is the congressional franking privilege, an American practice dating back to the Continental Congress. It permits a member of Congress to transmit "official correspondence" through the mails without having to pay for postage. While a congressman is not privileged to use the frank in his capacity as a political candidate, the line of separation is quite fuzzy. In addition to mail addressed to individuals, members of the House (but not the Senate) have extended the frank to include bulk mailing to their respective home districts, addressed simply to "occupant" or "postal patron." Under these circumstances, the utility of the frank as a political asset becomes even more obvious. For example, the franking privilege enables a congressman to send a newsletter to every postal patron — that is, to every household in his district — without having to pay anything for postage. Thus, on a continuing basis, Brademas sought to keep his constituents informed in part through the use of meticulously prepared newsletters, a practice engaged in by virtually every member of the House. In an election year, such newsletters assumed additional significance.

*Mobilizing Allies.* Gaining and maintaining group support is an invariable campaign strategy. In Brademas' case, there were many organizations and less formal groups whose favor he sought during the course of the campaign: church groups, veterans organizations, ethnic groups, chambers of commerce, farmer organizations, rural electrification associations, and many others. With friendly groups, Brademas sought to urge all allies to be sure to vote; with less friendly or hostile ones, he tried to neutralize expected opposition. A brief examination of Brademas' relationship with labor groups and with the apparatus of the Democratic party will help demonstrate the principle of activating allied forces. (Brademas' efforts to rally the "education community" on his behalf is examined in detail in a later section.)

Organized labor was a very important political force in the Third District, especially in the South Bend area. Two of the first locals of the United Automobile Workers of America (UAW) had been organized in South Bend, and in the 1968 election, as in many previous ones, they exercised considerable political influence through the UAW's political action arm. Likewise, the AFL–CIO's political action instrumentality — the Committee on Political Education (COPE) — was very active. Brademas worked closely with these groups, at both national and local levels. As the second-ranking officer in the Democratic Study Group (DSG) — the loose-knit coalition of House liberals — Brademas and other DSG leaders collaborated with COPE officials in devising priorities for the allocation of COPE resources. Their joint efforts were directed, first, at identifying House liberals whose reelection prospects were uncertain (or liberal challengers to incumbent conservatives) and who therefore needed and merited the investment of COPE resources and, second, at planning a massive COPE-directed voter registration effort on behalf of liberal congressional candidates. In all, Brademas' ten-year voting record, both within the House Education and Labor Committee and on the floor of the House, had shown consistent support for labor. And in the 1968 campaign, as in past elections, organized labor returned the favor through providing crucial support — campaign contributions and, particularly, manpower — for Brademas as well as for many other Democratic candidates and an occasional prolabor Republican.

The Democratic party itself was a major resource for Brademas only at the local level. The Democratic National Committee was perceived as being too preoccupied with the presidential race and, in some instances, with Senate races, and as having too limited funds and manpower to be of very much importance in House contests. The Democratic Congressional Campaign Committee in 1968 likewise had insufficient resources to be of much help.

Closer to home, the Indiana State Democratic Central Committee, with head-quarters in Indianapolis, was subdivided into district-wide organizations for each of the eleven congressional districts. The Third District Democratic Committee in turn consisted of representatives from the Democratic Ceneral Committees in each of the four counties comprising the district. The key troops were the precinct committeemen of the voting precincts within the cities and townships. They had principal responsibility within the party structure for registering Democratically inclined voters, for distributing campaign literature, and for getting out the vote.

Brademas clearly needed the support of this party apparatus during his 1968 campaign, but the Democratic party within the Third District needed Brademas as well. Brademas habitually led the Democratic ticket in Third District balloting, even compared to Democratic presidential and Senate candidates. The electoral fate of local Democratic candidates often seemed to be related to the length of Brademas' coattails. The party, in sum, desired Brademas' open identification as a Democrat as a key element of his and their campaign.

But life within the party had become complicated in 1968. Young insurgents — presidential primary supporters of McCarthy and Kennedy — were intent on wresting control of the party apparatus in St. Joseph County from the "old guard," and they hoped for encouragement from Brademas. The long-time party regulars, who were just as determined to maintain their leadership, had supported Brademas enthusiastically through six previous congressional campaigns and expected Brademas to be loyal to them. During these months Brademas emerged as a kind of mediator between the two factions. He sought to keep alive the spirit and idealism of the badly outnumbered young Democrats while discouraging any attempt at a party coup. He also urged party regulars to be sensitive to the values expressed by the McCarthy and Kennedy supporters. As a party man, in many meetings with the party leadership and precinct committeemen, Brademas indicated his appreciation for past support and exhorted party workers to renew their efforts on behalf of the candidates and the principles for which the party stood. The factions managed a tenuous accommodation, and despite the complexities of intraparty relations, the party apparatus served as Brademas' strong ally throughout the campaign.

*Image and Party.* Walter Bagehot, the eminent English constitutional scholar, once said of the House of Commons: "Party is inherent in it, is bone of its bone, breath of its breath." The American political party system differs significantly. To be sure, party is the salient feature of congressional behavior, but the party loyalty exhibited by members of Congress often falls far short of that displayed by a Member of Parliament. Because of the differences in the two electoral systems, the fate of the M.P. is more intimately tied to his party's overall success at the polls than is the case with his American counterpart. Professors Hugh A. Bone and Austin Ranney observe of the

American office-seeker: "A candidate's use of and relationship to the rest of the ticket is likely to be determined by pragmatic and expedient considerations. There is a team emphasis where candidates see profit in it, otherwise strategy and campaigning are individualistic matters and follow the dictum 'vote for the man.' "

In 1968 there were considerable risks for Brademas in being identified too closely with the Democratic party. Compare 1964, when all signs pointed to a lopsided Democratic presidential victory. Then, the prospects for Democratic candidates, *qua* Democrats, were good at all levels; it was one of those infrequent years in which it was politically advantageous to be perceived by voters as an Indiana Democrat. (The election results, a disaster for Indiana Republicans, more than justified the Democratic strategy of stressing party identification: Goldwater was swamped in Indiana, GOP candidates for governor and Senator were defeated, two of their seven House seats were lost, and, for the first time in twenty-eight years, control of both houses of the Indiana General Assembly went to the Democrats.) But in 1968 a comparable emphasis on partisan Democratic identification was a high-risk strategy. Brademas needed to broaden his appeal to the political middle, to the swing voters, to the thousands of politically "unstable" voters who cast ballots in presidential contests but often not in off-year elections.

Brademas' efforts to moderate his image as a liberal Democrat was no easy task. After all, he had campaigned vigorously as a Democrat for fourteen years, unequivocally and almost invariably on the side of "liberal" domestic and foreign aid programs and civil rights. Moreover, his roll-call voting record was indisputably very liberal. Throughout his time in Congress, Brademas had consistently received high ratings from liberal groups and low ratings from conservative organizations, and 1968 provided no exception. (For example, the liberal *New Republic* rated Brademas as having voted "correctly" on eleven of twelve key votes in 1967–68; only nine congressmen received perfect *New Republic* ratings, and Brademas was one of the next tier of thirty (twenty-nine of them Democrats) with eleven "correct" votes. By contrast, the conservative Americans for Constitutional Action rated Brademas' performance at only 4 percent "correct" key votes for the same 90th Congress.)

Brademas' voting record reflected the fact that, generally, congressmen enjoy very wide latitude to vote as they wish. After all, legislative issues are commonly very complex, and constituents are mostly perplexed by or indifferent to the intricacies of the legislative process. Indeed, the electorate for the most part is simply disinterested in how their representatives in Washington vote on most issues. Moreover, local press coverage of how a congressman votes, with the exception of a handful of newspapers across the nation, is skimpy or nonexistent. In all, the vast majority of voters have only the vaguest notion of the specific positions their representatives have taken in Washington. Typical is the finding by Warren E. Miller and Donald E.

Stokes that, "Far from looking over the shoulders of their Congressmen at the legislative game, most Americans are almost totally uninformed about legislative issues in Washington." As the late Congressman Herman Eberharter (D., Pa.) put it: "A Congressman can do pretty much what he decides to do and he doesn't have to bother too much about criticism."

In most instances, therefore, a congressman is relatively free either to follow Edmund Burke's famous injunction (as Burke put it, a representative owes his constituents "his unbiased opinion, his mature judgment, his enlightened conscience" which "he ought not sacrifice . . . to any man") or to be guided more by the wishes of his constituents as he perceives them. But a congressman's constituents, when they speak at all, seldom speak with a single voice, thereby allowing the representative even further leeway to follow his own will. In all, a congressman is relatively free to vote as he pleases on many issues.

But with strong antiliberal sentiments in the winds, Brademas' voting record, if attacked by his opponent, could prove to be a serious political handicap. The political complexion of the Third District was not by any criterion as liberal as his voting record. Indeed, Erwin, his opponent, repeatedly attacked Brademas' record, attempting to portray him as a member of the "liberal establishment," and to maneuver him into a defensive posture. "John Brademas," the Etna Green Republican charged, "would probably be a fine representative of the Eastern Establishment and New York City, but . . . there is more than ample evidence that the present congressman has lost touch with the people of the Third District."

Pursuing a less partisan image, Brademas capitalized on opportunities to be identified with Republicans. In late April 1968, he cosponsored a conference on "The Community Response to Crime" at the University of Notre Dame. Displaying concern for increasing crime rates was certainly sound politically. But Brademas went a step further; he prevailed upon New York City Mayor John Lindsay, then still a Republican, to be the principal conference speaker. In his opening remarks, Lindsay said some very complimentary things about his former House colleague, Brademas, and later Brademas made frequent use of those remarks in his campaign literature. Moreover, Brademas prominently displayed a photograph of Lindsay (as well as one of Brademas shaking hands with FBI Director J. Edgar Hoover) in a special newsletter to constituents on the topic of crime and the Notre Dame crime conference. In organizing his Campaign Kick-Off Banquet in South Bend in June (described in more detail later), Brademas enlisted his friend John Gardner, a Republican who had just resigned as Secretary of Health, Education and Welfare, as the main speaker. Gardner began his remarks by saying, "John Brademas is a Democrat and I'm a Republican, but we stand together on all important issues affecting the life and future of this nation." Brademas made good use of that bipartisan-flavored tribute in subsequent campaign literature.

Brademas also maintained his own separate headquarters rather than sharing space with other Democratic candidates in a large building rented by the local Democratic party. He had regularly followed that practice, although it was resented by some party regulars. In "Citizens for Brademas" headquarters in 1968 — a vacant store on South Bend's main street, two blocks from party headquarters — there were no large Humphrey-Muskie posters, no huge "Vote Democratic!" banners, no posters or literature promoting local candidates. It was, purely and simply, John Brademas' headquarters. Within was ample space for Brademas' own staff, as well as volunteers, many of them students who felt strongly about Brademas but were not drawn to the other Democratic candidates. Although a separate headquarters was a luxury, expensive to rent and operate, it provided an identification of the candidate in personal rather than chiefly party terms.

*An Exhausting Pace.* Another "strategy" was embodied in the intensive pace of the campaign. Considerable evidence indicates that most voters, perhaps the overwhelming majority, have decided how they will vote before the campaign begins; these voters decide in accord with their party identification and are not open to conversion by the campaign itself. Nevertheless, as William H. Flanigan points out, campaigning may well influence a "small but crucial proportion of the electorate," the so-called swing voters. Many elections are sufficiently close so that the winning margin could indeed be achieved late in a political campaign. And there is the perennial problem, most acute for the Democrats, of securing high rates of turnout among one's partisans in the citizenry.

Brademas acted on the belief that the contest might not be decided until the last few days of the campaign. Yet time for him to campaign in the district was hard to come by, for Congress did not adjourn until October 8. Although he campaigned on most weekends in the several months prior to congressional adjournment, his opponent had been campaigning vigorously since well before the May primary. (Here is one of the few *disadvantages* of incumbency.) In his weekend barnstorming, Brademas stressed to his audiences his need to be in Washington to tend to national affairs, but that hardly compensated him for electioneering time "lost" while in Washington and away from the district. The only offset was to maintain a furious campaign pace. Headquarters operated seven days — and evenings — a week for the last six weeks of the campaign. And Brademas' own schedule was grueling, as reflected in his official itinerary for a three-day period late in the campaign:

*Tuesday, October 22*
6:45 A.M.   Speaks at Breakfast Optimist Club, Victorian Room, Hotel Elkhart
9:30 A.M.   Speaks at Grace College Convocation, Winona Lake
4:30 to 6:30 P.M.   Walking tour in Elkhart

*Jack H. Schuster*

8:30 P.M.   Speaks to Elkhart Lodge, 1402 B'nai B'rith, Temple Israel, 430 North Second Street, Elkhart

*Wednesday, October 23*

8:15 A.M.   Speaks at Eagle Ethics Assembly, John Adams High School, South Bend

12:00 noon   Speaks at Elkhart Lions Club luncheon, Hotel Elkhart

2:15 to 2:45 P.M.   Speaks to Pioneer Womens Organization, Sons of Israel Synagogue, 415 South William Street, South Bend

3:00 to 3:45 P.M.   Greets workers at Kaiser Jeep plant factory gate and presents U.S. flag to Local 5, UAW

5:00 to 6:30 P.M.   Walking tour, South Bend

8:00 to 8:45 P.M.   Speaks at rally at Schori's Restaurant, 314 East Jefferson, Plymouth

9:30 P.M.   Attends rally at DiLoretto Society, 914 East Division, Mishawaka

*Thursday, October 24*

9:30 A.M.   Coffee with faculty and administrators, Bethel College, Mishawaka

10:00 A.M.   Address Bethel College Convocation

12:00 noon   Address St. Joseph Council of Churches, YMCA, South Bend

4:30 P.M.   Meets Adlai E. Stevenson III at St. Joseph County Airport

4:50 P.M.   Stevenson and Brademas press conference at Indiana Club, South Bend

5:00 to 6:00 P.M.   Reception for Stevenson and Brademas at Indiana Club

6:25 to 6:45 P.M.   Stevenson and Brademas fly to Warsaw Airport

7:00 to 7:30 P.M.   Brademas introduces Stevenson who speaks at fund-raising dinner at Shrine Building, Kosciusko County fairgrounds, Warsaw

7:45 to 8:00 P.M.   Stevenson and Brademas fly to Elkhart Airport

8:00 to 9:30 P.M.   Brademas introduces Stevenson who speaks at fund-raising dinner, Fourth Annual Rally 'Round, sponsored by Elkhart County Democratic Central Committee, Parkway Inn, 2220 South Nappanee Street, Elkhart

In sum, as Election Day, November 5, loomed ever larger, Brademas was finding his prospects for a sixth term complicated by the menace of redistricting, by dissension within Democratic ranks throughout the state (including the Third District), by the candidacy of Richard Nixon, a proven vote-getter in Indiana, and by the specter of Alabama's Governor George Wallace, who had run well in Indiana's 1964 presidential preferential primary. The South Bend Democrat could ill afford to bypass any political opportunity.

## Mobilizing the Education Community

The relationships between lobbyists and their allies in Congress acquire a sharper focus when viewed in the context of electoral politics. To what degree will an interest group commit itself in trying to assist a friend in Congress whose career may be in jeopardy? And, conversely, to what extent will a politician, locked in a tough fight for reelection, attempt to mobilize his "special interest constituency"? Such questions relate to important but little examined aspects of the national policy-making process.

This section focuses on the interaction between John Brademas (an "education congressman") and the "education community" (especially education associations and federal educator-administrators, but also university faculties, education-conscious noneducators, and students). John Brademas for ten years had been a strong congressional ally of education. In 1968, because of the uncertainty of success in his reelection bid, he was determined to marshall every possible political resource. Toward that end, much of his campaign effort was directed at mobilizing an "education constituency" at national, state, and local levels.

The point was previously made that a congressman, facing a political life-or-death struggle, attempts to activate all the allies he can find. But the "education community," theoretically Brademas' natural ally, traditionally has been apprehensive about engaging overtly in partisan politics and has never been easily activated. That situation has been changing in recent years; the federal government's increasingly influential role in shaping education policy and providing support for schools and colleges has led more educators to recognize their stake in cultivating favor on Capitol Hill.

*The Washington "Education Lobby."*    At one end of this lobbyist-politician relationship is the diverse sprawl of education interest groups in Washington. Dozens of education associations — some powerful, others barely visible — constitute a very loose-knit education "lobby." Reflecting American education's rich pluralism, the interests of these education groups differ markedly. Some, like the American Library Association, have relatively narrow policy objectives; others, like the National Education Association, concern themselves with a wide range of education issues. Some represent the interests of a single institution (the University of California maintains a Washington office) ; others are large "umbrella" organizations (the American Council on Education purports to speak for over 1,300 member colleges and universities). Some, like the United States Catholic Conference, represent religious interests; others, such as Protestants and Other Americans United, seek to preserve secularism in public education. Some, like the AFL–CIO or the NAACP, are not primarily education oriented, though they engage in education lobbying. Almost all represent nonprofit institutions, but a few, such as the National Audio-Visual Association, speak for the interests of a group of profit-making businesses. Some represent the interests of states (the

*Jack H. Schuster*

Education Commission of the States or the Council of Chief State School Officers) and the cities (the Research Council of the Great Cities for School Improvement).

Diverse as their interests are, most Washington-based education groups perceive at least one common cause: to expand education's share of perennially scarce federal funds, with as few strings attached as possible. (Other claimants on federal funds are of course numerous — highway builders, defense contractors, urban renewers, health researchers, ad infinitum.)

To protect the interests of their respective clienteles, these interest groups monitor developments in the federal government, seeking to influence policy outcomes. To accomplish this, they must focus attention on the critical stages in the policy formulation process — when an education proposal is being drafted by the U.S. Office of Education or elsewhere in the executive branch or by an ad hoc presidential task force, when a congressional hearing is underway on an education bill or an appropriations measure, when a vote is about to be taken in an education subcommittee or full committee or on the floor of the House or Senate, or when the Office of Education or Department of Health, Education and Welfare formulates guidelines for the implementation of newly enacted legislation.

The "education community" has experienced some moments of success in Washington, such as when a recently formed education coalition — the "Emergency Committee for Full Funding of Education" — influenced Congress in late 1970 to override President Nixon's veto of a major education appropriations bill. Observers have often concluded, though, that the educators, plagued by internal dissent and their ambivalence toward politics caused by their self-perception as professional educators, have been largely ineffective in their lobbying efforts at the national level.

The lack of cohesion stems, almost inevitably, from the very different education interests that the various associations represent. And at education's grass roots, most classroom teachers and university faculties have heretofore been reluctant to compromise their professionalism by becoming involved in partisan politics. This posture is eroding in the face of widespread collective bargaining among educators and growing bands of aggressive political activists within their ranks. But in 1968 — at best a transition period with respect to these attitudes toward political involvement — it was not at all clear whether the Washington education lobby had the capability to "deliver," assuming it wanted to do so in the first place.

*The "Education Congressman."* Brademas' credentials as an education-minded legislator began with his assignment to the House Education and Labor Committee. (He tells the story of driving to Bonham, Texas, on his way back to Indiana from a trip to the West Coast following his election in 1958, in order personally to ask House Speaker Sam Rayburn that he be assigned to that committee. His request was subsequently granted.) As the 1968 election drew near, Brademas was nearing the completion of ten years on that House committee, the focal point of his legislative energies. At that time, he was eighth-ranking majority member (among eighteen Democrats) on the committee, and, more importantly, sat as the "ranking majority member" (that is, junior only to the chairman) of two key education subcommittees: the Special Subcommittee on Education (with jurisdiction for higher education legislation) and the General Subcommittee on Education (with jurisdiction for elementary and secondary education).

As a member of the full committee, Brademas had sponsored or cosponsored virtually every major education law enacted since 1959. In varying degrees, he contributed to the writing or passage of the Higher Education Facilities Act of 1963, the Technical Education Program of 1963, the Teacher Fellowship and Teacher Corps Program of 1965, the landmark Elementary and Secondary Education Act of 1965 and the 1967 amendments, the Higher Education Act of 1965 and the 1967 amendments, the International Education Act of 1966, and the Education Professions Development Act of 1967.* Education and Labor Chairman Adam Clayton Powell had named Brademas in 1961 to chair an ad hoc advisory group on higher education and in 1966 to lead a special House task force on international education.

His support of education had earned him widespread recognition from education groups, including an "Award for Distinguished Service in International Education" from the Institute of International Education, and, during the course of the campaign, an award for distinguished service from the Legislative Commission of the National Education Association. By 1968 he had received honorary doctoral degrees from four universities; the citations usually emphasized his contributions to American education.

Another facet of Brademas' involvement with education was his active service on education boards and councils. He sat as a member of the Board of Visitors to Harvard University's John F. Kennedy School of Government and to its Department of Romance Languages and Literatures; was a member of Advisory Councils of the College of Liberal Arts, University of Notre Dame; the School of International Service, American University, Washington, D.C.; and the Institute of Urban Affairs, Boston College; and was also a trustee of Saint Mary's College in Notre Dame, Indiana (where he had taught in 1957–58) and of the Educational Testing Service, Princeton, New Jersey.

By 1968, then, John Brademas' exceptional academic background and his immersion in education legislation for a decade had distinguished him above all but a few of his congressional colleagues as "an education congressman."

*Education as a Campaign Issue.* Brademas was aware that voters only infrequently are able to identify issues as the basis for voting *for* a congressman; a reliance on issues as grounds for voting *against* a candidate for

---

* Editor's note: Brademas' contribution to the passage of the Elementary and Secondary Education Act (ESEA) of 1965 is touched on in the study by Murphy in this volume. See p. 166.

Congress is somewhat more common. Moreover, it is rare, at least according to Brademas' judgment, that voters will cite "support of education" as a reason for voting for a congressman.

Why, then, were all the time and resources invested in reinforcing Brademas' image as an "education congressman"? At the time and again in retrospect, Brademas recognized that his 1968 campaign for reelection may have siphoned off a disproportionately large amount of his resources for the purpose of wooing both the educators and, through his identification with education, the general electorate. Nevertheless, Brademas believed the strategy was sound, especially in light of his commitment, independent of the campaign, to promote public support for American education.

Further, many people other than educators find education to be one of their salient interests and recognize that education is a "good thing." More important, education is often a less controversial and hence less vulnerable issue than most, characteristics which are especially attractive to a liberal congressman representing a more conservative district. A legislator's strong identification with education is less likely to repel a conservatively disposed voter than is, say, a strong identification with the labor movement, with civil rights, or with foreign economic assistance.

True, a conservative voter can find fault with a congressman's preference for retaining significant federally centralized prerogatives which establish education priorities. But virtually no voter (excepting perhaps a few educators) makes sophisticated distinctions between federally determined categorical aid programs and more decentralized, state-oriented general aid programs. Indeed, a strong identification with "education" in general can deflect attention from a congressman's "liberal" record on such highly charged education issues as busing to achieve racial balance or opposition to the "student unrest amendments" which would suspend federal assistance to students who engage in illegal disruptive activities. Similarly, popular perceptions of a legislator as primarily "pro-education" can help to temper his larger record on issues unrelated to education. On balance, then, a congressman who develops a reputation as a promoter of education policy and interests may or may not win many committed friends, but he is not likely thereby to make many dedicated enemies.

*Cultivating the Education Interest Groups.* During his five terms in Congress, Brademas had developed a close working relationship with representatives of the most influential national education groups. To use the political vernacular, he had "delivered," that is, he had fought the educators' battles on Capitol Hill and unquestionably had contributed considerably to advancing the interests of education. Now, faced with a difficult reelection campaign in 1968, Brademas sought the support of some of these educational colleagues. The response was varied, given the wariness of education groups of becoming identified with partisan politics. Nevertheless, the Legislative Commission of the million-member National Educational Association (NEA) decided to award Brademas its Distinguished Service Award. John Lumley, NEA's assistant executive secretary for legislative and federal relations, wrote:

> In recognition of your distinguished record in promoting educational legislation during the Ninetieth Congress, the Legislative Commission of the National Education Association has voted unanimously to award you their distinguished service plaque.
>
> We will be pleased to make this presentation to you in your home district or at your Washington office as you prefer. I will appreciate hearing from you at your earliest convenience.
>
> I want to express my personal appreciation to you for your dedication to improving the educational opportunities of the youth of this country. Best wishes for your continued success.

A representative from the Legislative Commission office in Washington flew to South Bend to present this award. That the presentation ceremony, with appropriate fanfare, took place just five days prior to the election was hardly coincidental. For the occasion, Brademas' staff arranged a reception at the University of Notre Dame's Faculty Club. Numerous local school and university educators were invited and a top-ranking Department of Health, Education and Welfare official was also on hand to make kind remarks about Brademas.

During the course of the event, a letter was read from Robert Wyatt, executive secretary of the Indiana State Teachers Association (the NEA affiliate). Wyatt had been national president of the NEA at the time the landmark Elementary and Secondary Education Act of 1965 was enacted and had developed a close working relationship with Brademas. Wyatt's timely letter of October 14 lavished praise on the congressman:

> As the 90th Congress adjourns, I want to take this opportunity to express to you, on behalf of the teachers of Indiana, our great appreciation for the outstanding contribution you have made to the progress of education in Indiana and throughout the Nation.
>
> Your role in the 90th Congress has been especially commendable in two respects: First, in your effort to prevent damaging cutbacks in appropriations for school aid programs authorized by earlier Congresses; second, in your sponsorship of new education laws sponsored by our organizations and enacted by the 90th Congress, including the Education Professions Development Act, the Elementary and Secondary Education Amendments of 1967, and the Vocational Education Amendments of 1968.
>
> We in Indiana take pride in your being the only member of Congress from our state on the House Committee on Education and Labor. Your leadership and hard work on these and other educational mea-

sures fully merit the description in *Look Magazine* as "Mr. Education in Congress."

The media were invited to attend, and considerable print and television coverage resulted — which was, of course, the point of the whole exercise.

The American Federation of Teachers (AFT), an AFL-CIO affiliate and the NEA's principal rival nationally, was quite helpful at the local level through the South Bend Federation of Teachers (SBFT), bargaining agent for South Bend classroom teachers and the local AFT affiliate. A telephone call from David Selden, national AFT president, to the president of the SBFT, Larry Bishop, helped stimulate the local organization's political activity. Bishop, with whom the Brademas staff had been in close contact, subsequently circulated a mimeographed memorandum entitled "Political Participation" to every AFT member in South Bend. It commented on Selden's call as follows:

> Dave pointed out that there isn't another congressman as dedicated to furthering the cause of education than Congressman Brademas and it would be a real tragedy to lose him. Since I received that call from Mr. Selden I have been in contact with Brademas Headquarters in South Bend to find out what we as teachers can do to help.
>
> There are several ways. First, they are in need of people to answer the phones in the afternoon. Second, on November 3rd from 1:30–5:30 they would like volunteers to knock on doors in different parts of the city to drum up support. Third, they would like to have an ad in the [*South Bend*] *Tribune* sponsored by teachers. Finally, they can always use people to stuff envelopes and similar tasks. . . . I hope you will give this request for help very careful consideration.

As a result of Bishop's recruiting, a small group of eighteen teachers, all SBFT members, volunteered to canvass for Brademas on the Sunday preceding the election. Brademas' staff briefed the group on two occasions, equipped them with badges prominently identifying them as "Teachers for Brademas," and dispatched them to crucial "swing" precincts. When they were "debriefed," the staff judged that their door-to-door salesmanship had met almost invariably with respect and, occasionally, enthusiasm, presumably reflecting the credibility generally accorded schoolteachers. Their apparent success could be contrasted with the somewhat less receptive attitudes often encountered by Brademas' student canvassers. In all, this small band of teacher-activists succeeded in blanketing fifteen key precincts two days prior to the election. Though the impact was not susceptible to measurement, it was thought to have been quite helpful.

Concurrently, a written appeal for support of Brademas was initiated within the Department of Audiovisual Instruction (DAVI) in Washington, a highly autonomous division of the NEA. These individually addressed letters, written by DAVI's assistant executive secretary, but signed in her individual capacity, were sent from Washington to all DAVI members in the South Bend area, i.e., to audiovisual specialists in the schools. Technically, the letters were sent neither by DAVI nor the parent NEA, but their impact likely was not too different than if they had been:

> I make this appeal to you as a private citizen, not as a staff member of your national organization nor even as a fellow I.U. [Indiana University] alumnus. I've never been active in politics but it seems to me it's time to become active and ask my colleagues to cross party lines, if necessary, to vote for a man who so ably represents our profession.
>
> As an educator, how many times have you said to yourself: Why can't we get educated, intelligent men to run for office — thinking men who will bring *honesty* and *integrity* into politics! Well, you people in the Third Congressional District of Indiana gave Congress just such a man, a Rhodes Scholar, a man who values education, who fights for your interests on the floor of Congress. He has supported our case; now let's support his.
>
> Maybe you have never been active in politics either because it's been a forbidden area for teachers. Now that we have teacher power, let's use it. Let's do more than just cast a vote on election day. It's time to actively campaign for men like John Brademas. Urge everyone you meet to vote for him — if not for yourself, then for the kids. Keeping men like Brademas in Congress is our only hope for tomorrow.

*The Federal Educators — Legislative-Executive Coordination.* Several key HEW officials were quite helpful, although not in any highly organized or particularly visible way. Most notable was the assistance of two political scientists-turned-HEW-officials: the assistant secretary for legislation and his deputy for education legislation, both key figures in the federal education network. Brademas had fought their fights on Capitol Hill for a decade; they recognized that he now needed help, and they were responsive when he outlined his plight.

The assistant secretary, who was to be in the Midwest in late October, had volunteered to help in any way he could. He flew to South Bend for the NEA award presentation (discussed earlier), where he made some highly flattering remarks about Brademas' contributions to American education. That evening he accompanied Brademas to a meeting of St. Joseph County Democratic candidates and party workers. Following remarks by the county chairman, the party's nominee for governor, and Brademas, he gave a short, spirited pep talk in which he sang hymns of praise for Brademas. He had also been very helpful some months earlier in suggesting the names of persons, within and outside the education community, who could be solicited by Brademas for contributions to his campaign fund.

*Jack H. Schuster*

The deputy assistant secretary, with whom Brademas had often collaborated in legislative matters, went one step further and personally wrote letters of solicitation to fifty or sixty potential contributors, many of whom worked within the federal education establishment. He did not, of course, write in his capacity as an HEW official.

*Rallying the Local Educators.* Brademas was hopeful that the local educators would rally to his banner. Indeed, he hoped that they could be tapped for campaign contributions and other support on the assumption, not unreasonable, that they would be willing to so express their appreciation of his efforts in Congress on their behalf.

Brademas' principal fund-raising device was a campaign kick-off banquet. Volunteers, frequently wives of Notre Dame professors, customarily compiled a list of persons to be invited and tended to the laborious task of sending out hundreds of letters. These affairs commanded the attention of the local press. For example, in April 1960 the principal speakers were presidential aspirant John F. Kennedy and Congressman Stewart L. Udall (D., Ariz.); in 1966 the featured speaker was Secretary of Labor Willard W. Wirtz. For the June 1968 affair Brademas achieved another coup. The speaker was John W. Gardner, who had very recently resigned as HEW secretary to become chairman of the newly organized Urban Coalition. Gardner was especially attractive for this occasion, for, in addition to being a political celebrity, he was a Republican, and, as suggested earlier, every ounce of bipartisan identification that Brademas could muster was thought to be helpful. Banquet tickets were priced at $25 for "sponsors" and $100 for "patrons." The general response was enthusiastic; more persons bought tickets than ever before.

Ah, but the teachers. . . . Although a special letter of invitation had been mailed to each of the several thousand schoolteachers in the area, so few of them bought tickets that the idea of trying to rouse the education community seemed a dismal failure. Partly because of the disappointing turnout among teachers in June, some earlier plans to enlist the education community were abandoned, such as arranging fund-raising luncheons or teas for area teachers or running a newspaper advertisement to be sponsored and signed by schoolteachers.

One time-consuming project, however, was pursued. A special "Dear Educator" letter was mailed to each of the 9,000 school and college personnel in the Third District. In a brief cover letter, on congressional letterhead, Brademas underscored his intimate connection with education policy:

> Because we have a common interest in education, I am taking the liberty of sending you a summary of the major education bills enacted into law by the 90th Congress.
>
> As you may know, I have been a member of the House Committee on Education and Labor for the past ten years, and am presently ranking

member of the two subcommittees that handle elementary and secondary school legislation and higher education bills.

The 90th Congress has built constructively on the education measures passed by the historic 89th Congress. Most of the measures we have approved in the last few years are already benefiting schools and colleges and universities, students and teachers and professors, throughout Indiana and the nation.

My own view is that we must maintain and strengthen American education at every level, from pre-school through graduate school, in both public and private institutions, if our country is to be able to cope effectively with the challenges that history has thrust upon us.

I hope that you find this summary helpful and that you will feel free to send me any questions or suggestions you may have.

A four-page mimeographed enclosure enumerated the education accomplishments of the 90th Congress. Drafted over a period of many weeks, the enclosure described the Education Professions Development Act of 1967, the Elementary and Secondary Education Act amendments of 1967, the Vocational Education Act amendments of 1968, the Higher Education Act of 1968, and five lesser bills.

Brademas' nonpartisan cover letter was sent as franked mail. The letters were mailed on October 24 and 25, less than two weeks before the election, triggering an outcry from the camp of his Republican opponent, Erwin, alleging misuse of the congressional frank. But the issue, not pressed vigorously by the opposition, quickly faded from view; indeed, the practice of using the frank for such purposes is commonplace. So, for relatively little capital outlay, Brademas was able to remind 9,000 educators, in their homes, of their community of interest in a not-so-subtle preelection message.

Further efforts to energize the local higher education community centered around a project initiated during the last weeks of the campaign. Faculty wives from Notre Dame spent many hours contacting area college and university teachers to request from each the inclusion of his or her name and a contribution of a few dollars to run a newspaper advertisement in support of Brademas. On November 4, the day before the election, a nearly full-page ad, costing approximately $550, appeared in the *South Bend Tribune*. Its banner headline proclaimed:

350 COLLEGE AND UNIVERSITY EDUCATORS FROM
THE THIRD CONGRESSIONAL DISTRICT ENDORSE
CONGRESSMAN JOHN BRADEMAS' BID FOR REELECTION

The copy listed all 350 "Faculty Friends of John Brademas" and praised his support of education.

Despite the great time and energy directed at cultivating local educators to support and work for Brademas, the results, to the extent that they were tan-

*Jack H. Schuster*

gible, were mixed at best. Little hard cash was raised. On the other hand, the assistance of the canvassing schoolteachers, and especially the help of the handful of Notre Dame wives, was valuable. Were votes changed by this special campaign within a campaign? No attempt was ever made to determine how this sizable number of local educators actually voted or whether they were influenced by Brademas' special attentiveness. Such a survey would have been revealing — but costly to conduct. In any event, it is clear that a mere handful of educators — perhaps forty at most — were actively involved in the campaign, investing, on the average, several hours of their time. A hard-nosed cost-benefit analysis of this aspect of the campaign probably would yield disappointing conclusions.

*Seeking an "Education Community-at-Large."*    Brademas had come to know well many university presidents and scholars. Through friendships formed at Harvard, Oxford, and Notre Dame, through contact with the Stevenson "braintrust," through persons he had met over a decade as a member of the House Education and Labor Committee and as an inveterate conference-goer, and through his membership on a number of education boards and councils, Brademas had become acquainted with a great many persons prominent in American education. In the 1968 election year, facing a close race, Brademas decided for the first time to try to harness this potential resource through an organized effort. Two endeavors are worth special mention: the "National Friends of John Brademas" fund-raising effort and a national education conference held at the University of Notre Dame. In early 1968, following the congressional redistricting, Brademas determined that he would have to spend substantially more money on his 1968 reelection than he had on any of his previous campaigns. The major fund-raising activity was the campaign banquet referred to previously. In addition, friends of Brademas ordinarily organized cocktail receptions in Washington, Chicago, and New York to help raise funds for him. But these smallish affairs could yield only a portion of the money needed for this campaign.

Now, for the first time in his eight campaigns for Congress, Brademas sought to make direct use of his national reputation in education circles by trying to tap an amorphous, elusive national education constituency. He reasoned that educators across the country and prominent persons sensitive to the needs of American education would be receptive because of his efforts for education during a decade in Congress. But did such a constituency in fact exist? And how might these fresh potential contributors be motivated to contribute to a relatively obscure political campaign in Indiana?

Over a period of months, the idea of organizing a special committee to solicit funds had been discussed. Brademas was in sporadic contact with friends to seek advice concerning potential contributors and how to reach them. However, with the press of other business, final decisions on how to organize this special appeal had been deferred. In May, Brademas met in New York with Francis Keppel and Peter H. Gillingham. Keppel, chairman of the board and president of the General Learning Corporation, was one of the most distinguished names in American education: youthful dean of Harvard's Graduate School of Education (1948–62) and U.S. commissioner of education (1962–65). Gillingham, an executive at the Education and World Affairs foundation in New York, had served as staff director of the Special House Committee Task Force on International Education which Brademas had chaired in 1966. They agreed upon a general strategy: a dozen or so persons would be recruited to serve as solicitors, who, in turn, would send personalized letters and a brochure to potential contributors whom they felt they could contact personally. Brademas lined up the solicitors, for the most part friends who were strongly identified with education policy. In addition to Keppel, they included, among others: Stephen K. Bailey, dean of the Maxwell School of Citizenship and Public Affairs, Syracuse University; Douglass Cater, special assistant to the president of the United States (specializing in education policy); Allan Cartter, chancellor and executive vice president, New York University; Charles U. Daly, vice president for development and public affairs, University of Chicago, a former Kennedy administration official; and Samuel Halperin, deputy assistant secretary for legislation, HEW.

Brademas and his advisers had discussed for some time how a national committee might be organized. Not until early August, however, was a name selected — "National Friends of John Brademas" — and membership on the "executive committee" decided upon. Two of the "solicitors" were designated as members of the Executive Committee: Francis Keppel, who served as chairman, and Stephen K. Bailey. In addition to those two, there were sixteen other committee members, including two prominent South Bend businessmen. Members of the Executive Committee, and their positions at the time were: William Benton, chairman of the board, Encyclopaedia Britannica and former U.S. senator from Connecticut; Edward E. Booher, president, McGraw-Hill Book Company, Inc.; Paul H. Douglas, former U.S. senator from Illinois; J. Wayne Fredericks, a foundation executive and former Department of State official; J. Kenneth Galbraith, professor of economics, Harvard University, and former ambassador to India; Arthur J. Goldberg, U.S. representative to the United Nations, formerly secretary of labor and associate justice, U.S. Supreme Court; Richard G. Hatcher, mayor of Gary, Indiana; Walter W. Heller, professor of economics, University of Minnesota, former chairman, Council of Economic Advisers; Bert Liss, South Bend businessman and civic leader; George C. Lodge, lecturer, Harvard Business School, previously a federal official and in 1962 the Republican senatorial candidate from Massachusetts; Newton N. Minow, Chicago attorney (Adlai E. Stevenson's firm) and former chairman, Federal Communications Commission; Daniel P. Moynihan, director of the Harvard-M.I.T. Joint Center for Urban Studies, formerly a Labor Department official; George N. Shuster, assistant to the president, University of Notre Dame and former president of Hunter College, New York City; Adlai E. Stevenson III, Illinois state treasurer; Frank E. Sullivan,

South Bend businessman and civic leader; and Marietta Tree, former U.S. representative to several United Nations agencies.

A special letterhead and brochure were designed for distribution exclusively outside the Third District; layout and copy emphasized that John Brademas was "A Congressman for the Nation." In September and October about 2,500 letters were sent to persons whose names had been suggested by solicitors or culled from various membership lists. The great bulk of these letters — about 1,800 of them — were signed by Keppel; the remainder were signed by the various solicitors on the basis of their personal contacts. The appeal was cast chiefly in terms of Brademas' education ties:

> For ten years, Congressman John Brademas of South Bend, Indiana has been one of the ablest, most intelligent and effective members of the House of Representatives.
>
> He has earned a reputation as a top authority in Congress on education. Indeed he has either sponsored or helped write nearly every major education bill enacted into law in the past several years.
>
> You may know John Brademas because of his particular interest in higher education . . .

Only a portion of these several thousand addressees were educators per se. However, most of the names were drawn from membership or board of director lists of elite organizations such as the Council on Foreign Relations, the Committee for Economic Development, the Institute for International Education, and numerous university and foundation boards. The assumption was that many of the persons solicited would at least recognize Brademas' name and, it was hoped, would be favorably impressed by the endorsement of the National Friends Committee.

A parallel endeavor was the mailing of slightly different letters to Americans who had attended Oxford University. Brademas asked three friends, Rhodes Scholar classmates, to constitute "American Oxonians for Brademas." This committee consisted of John W. Dickey, attorney, Sullivan and Cromwell, New York City; James H. Billington, professor of history, Princeton University; and Lawrence C. McQuade, assistant secretary of commerce for domestic and international business. Because of poor planning and the press of other campaign priorities, these letters were not mailed until October 23, a bare two weeks before the election.

Brademas' effort to raise money from a specialized constituency was not a unique congressional fund-raising technique; congressmen often receive campaign funds from trade associations, labor groups and other interests whose welfare is affected by the recipients' activity in Congress. But Brademas' attempt to mobilize an education constituency on a national basis was distinctive and perhaps unprecedented for a congressional campaign. As part of a total effort aimed at drawing support from educators and education-minded citizens, the National Friends campaign served reasonably well as a first effort, attracting contributions of about $5,000. More, doubtless, would have been raised if the National Friends' letters had been mailed earlier; nevertheless, the money constituted a helpful and welcome increment to the total campaign budget.

*A Well-Timed Education Conference.*   Still another venture calculated to enhance Brademas' credentials as a public servant committed to education took the form of an education conference held at the University of Notre Dame on October 25–26, just days before the election. The conference was Brademas' idea: an event that would focus attention on policy questions in American education and, not coincidentally, on his own increasingly important role in federal education policy-making.

The conference, titled "Major Tensions in American Education: Shaping Policies for the '70's," was sponsored jointly by Brademas and the Department of Education at the University of Notre Dame. (His relationship with Notre Dame could best be described as symbiotic. As their "lobbyist" in Congress, he provided University scholars and administrators information about federal programs, helped to put federal agency officials in touch with University officials to facilitate grants, inserted in the *Congressional Record* an occasional article about the University or a speech by its dynamic president, the Reverend Theodore Hesburgh.) Several thousand invitations were mailed throughout northern Indiana to school administrators, teachers, university faculty and officials, guidance counselors, government and labor officials, and other community leaders. Brademas alone was responsible for securing commitments from the speakers, who included Francis Keppel, McGeorge Bundy (president of the Ford Foundation), Richard A. Graham (director of teacher corps of the U.S. Office of Education), Paul W. Briggs (superintendent of the Cleveland schools), and Harold Howe II (U.S. commissioner of education).

With a line-up of national education luminaries, several hundred local educators and civic leaders were attracted to the conference. Brademas was careful not to use the conference as a partisan platform. He did not solicit kind remarks from the speakers, but each of them praised him warmly, some even extravagantly, in his opening remarks. (The speakers, after all, were political allies or personal friends of Brademas.) Ample coverage in Sunday's *South Bend Tribune* was given to the conference in general and, especially, to Brademas' key role in organizing it.

*Recruiting Student Support in the Year of Disaffection.*   Early in the campaign, during the late spring and summer, it became clear to Brademas that he would need to mount the most extensive campaign of his career. A lot of manpower would be needed for anticipated projects: door-to-door canvassing, telephone "blitzes," stuffing envelopes, and so forth. Hence

Brademas decided to harness as much student energy as possible for the campaign. The efforts of hundreds of student volunteers in the early McCarthy presidential primaries, especially New Hampshire, had dramatized the effectiveness of student campaigners. Student activism in the Indiana primary, both for McCarthy and Kennedy, dispelled any remaining skepticism regarding this potentially potent political resource.

But the Third District race was no glamour-filled, issue-packed presidential campaign. Could Brademas mobilize student support on his behalf? He was not a national figure (except perhaps among education's cognoscenti) and, though he related extremely well to students, he had neither the electrifying appeal of Robert Kennedy nor the White Knight image of Eugene McCarthy. And Brademas had opted against taking a strong, unequivocal position on the one issue that had galvanized student participation in the presidential race — the war in Vietnam. From opinion surveys of the Third District and discussions with advisers and constituents, Brademas concluded that prudence required his avoidance of a "super-dove" label. Would his solid credentials as a liberal and his leadership role within the Democratic Study Group offset — for students — his imperfect position on the Vietnam War?

An extensive recruiting effort was launched during the summer months. Hundreds of letters were written to students who attended several of the colleges in the Third District — the University of Notre Dame, the South Bend Regional Campus of Indiana University, Saint Mary's College, Goshen College, and Bethel College. In some cases, the letter soliciting help was sent over the signature of Brademas himself, in others, over the signature of a student or student-faculty committee which Brademas had helped to establish. In some instances, the letter was sent to every student who attended a particular institution. In other cases, more selective appeals were mailed by Brademas to "probable sympathizers" identified from lists, where available, of Kennedy and McCarthy volunteers. For example:

> Dear _____ :
>
> I am taking the liberty of writing to you at the suggestion of a number of people who worked closely with Senator Robert F. Kennedy in the Indiana Presidential Primary. For the last week or so I have been getting in touch with leaders on college campuses in Northern Indiana who might be willing to help me this fall in what will probably be the toughest campaign I have ever faced.
>
> To be specific, since early March of this year, my staff has been working on a registration and turnout strategy for the fall. I am pleased that Miss Gayle Stack, who was the office manager for the Kennedy Headquarters in the Primary, had joined this effort. The end product of this planning will be to define clearly the target population for the fall registration drive. . . .

As an example of a more generalized appeal, on August 22, 1968, several hundred letters were mailed from Washington to students who attended Indiana University at South Bend. In this letter, Brademas emphasized his connection with education, and concluded:

> I am firmly convinced that the energies and abilities of college students in my campaign can be decisive in November. If you are willing to work for me this fall, please return the enclosed application to Professor James Conley, Department of Government, Indiana University Extension, South Bend, Indiana. Professor Conley is one of my campus organizers, and he will be responsible for organizing Indiana University Students for Brademas on the South Bend campus. We need to complete plans for a mass canvassing operation during the first few weeks of school.

Student leaders at the University of Notre Dame and Saint Mary's College, principally those who had been active in the McCarthy and Kennedy primary efforts in Indiana, signed letters similar to those sent by Brademas himself.

When students returned to their campuses in September, a series of organizational meetings were held to discuss techniques for recruiting students and to determine the most effective use of student help. Principal responsibility for recruiting was vested in one Brademas staffer, herself a very able graduate student on temporary leave from Princeton University's Woodrow Wilson School, and in several student contacts on each campus. Brademas headquarters provided mimeograph machines and telephones. Mimeographed notices and handouts distributed on campus underscored Brademas' role in education and entreated: "John Brademas needs your help."

In mid-September, an "All-Campus Rally" was organized to recruit a wider circle of college student support. The site was the South Bend Regional Campus of Indiana University. The featured speakers were Richard E. Neustadt — professor of government and director of the Institute of Politics, Harvard University, a man whose scholarship would be familiar to many college students — and Brademas himself. Professor Neustadt flew from Boston to South Bend for this occasion. Following Neustadt's warm introductory remarks, Brademas spoke informally and then responded at length to student questions. The turnout of several hundred students was mildly disappointing, especially in view of the proliferation of publicity on the local campuses. Even so, if any significant proportion of these students could be enlisted as campaign volunteers, something very useful would have been accomplished.

The campaign seemed to be working; several highly favorable columns appeared in the University of Notre Dame's daily paper, *The Observer*. Then, on October 16, that paper ran a long editorial entitled "The Essential Brademas," which concluded by urging students to

> . . . devote a few hours of your time in helping this man who sym-
> bolizes the hopes and aspirations of many of us. We urge that you
> vote for him and moreover that you work for him. He needs student
> help.

The recruiting campaign intensified. Meetings were held almost daily either at Brademas' headquarters or on the various campuses. Brademas' staffers worked hard to inspire hard-core enthusiasts to spread the word on their respective campuses. A recruiting campaign was mounted through the student press. Two advertisements underscoring Brademas' credentials as a liberal were placed in *The Observer*, both paid for by the contributions of "Notre Dame Faculty Friends of John Brademas." The first, a full-page ad with 108 faculty names listed at the bottom of the page, borrowed for a headline the title of the *Look* magazine article which had appeared three days before: "John Brademas: A Liberal Fights for Survival." Aimed at potential volunteers, the advertisements featured letters from Senator Eugene McCarthy and Senator Edward M. Kennedy (D., Mass.) urging support of Brademas. A subsequent, smaller advertisement featured one-sentence endorsements from the *New York Times*, the *New Republic*, McCarthy, Kennedy, and *Look*.

The results of these extensive efforts were less than overwhelming. College students did report to Brademas' headquarters in small clusters for stamp-licking and similar tasks. More often than not, though, the students who turned up at headquarters were more disposed to help formulate global strategies than to stuff envelopes. Ultimately, most of the necessary menial work was performed by women volunteers (especially the Notre Dame faculty wives), or, on occasion, by high school students.

The most effective potential use of college students, as seen by the Brademas staff, was door-to-door canvassing. A computer had been used to help identify key precincts. The staff's strategy was to mount "blitz" canvassing campaigns for as many as possible of the last six or seven weekends prior to the election. Unfortunately for the campaign, Notre Dame played three of its first four football games at home; on those Saturdays, any activity not involving the "Fighting Irish" was doomed. However, in the closing weeks of the campaign small groups of college students did cover a lot of territory. Whereas the staff at one time had hoped to recruit fifty to a hundred college students for an afternoon's canvassing activity, the actual turnout on any one weekend afternoon turned out to be closer to ten to fifteen students. As it developed, fifteen collegians, joined by an equal number of adults and high school students, could effectively cover a number of key precincts in an afternoon.

A final dividend of the recruiting efforts was student assistance in a telephone blitz operation. With seven days of the campaign to go, a bank of thirty telephones was installed in rented office space. Most of the telephones were operated by college students, some of them volunteers, others receiving a nominal hourly wage. A Notre Dame graduate student worked as a volunteer for five straight days and evenings overseeing and coordinating the operation. Calls were placed to all residents in high priority precincts and townships. Telephoning from 10:00 A.M. to 10:00 P.M., these workers dialed nearly 40,000 homes in the closing days of the campaign.

On balance, then, local students did make a significant contribution to the outcome of the campaign. The actual impact, of course, could not be measured. In one respect, perhaps the most important product of student activity was the image that their enthusiasm projected. In a national campaign notable for widespread student disaffection, residents of the Third District were made aware of student efforts on behalf of Brademas. Some adult voters may have appreciated the fact that, not unlike Senators Kennedy and McCarthy, Brademas had been able to inspire the confidence and support of at least some of America's young people.

*National Mass Media Endorsements.* In the closing days of the campaign, Brademas received an unusual degree of attention from the national press, typically focusing on his contribution as an education-minded legislator. The three-page article in *Look* cited previously — "Congressman John Brademas: A Liberal Fights for Survival" — hit the newsstands on October 15. The author, a *Look* senior editor, described Brademas as ". . . 'Mr. Education' in the U.S. Congress." An editorial in the same issue of *Look* endorsed Brademas' bid for reelection: ". . . the House of Representatives needs . . . more Democrats like John Brademas of Indiana. . . ." In a November 1 editorial, *Life*, which supported Nixon for president, singled out eight House incumbents and nine candidates for the Senate and encouraged its readers to vote for them. Brademas was one of three Democratic representatives so anointed:

> In Indiana, the conservative trend, plus redistricting, threatens to unseat one of the House's most intelligent and effective Democrats, John Brademas, an experienced specialist in education. We hope Brademas makes it.

Brademas also received the endorsements of the *New York Times* (October 23, 1968) and the *New Republic* (October 26, 1968).

### The Election Outcome

As Election Day, November 5, grew nearer, Brademas' campaign staff was wary. On the one hand, there was no solid evidence that Brademas was in fact trailing his opponent. On the other hand, there were a number of imponderables whose impact could not easily be measured. Nixon would carry Indiana big, that seemed certain. But how strong would his coattails be? George Wallace would siphon off a sizable number of votes. But how many Wallace-voting Democrats, disaffected with the Democratic presidential ticket, would split their ballot to vote for John Brademas? "Will" Erwin had campaigned vigorously for months, conducting a clean, aggressive campaign. Had he shaken enough hands and identified Brademas closely enough with "the mess in Washington" and East Coast liberalism to attract many swing voters? Brademas, thinking himself to be the front-runner with more to lose than to gain by appearing on the same platform as Erwin, had consistently refused to debate his opponent directly. Erwin had pounded away at Brademas for his reluctance to meet head-on. Had Brademas' strategy alienated the electorate?

The *South Bend Tribune* summed it up, somewhat melodramatically, two days before the election:

> U.S. Rep. John Brademas . . . will be struggling for his political life Tuesday. Despite enough woes to bring tears to a stone statue of Andrew Jackson or any other Democratic patriarch, Brademas appears to hold a precarious lead in his race for a sixth term in Congress.

A short while after the polls closed, the returns began to flow in. The first returns that night were from South Bend and St. Joseph County — Brademas' usual bastion of strength — and they were reassuring. He was off to an early lead. Significantly, Erwin's edge in key Republican precincts in South Bend was not cutting deeply into Brademas' big leads in predominantly Democratic precincts; it looked as though a lot of ticket-splitting had taken place, the sine qua non for a Brademas win. Indeed, Brademas' plurality in St. Joseph County kept mounting until it reached 20,000, a margin that simply could not be overcome by Erwin in the remaining three counties of the district. By 10 o'clock that night the outcome was clear, and a weary, but beaming Brademas made the rounds of several of the television studios in the district to be interviewed, then returned to his campaign headquarters to the cheers of his supporters. Later results that evening and the next morning showed that Brademas had lost each of the other three counties; in one, Kosciusko, he barely managed 30 percent of the vote — a whopping net loss of almost 8,000 votes. Brademas held the loss in Elkhart County to a 3,600-vote deficit, and in much smaller Marshall County to 1,650 votes. In all, Brademas was reelected to a sixth term by a close vote of 94,452 to 86,354 (52.2 percent). In contrast to Brademas' 8,100 vote margin, Nixon carried the Third District handily — by 21,000 votes — and swept to a victory in Indiana with a 261,000 lead, his greatest plurality in any state. In the three-way presidential race, Nixon received 50.3 percent of the Indiana vote and Humphrey only 38.0 percent, with Wallace drawing 11.4 percent. (Nixon, it should be recalled, got but 43.4 percent of the national popular vote in 1968; Humphrey's share was 42.7 percent and Wallace's 13.5.) In the Third District, Nixon got 50.6 percent,

Humphrey 39.2 percent — in contrast, as noted above, to Brademas' 52.2 percent — and Wallace 10.2 percent.

Indiana Democrats lost one of their five House seats. The Republicans regained the Statehouse with a clean sweep of all state offices. Senator Birch Bayh barely survived a stiff challenge, receiving 51.8 percent of the vote.*

Given these circumstances, Brademas' victory was clearly one he had in good part earned by his own strength. The *South Bend Tribune* was justified in terming his reelection "the most impressive win of his political career."

### Concluding Observations

To what extent did Brademas' efforts to mobilize the "education community" on his behalf pay off? Although the answer will never be known with any precision, speculation about the "cost-effectiveness" of this particular dimension of the campaign is possible.

With respect to the national education interest groups, the award presented by the National Education Association attracted some favorable attention from the local media. Of greater importance, however, was the support of national AFT headquarters which prompted the canvassing activity of a score of South Bend teachers. This participation yielded over one hundred man-hours of work "in the field," ringing doorbells and talking to voters in "swing" precincts. Brademas' efforts to energize this particular interest group was minimal; the local impact of their efforts surely was helpful. Apart from the canvassing assistance provided by these activist members of the South Bend Federation of Teachers, the rather extensive efforts by Brademas to recruit volunteers and solicit contributions from among several thousand elementary and secondary school teachers in the Third District went virtually for naught.

Brademas did not expend much energy in contacting a handful of educator friends in the Executive branch. He placed telephone calls to several and hosted a few brief meetings. These efforts yielded the names of potential contributors, a few of whom he subsequently contacted personally. In addition, these friends sent out about a hundred letters soliciting contributions for Brademas. The payoff was minor in terms of money contributed to the campaign, but so, too, was the amount of time Brademas had to invest. On balance, then, a successful effort.

At the college level, a handful of faculty — and especially a few wives — contributed their time generously. In fact, campaign headquarters would have been substantially less productive without the consistent and effective work of three or four faculty wives. But, again, to the extent that Brademas' staff once envisioned squads of professors turning out the vote and "turning

* Editor's note: Birch Bayh was the major congressional leader pushing for direct election of the president in 1969–70. See the case study by Sindler in this volume.

on" their students, the ultimate results were disappointing. Perhaps the staff should have concentrated in the beginning on trying to develop a small nucleus of enthusiasts on each college campus to function with more autonomy rather than trying to oversee the operation from headquarters. In sum, local college and university educators may well have voted for Brademas and several hundred of them did contribute a few dollars each to sponsor several newspaper advertisements. Quite clearly, however, the education community in the Third District did not rise as one to demand that "Mr. Education in Congress" be returned to Washington.

The energies devoted to recruiting college students absorbed a great deal of staff time. The output was far from negligible. College volunteers rang many doorbells and dialed thousands of telephones throughout the district. But whether the staff time invested in recruiting and deploying college students was worth the results could be argued either way. A more modest effort was made to recruit high school students. Their assistance proved very valuable to the Brademas campaign. High school volunteers stamped and stuffed many an envelope and called at many a door. High school students had proven their value during the Kennedy and McCarthy primary races in Indiana. In retrospect, perhaps the Brademas staff should have given more attention to recruiting high school volunteers.

Finally, there was the effort to raise funds from a national educational constituency if, indeed, one existed. Many of the contributions raised through the "National Friends of John Brademas" were no doubt made in response to the interest in education demonstrated by Brademas and the National Friends Committee. The financial gleanings, at least in 1968, were rather thin.

On balance, then, the efforts made to harness educators at the local and national levels yielded visible but modest results. A cost-benefit analysis might well indicate that Brademas should have invested much of that campaign energy in ways other than those calculated to win minds, money, and manpower from within the education community. At the same time, the expected closeness of the election outcome would seem to have justified Brademas' every effort to mobilize his natural allies.

*Postscript.* John Brademas was returned to Congress in 1970 for his seventh term by 57.5 percent of the district vote; beset by fewer complications than had confronted him in 1968, he won by 23,000 votes. (Meanwhile, the "National Friends of John Brademas" has expanded its fund-raising activities and has been more successful than the initial, hurried effort. Wilbur Cohen, dean of the School of Education at the University of Michigan and former HEW secretary, has succeeded Francis Keppel as chairman for the 1972 campaign. Keppel, who invested a considerable amount of his time as chairman through two campaigns, remains as vice-chairman; other "glamour" names have been added to the committee.)

John Brademas' congressional career has prospered. In 1969, he became chairman of the House Select Subcommittee on Education. Gradually expanding its jurisdiction, he has led the subcommittee to produce many bills that have been enacted into law, most notably the milestone legislation in 1972 to create a National Institute of Education. Also in 1972 he was appointed by the Speaker of the House to serve as a member of the President's National Commission on the Financing of Postsecondary Education. Of special importance, in January 1971 when the Democrats organized the 92nd Congress, Brademas was named to a new House leadership post as one of two deputy majority whips (the youngest member of the leadership team consisting of the Speaker, the majority leader, the majority whip, and the two deputies).

Brademas' "extracurricular" education activities have continued apace. In 1969 he was elected to a six-year term on Harvard's Board of Overseers (its senior governing board) and was selected a Fellow of the prestigious American Academy of Arts and Sciences. Other honors and national education awards have accumulated, including election to the national Senate of Phi Beta Kappa.

At this writing, John Brademas once more is campaigning very vigorously for reelection to an eighth term. For the third time in twelve years, he is confronted with a Nixon presidential campaign that threatens to sweep Indiana and Brademas' own district; once again, John Brademas' fate will probably hinge on the willingness of voters to split their tickets on his behalf.

*Some Larger Questions.* John Brademas' 1968 campaign raises some basic questions concerning American national politics. In Brademas' political life, the challenge of serving two very different constituencies — Indiana's Third District and educators across the land — looms ever large, illustrating a debate in progress since the inception of the American nation: should our national representatives function in Congress primarily as independent trustees (mindful of Burke's injunction to vote one's conscience) or should they assume more the role of their constituents' delegate, intent on reflecting as perfectly as possible their constituency's preferences? Of course, no simple answer exists; some balancing of these interests, when they clash, is inevitable. While John Brademas enjoys a great deal of latitude in Congress and increasing influence in shaping national policy, he knows that to secure that freedom — to be returned to Congress every two years — he and other congressmen from tough, marginal districts, must pay incessant attention to the needs of their constituents. Brademas must never let up in the constant — and fatiguing — campaign for reelection. We must inquire: Do the pressures on marginal-district House members continually to campaign distort or enhance the democratic process? Would a four-year term make more sense for U.S. representatives?

The Brademas campaign raises a number of other questions concerning the relationships between politicians and interest groups. Was his interaction with his "special interest constituency" typical of the way other national legislators seek the assistance of interest groups? Was there any compromise of integrity by either politician or lobbyists? Is it significant that the education lobby represents a predominantly nonprofit, service-oriented sector of society (with relatively little money available for lobbying purposes) while many other congressmen have similarly strong ties with more affluent profit-oriented constituencies (bankers, homebuilders, defense suppliers, cotton growers, oil producers, bulk-rate mailers, and so forth)? Does the pluralistic nature of American education preclude cohesive, effective lobbying efforts in Washington on behalf of education?

Upon reflection, the reader should find that the issues raised by these questions about political campaigning lie very close to the heart of the American democracy.

## SOURCES AND READINGS

This study was stimulated by my experience initially as legislative assistant and then as administrative assistant to Congressman John Brademas, from July 1967 to January 1970, and especially my activity as director of his Third District campaign headquarters in 1968. While no amount of reading can take the place entirely of personal immersion in a political campaign, there are many studies highly useful to serious students and practicing politicians alike.

Congressional campaigning and, more generally, a congressman's relations to his constituents are explored from the congressman's vantage point in Charles L. Clapp, *The Congressman: His Work as He Sees It* (Garden City, N.Y.: Doubleday, Anchor Books edition, 1964), and Donald Riegle, with Trevor Armstrong, *0 Congress* (Garden City, N.Y.: Doubleday, 1972). Both Lewis A. Froman, Jr., *Congressmen and Their Constituencies* (Chicago: Rand-McNally, 1963), and M. Kent Jennings and L. Harmon Zeigler (eds.), *The Electoral Process* (Englewood Cliffs, N.J.: Prentice-Hall, 1966), provide helpful insights into legislator-constituency relationships.

Three explorations of contemporary, big-time political campaigning are found in Dan Nimmo, *The Political Persuaders: The Techniques of Modern Election Campaigns* (Englewood Cliffs, N.J.: Prentice-Hall, 1970), James M. Perry, *The New Politics: The Expanding Technology of Political Manipulation* (New York: Clarkson N. Potter, 1968), and Ray Hiebert, Robert Jones, Ernest Lotito, and John Lorenz, *The Political Image Merchants: Strategies in the New Politics* (Washington, D.C.: Acropolis Books, 1971).

Voter behavior is explored in two brief, readable studies, Hugh A. Bone and Austin Ranney, *Politics and Voters* (New York: McGraw-Hill, 1971), and William H. Flanigan, *Political Behavior of the Ameri-*

*can Electorate* (Boston: Allyn & Bacon, 1972). More detailed are the studies of Angus Campbell, Philip E. Converse, Warren E. Miller, and Donald E. Stokes, authors of both *The American Voter: An Abridgement* (New York: John Wiley & Sons, 1964) and *Elections and the Political Order* (New York: John Wiley & Sons, 1966). See also Milton C. Cummings, Jr., *Congressmen and the Electorate: Elections for the U.S. House and the President, 1920–1964* (Glencoe, Ill.: The Free Press, 1966), for a systematic treatment of House district voting patterns for congressmen and president.

A good account of national education politics is Eugene Eidenberg and Roy D. Morey, *An Act of Congress: The Legislative Process and the Making of Education Policy* (New York: W. W. Norton & Company, 1969), which treats the enactment of the Elementary and Secondary Education Act of 1965. Teachers as lobbyists are scrutinized by Alan Rosenthal, *Pedagogues and Power: Teacher Groups in School Politics* (Syracuse: Syracuse University Press, 1969), and Harmon Zeigler, *The Political Life of American Teachers* (Englewood Cliffs, N.J.: Prentice-Hall, 1967).

John Brademas, "The Role of the Intellectual in Politics," *Texas Quarterly* (Winter 1965) is a provocative essay on the collision of two worlds.

# NOTES ON THE CONTRIBUTORS

EDWARD C. BANFIELD has written case studies on the efforts of the federal government to establish a cooperative farm in the Arizona desert, politics in Chicago, and the organization by IBM of a factory to employ "hard core" workers in the Bedford-Stuyvesant section of New York City. His books include *City Politics* (1963) with James Q. Wilson, *The Moral Basis of a Backward Society* (1958), and, most recently, *The Unheavenly City* (1968). Now a professor at the University of Pennsylvania, he was in 1969 the chairman of a task force which made recommendations on the Model Cities program to President Nixon. The task force's report was published by the White House in August 1970 under the title: *Model Cities: A Step Towards the New Federalism*. He hopes eventually to write a sequel to his present contribution, carrying the story through the Nixon administration.

DAVID L. KIRP, a lawyer who teaches at the Graduate School of Public Policy and the Law School, University of California at Berkeley, was previously Director of the Center for Law and Education, Harvard University. In that post, he was directly involved in a variety of education policy issues, including school desegregation and federal education program administration. He continues to mix practice, teaching, and writing, and has published articles in such scholarly and popular journals as the *Michigan Law Review, Harvard Educational Review, Social Policy*, and the *Christian Science Monitor*. His current research interests include the labeling and sorting of students, and the provision of legal services to the near-poor.

THEODORE R. MARMOR, who contributed a study of Medicare to this volume's predecessor (A. P. Sindler, ed., *American Political Institutions and Public Policy*), teaches public-policy courses at the University of Minnesota. Author of *The Politics of Medicare* and editor of *Poverty Policy*, he has been involved in welfare-reform issues as a writer and consultant. He prepared, with Martin Rein, a report on European welfare state experience for the President's Commission on Income Maintenance Programs (1968–70), and has worked on health and welfare issues for various state and federal government organizations.

JEROME T. MURPHY has been close to the subject of his study for some years. He was a legislative assistant in the Office of Legislation of the U.S. Office of Education (1964–66); a special assistant to the assistant secretary for legislation, Department of Health, Education and Welfare (1966–68); and associate staff director of the National Advisory Council on the Education of Disadvantaged Children (1968–69). He is currently completing work for an Ed.D. at the Graduate School of Education at Harvard University, and is a member of its Center for Educational Policy Research. He has written several articles on education, poverty, and consumer policy and politics.

MARTIN REIN is a professor in the Department of Urban Studies and Planning at Massachusetts Institute of Technology. Author of many works on public policy, poverty, the welfare state, and housing, his most recent book is *Social Policy: Issues of Choice and Change.* He has collaborated with Theodore Marmor on studies of the fate of welfare reform in the United States and on welfare policy in European nations.

JACK H. SCHUSTER is assistant to the chancellor and lecturer in political science at the University of California at Berkeley. His teaching and writing have focused on national education politics. Formerly an administrator at Tulane University, he was in Washington from 1967 to 1970, first as legislative assistant, and then as administrative assistant to Congressman John Brademas of Indiana. For the latter's reelection bid in 1968, which is the subject of Schuster's study in this volume, he served as director of Brademas' campaign headquarters. A lawyer by training and a member of the District of Columbia bar, his current research interest is in collective bargaining in higher education.

ALLAN P. SINDLER, who has taught at Duke, Yale, and Cornell, has since 1970 been with the Graduate School of Public Policy, University of California at Berkeley. A political scientist with broad interests in the American political process, he is particularly concerned with the interplay of the political environment, institutions, and the making of public policy and its subsequent implementation. His writings include books and articles on southern politics, political parties, race and politics, and political institutions. He edited this volume's predecessor, *American Political Institutions and Public Policy.*